Genocide of Indigenous Peoples

Genocide of Indigenous Peoples

Genocide: A Critical Bibliographic Review
Volume 8

Samuel Totten and Robert K. Hitchcock
editors

Transaction Publishers
New Brunswick (U.S.A.) and London (U.K.)

Library of Congress Catalog Number: 2010024225
ISBN: 978-1-4128-1495-9
Printed in the United States of America

Library of Congress Cataloging-in-Publication Data

Genocide of indigenous people : a critical biographical review / Samuel Totten
and Robert K. Hitchcock, [editors].
    p. cm. -- (Genocide : a critical biographical review ; v.8)
Includes bibliographical references and index.
ISBN 978-1-4128-1495-9 (alk. paper)
    1. Genocide. 2. Crimes against humanity. 3. Indigenous peoples--Violence against. 4. Indigenous peoples--Crimes against. I. Hitchcock, Robert
K. II. Totten, Samuel.

HV6322.7.G4556 2010
364.15'1--dc22

                                                                      2010024225

Contents

Introduction
The Genocide of Indigenous Peoples

Samuel Totten and Robert K. Hitchcock

This volume of Genocide: A Critical Bibliographic Series focuses on the genocides of indigenous peoples across the globe. With the exception of Leo Kuper's chapter ("Other Selected Cases of Genocide and Genocidal Massacres: Types of Genocide") in the first volume of the series, very few chapters in the various volumes have addressed, at least in any detail, the plight and fate of indigenous peoples. In part, this volume was developed to rectify this oversight.[1]

Indigenous peoples—those groups who consider themselves or are considered by others to be aboriginal, "First Nations," "native peoples," "Fourth World peoples," or "original occupants" of specific places on the planet—have faced genocide, cultural destruction, and forced removal from their ancestral areas for thousands of years. These processes intensified with colonization—the expansion of European nations into Asia, Africa, the Americas, Australia, New Zealand, the Pacific, and, more recently, the Arctic—over the past 500 years. Colonization had a variety of impacts, including purposeful as well as unintentional destruction of indigenous peoples, the spread of epidemic diseases, dispossession of indigenous lands, the exploitation of natural and cultural resources, slavery and forced labor, and the transformation and modification of indigenous cultures, practices, and belief systems.

An estimated 350,000,000 to 600,000,000 indigenous people reside across the globe today. Numerous governments, however,

1

fail to recognize indigenous peoples living within their (the nation-states') borders. In Asia, for example, *only one country*, the Philippines, has officially adopted the term "indigenous peoples," and established a law specifically to protect indigenous peoples' rights. Only two countries in Africa, Burundi and Cameroon, have statements about the rights of indigenous peoples in their constitutions.

Conflicts between governments and indigenous peoples arose in many different parts of the world, including what is now Australia, Bangladesh, Brazil, Canada, Guatemala, India, Indonesia, New Zealand, Paraguay, the Philippines, and the United States. It was not until the latter part of the twentieth century that the genocide of indigenous peoples became a major focus of human rights activists, non-governmental organizations, international development and finance institutions such as the United Nations and the World Bank, and indigenous and other community-based organizations. A key reason for such attention was the advent of the human rights movement that followed the Second World War and the passage of the Universal Declaration of Human Rights and the UN Convention on the Prevention and Punishment of the Crime of Genocide in 1948. At one and the same time, it is also true that the expansion of interest in genocides of indigenous peoples came about as a result of the massive increase in conflicts involving states and indigenous peoples, characterized by Bernard Neitschmann as "the Third World War."[2]

Scholars and activists began paying greater attention to the struggles between Fourth World peoples and First, Second, and Third World states because of what they saw as illegal actions of nation-states against indigenous peoples, indigenous groups' passive and active resistance to top-down development, and concerns about the impacts of transnational forces, including what is now known as globalization.

The indigenous peoples' rights movement also began to take shape after the Second World War, and especially in the latter part of the 1960s, partly as a response to the rising concerns and activism of indigenous peoples such as Australian Aboriginals who voiced concerns about their disenfranchisement and sought

Table I.1

**International Human Rights Institutions Relating to Indigenous Peoples' Rights
International Covenant on Civil and Political Rights (ICCPR).**

This covenant was based on the Universal Declaration of Human Rights (UDHR) and was adopted by the United Nations General Assembly in 1966. The Human Rights Council is the body of independent experts that monitors the implementation of the ICCPR by states.

International Covenant on Economic, Social, and Cultural Rights (ICESCR).
This covenant was adopted by the United Nations General Assembly in 1966, and it came into force in 1976. This covenant commits states to promote and protect a wide range of economic, social and cultural rights, including the right of individuals to work in economically just and healthy conditions, to an adequate standard of living, to social protection, to education and to enjoy the benefits of cultural freedom and scientific progress. The implementation of this covenant is monitored by the Committee on Economic, Social, and Cultural Rights (CESR), a body of independent experts.

International Labour Organization Convention 169 concerning Indigenous and Tribal Peoples in Independent Countries
This multilateral convention, which consists of 34 articles, was opened for ratification in 1989.

The United Nations Declaration on the Rights of Indigenous Peoples (UNDRIP).
This important declaration, 23 years in the making, was passed by the United Nations General Assembly on September 13th, 2007.

United Nations Expert Mechanism on the Rights of Indigenous Peoples (UNEMRIP)

This group of experts was created by the Human Rights Council in 2006. Consisting of 5 experts, the Expert Mechanism focuses primarily on studies and research-based advice to the High Commissioner for Human Rights and the Human Rights Council.

United Nations Permanent Forum on Indigenous Issues (UNFPII)

This forum was created by the United Nations in 2000. It meets annually in New York.

Special Rapporteur on the Situation of Human Rights and Fundamental Freedoms of Indigenous Peoples

This special rapporteur position was created by the Commission on Human Rights (the predecessor to the Human Rights Council) in 2001.

a greater voice in Australian government policy and American Indians who were dissatisfied with the treatment of Indians, past and present. Several of the major indigenous peoples' human rights organizations were founded at the end of the 1960s and the beginning of the 1970s, including the International Work Group for Indigenous Affairs (1968), Survival International (1969), and Cultural Survival (1972). Numerous organizations were also formed by indigenous peoples themselves, such as the American Indian Movement (AIM), founded by Indian activists in 1968, and various indigenous regional organizations such as those in the Amazon and Andean regions of Latin America. The objectives of these groups varied considerably, but one overarching goal was the protection and promotion of the human rights of indigenous peoples.

Social and political movements in the developing world gained traction in Southeast Asia, Africa, Latin America, and the Pacific in the latter part of the twentieth century. Governments opposed to these movements often perceived such activism as being secessionist in nature, something that, in fact, was rarely the case. In Central and South America, as Jackson and Warren note, "During the past three decades, armed conflict, especially in Guatemala, Peru, and Colombia, has produced severe political repression, hundreds of thousands of indigenous deaths, and over a million indigenous refugees and internally displaced persons."[3]

In May 1992, a declaration and charter (The Kari-Oka Declaration and the Indigenous Peoples Earth Charter) was issued by representatives of indigenous peoples from around the world who attended the World Conference of Indigenous Peoples on Territory, Environment, and Development held in Brazil prior to the Earth Summit (the World Conference on Sustainable Development of the United Nations) in June, 1992, and both addressed the issue of genocide. More specifically, the Kari-Oka Declaration stated that "We continue to maintain our rights as peoples despite centuries of deprivation, assimilation, and genocide." The document concluded by asserting that the United Nations Convention on Genocide must be changed to include a discussion of the genocide of indigenous peoples.[4] Questions were also raised about the impacts of transnational corporations on indigenous peoples, an issue that was addressed by the United Nations Forum on Indigenous Peoples in 2008-2009.[5] Indigenous peoples also sought meetings with government officials regarding remedies for ways in which they had been treated, and they engaged in demonstrations, one example being the takeover in 1973 by American Indian activists at Wounded Knee on the Pine Ridge reservation in South Dakota where Lakota and other Indians were massacred by the U.S. Seventh Cavalry in December of 1890. Indigenous peoples in a number of countries sought apologies and restitution from the governments of the states in which they resided, as was the case, for example, in Australia, New Zealand, and Canada.[6]

At one point in time, the ethnocide and genocide of indigenous peoples were simply considered part and parcel of colonization.[7] Today, however, there are international laws and agreements that outlaw such practices. Be that as it may, these human rights instruments have not brought to an end the decimation of indigenous peoples. This is due in part to the fact that international conventions and declarations on indigenous peoples too often go unenforced, something that is also true for national laws and constitutional protections.

It is a disturbing fact that some governments refuse to recognize groups within their borders as indigenous or, alternatively, treat them differently from other peoples in their countries. Representatives of indigenous peoples are sometimes prevented from traveling to international forums dealing with indigenous peoples (e.g., to the meetings of the United Nations Permanent Forum on Indigenous Issues) or appealing to international agencies such as the World Bank Inspection Panel or the World Court for help. Many governments wish to avoid situations in which indigenous groups seek self-determination. Tellingly, indigenous peoples seeking self-determination and/or greater recognition of their rights often suffer human rights abuse at the hands of the state in which they reside, and some indigenous groups are targeted as "secessionists," "terrorists," or "enemies of the state" (see table 1 for some examples of indigenous groups that have been labeled negatively by governments in the twentieth and twenty-first centuries.) In some cases, genocides occurred when indigenous peoples resisted

Table I.2
Cases of Indigenous Peoples Involved in Liberation Struggles and Social Movements
that have been Defined by Some Nation-States as Terrorist or Secessionist

Conflict	Country, Region	Comments
Fur, Masalit and other black African groups	Darfur, Sudan. Africa	2003-present, war by Sudan and paramilitary units
Harkat-ul-Jihad-al-Islami (HUJI)	Bangladesh, South Asia	Chittagong Hill Tracts groups oppose government policies
Revolutionary Armed Forces of Colombia (FARC)	Colombia, South America	Some of the FARC victims have been indigenous peoples
Liberation Tigers of Tamil Eelam (LTTE), Tamils, Wanniyala-Aeto	Sri Lanka, South Asia	In 2009, LTTE was largely destroyed by Sri Lankan military campaigns
Abu Sayaaf, Moro Islamic Liberation Front, New Peoples Army (NPA)	Philippines, East Asia	Islamic/Maoist groups vs government
Maoists, Naxalites	India, South Asia	Struggle in the Tribal Belt of central and eastern India and other parts of the country
Karen, Hill Tribes	Burma (Myanmar), Southeast Asia	rebel groups, Buddhists, Muslims vs government
Tyua, Ndebele, Kalanga	Matabeleland Province, Zimbabwe, Africa	Zimbabwe state under Robert Mugabe vs opposition groups
Ogoni, Ibibio, Movement for the Emancipation of the Niger Delta (MEND)	Nigeria, Africa	Attacks on oil installations began in 2006
Hmong, Montagnards, Hill Tribes	Laos, Vietnam, Thailand	Vietnam (American) war for liberation, 1950s-1975
Quechua and other Andean Indians, Sendero Luminoso (Shining Path)	Peru, South America	Shining Path (Sendero Luminoso) vs government
American Indian Movement	United States	US defined AIM members as terrorists in the early 1970s
Haddad, Tuaregs	Chad, Africa	Haddad affected by war in Chad and Sudan
Eyle and others in al-Ittihad al-Islamia	Somalia, Africa	groups seeking autonomy and opposing governments
Lacandon Maya and others, Zapatistas	Chiapas, Mexico	January 1, 1994 - present

the take-over of their lands and resources or when they opposed development projects that governments were anxious to implement such as land resettlement programs or hydroelectric dams. In other cases, genocides occurred in the context of conflicts among groups seeking to eradicate potential opponents, as occurred in Guatemala. Indigenous peoples have often lost out in obtaining valuable resources (e.g., minerals, timber, and oil) due to the rapaciousness of governments, private companies, and individuals over the centuries.

Transnational corporations (or those corporations that operate in two or more countries, which are also often referred to as multinational corporations) have been blamed by indigenous peoples for serious human rights violations and for causing social, economic, political, and environmental problems in many parts of the world.[8] Private corporations have been implicated along with nation-states as having carried out genocidal massacres, targeted assassinations, forced resettlement, and ecocide (purposeful destruction of the environment aimed at destroying the resource base and livelihood of a group)

Even a cursory study of the history of contacts between indigenous peoples and other groups, government officials, transnational corporations, and non-indigenous organizations and institutions reveals that indigenous peoples are usually the losers and bear the costs of contact and incorporation into state systems. In relatively few cases have indigenous peoples been able to assume the reins of power in modern nation-states, though some progress is being made in this regard, notably in Latin America. Indigenous peoples, including the Inuit, have been able to assert themselves and to gain political power and autonomy in Greenland and in Nunavut in Canada.

On a different but related issue, it is extremely difficult to obtain accurate statistics on indigenous peoples, particularly those who live in remote areas, who are mobile, or who reside in places where conflict is rife. Obtaining facts on the attacks and decimation of indigenous peoples is even more difficult, and that is true, at least in part, because of the concerted efforts of perpetrators today to destroy evidence of their actions.

Numerous organizations—indigenous rights organizations and human rights organizations, alike (as well as individual activists and scholars)—work indefatigably to assist and report on those indigenous peoples caught in conflict situations and/or victimized by states, paramilitaries, or political groups contending for power. While some of this information includes eyewitness testimonies, other types include data collected from forensic investigations of places where massive human rights violations occurred. As some indigenous spokespersons have pointed out, it is usually the poorest and most marginal peoples who tend to suffer the most from the actions of governments and companies bent on exploiting natural and human resources without considering the social and environmental costs of such activities. If various organizations whose express purpose is the protection and promotion of the rights of indigenous peoples and the efforts of indigenous peoples themselves did not exist, it is surely a fact that many indigenous groups would be in far worse shape than they are at present.

Members of indigenous groups themselves are now learning how to carry out forensic human rights investigations, as is the case, for example, with the Guatemalan Forensic Anthropology team. These investigations serve a number of purposes, one of them being to identify the people who were murdered so that their families can be informed of what happened to them. Another is to compile evidence for use in criminal proceedings against governments or individuals alleged to have been responsible for the murders and disappearances.

To this day, there remains active, and sometimes acrimonious, debate over what to call the ill-treatment of indigenous groups. There are those scholars who view the entire 500 year long history of the expansion of European states into what are now called the Americas, Africa, and Asia, and more recently the Pacific and the Arctic, as a genocidal enterprise.[9] Not all, though, are inclined to agree with such a position.

Likewise, acrimonious debate and disagreement rage among analysts, governments, indigenous peoples' support groups, and indigenous peoples themselves, as to whether specific sets of events —not only modern but contemporary events—can be labeled genocide. Some of these debates have revolved around issues of "intent." This was the case, for example, in the discussions surrounding the treatment of the Ache in Paraguay, who were reported to have been victims of genocide as a result of the actions of the Paraguayan state and various non-state actors, including settlers and faith-based organizations.[10]

Concomitantly, debate continues unabated over which entities have been responsible for the destruction of indigenous groups. For example, governments of nation-states such as Indonesia, Paraguay, and the United States all deny, categorically, that they intentionally destroyed indigenous peoples on the basis of who they were. These same countries have also shown a marked unwillingness to apologize to indigenous peoples for how they were treated.

A number of the above issues are addressed in various chapters in this volume of *The Genocide of Indigenous Peoples: Genocide: A Critical Bibliographic Review*. A brief overview of the contents of the book follows.

Over the years, there has been considerable debate over whether the actions of the United States with respect to indigenous peoples constituted genocide. The varied interpretations of the facts of various events and their causes and consequences raise critical questions about the ways in which scholarship on the North American West and on genocides of indigenous peoples should be pursued (including the significance of documenting the perspectives of the various individuals and groups involved). In "Genocide of Native Americans: Historical Facts and Histriographical Debates," Brenden Rensink addresses these concerns and discusses some of the complexities in the historical debates about the genocide and ethnocide of Native Americans.

In the second chapter, "Genocide in Colonial South-West Africa: The German War Against the Herero and Nama 1904-1907," Dominik Schaller, an expert on the genocide of the Hereros, contributes a chapter that examines the plight and fate of the Hereros at the hands of German colonialists and soldiers in Southwest Africa in 1904. His chapter is particularly valuable as it includes recent research that provides a deeper understanding of the genocide than previously available.

In "Genocide of Canadian First Nations," Andrew Woolford and Jasmine Thomas assert that "There is little academic — and even less public discussion — of genocide in relation to Aboriginal experiences of the colonization and settlement of Canada.... Settler colonialism in Canada involved multi-layered and networked actions that stretched over several hundred years and a broad geographic expanse. The destructive impact of these intertwined assaults is undeniable. But the challenge remains of trying to understand them both in their historical and local specificity as well as through the universal lens of 'genocide.'" The authors take on this enormous challenge in their chapter.

In the next chapter, "The Destruction of Aboriginal Society in Australia," Colin Tatz, a noted genocide specialist based in Australia, observes that "The Australian case [of genocide] diverges from the 'classic' genocides of last century, but the uncommon aspects do not invalidate the case for the crime. Rather, they broaden our narrower Eurocentric templates of what constitutes genocide." In his chapter, he addresses the unique aspects of "Australia's genocidal history"; and in doing so, addresses (1) key controversies surrounding the issue of genocide as it relates to Australia, and (2) various policies, positions and actions of different Australian groups and governments that, according to the United Nations Convention on the Prevention and Punishment of the Crime of Genocide (UNCG), constitute genocidal actions. In his conclusion he states the following: "[Australian] historians writing in the 1970s and 1980s talked of pacifying, killing, cleansing, exterminating, starving, poisoning, shooting, beheading, sterilizing, exiling—but avoided talking about and using the term *genocide*. There is no need for synonyms. Some insist on a 'complete outcome' to warrant the 'g' label; some split hairs between cultural and biological absorption of children; some, however much in vain, chase after non-UNCG definitions of the crime and seek 'more appropriate nomenclature' for the Aboriginal experience; some make awkward and difficult-to-sustain analogies or parallels between Aboriginal and Holocaust victims; and a few insist that only the striped *musselmanner* hanging on the wire in Auschwitz represent 'the true meaning of genocide.' None seem to take into account that the

UNCG's Article III on conspiracy, incitement and complicity treats those actions as seriously as the physical crime itself."

In "Genocide in the Chittagong Hill Tracts, Bangladesh," Jennike Arens discusses a genocide little known about by most people. Therein, she examines the events leading up to the genocidal actions, including the militarization of the Chittagong Hill Tracts (CHT) of Bangladesh, transfer programs that involved the settlement of hundreds of thousands of Bengali in the CHT, and the relocation of indigenous people in strategic cluster villages that not only systematically denied the latter their livelihoods and cultures but resulted in massive killings and violations of their rights. To root out the indigenous peoples' existence, she asserts, their women have been specifically targeted: many have been systematically raped, abducted, and killed. Ultimately, Arens notes that "the indigenous peoples have been systematically robbed of their lives, livelihood, culture and religious freedom on a mass scale. Bengalis who have been victims of genocide themselves during the liberation war in 1971 have turned into perpetrators, inflicting deep traumas on the indigenous population." Concluding her chapter she makes a critical observation and then issues an equally critical warning: "The culture of impunity continues. Unless historical injustices are repaired, impunity is lifted and perpetrators brought to justice, both of the liberation war and of the armed conflict with the indigenous Jumma, a deep trauma on both sides will result in the continuance of this genocidal process."

In their chapter, "Genocide of Khoekhoe and San Peoples in Southern Africa," anthropologists Robert Hitchcock and Wayne Babchuck examine the complex ways in which those peoples who claim indigenous identity were treated over time. They note that there were concerted efforts to eradicate Khoekhoe and San peoples by settlers and by the colonial state governments in what was to become South Africa. While much scholarly attention has been paid to the genocide perpetrated by the Germans against the Herero and the Nama in the early part of the twentieth century, the purposeful destruction of San (Bushmen) in Namibia in the period immediately following the 1904-1907 Herero-Nama genocide is often overlooked, invisible even to the descendants of these peoples and the organizations working with them. Not only did San and other indigenous groups face genocidal campaigns in Zimbabwe in the 1980s, but the murder, disappearance, and rape of members of the Tyua, the VaDema, and other groups continue through the present day in Zimbabwe. One of the responses to the actions of southern African governments has been to take them to court for actions that violated the human rights of indigenous peoples.

In "Ache of Paraguay and other Isolated Latin American Indigenous Peoples: Genocide or Ethnocide?" Robert K. Hitchcock, Charles Flowerday, and Thomas E. Koperski primarily focus on the controversial case of the Ache of Paraguay. While originally said to be a genocide, over the years various scholars have debated the claim. The authors' examination of the debate is instructive and interesting in regard to how various scholars, all good-intentioned, disagree over both what transpired and what to deem it.

Samuel Totten contributes two chapters on genocide in Sudan. In his first contribution, "Genocidal Killings and Genocide by Attrition of the Nuba in Sudan," Totten discusses the root causes of the genocide, the way in which the genocide was carried out, and the ramifications of the genocide of the Nuba. As Totten points out, the very same government that carried out the genocide against the Nuba has more recently been accused of carrying out genocide against the black Africans of Darfur. One has to wonder whether the silence of the international community in response to the Government of Sudan's (GoS) acts of genocide against the Nuba emboldened the GoS to carry out its genocidal assault against the black Africans in Darfur.

In his second contribution on Sudan, "Genocide of Black Africans, Darfur, Sudan," Totten delineates the roots of the crisis in Darfur, presents an analysis of the genocidal actions, and discusses the many and varied ramifications of the first genocide of the twenty-first century. Totten argues that the international community has, once again, failed to act to stop a genocide. Instead of undertaking timely and effective action to quell the violence, the international community has largely engaged in talk, talk and more talk. When it did attempt to move beyond talk, it was quick to reach compromises with the Government of Sudan, most of which left the black Africans of Darfur at the mercy of Government of Sudan troops and the *Janjaweed* (Arab militia).

The volume concludes with another chapter by Totten, "Genocide of the Maya in Guatemala." In addition to addressing the antecedents to the genocidal actions carried out by the state of Guatemala against the Highland Mayas and the genocidal actions themselves, Totten addresses the culpability of the United States in both supporting the right wing dictatorships' genocidal actions (including, training Guatemalan military officials to carry out counterinsurgency efforts that, in effect, constituted a scorched earth program) and providing the Guatemalan government with both verbal praise for its policies and funds and weapons to carry them out.

It should be noted that the express purpose of the inclusion of the annotated bibliography following each essay is to provide readers with a handy reference tool vis-à-vis authoritative and valuable works (articles, chapters, monographs, books) on the subject at hand. Each author was asked to create an annotated bibliography that included the works by the most noted scholars in the field, classics in the field, the most cutting-edge works, and those that any researcher into the topic should not overlook.

When all is said and done, there is a clear message here for genocide scholars and others concerned with crimes against humanity and/or genocide: greater attention must be paid to the plight of all peoples, indigenous and otherwise, no matter how small in scale, how little known, how "invisible" or hidden from view. If such attention is not paid to these societies, they will disappear or will be absorbed into the sizable populations of rural and urban poor who themselves have few rights. "Invisible" and "silent" genocide is just as much genocide as those cases that claim the attention of the mass media and outrage the masses across the globe (if, in fact, that actually happens). Part and parcel of being human rights or genocide scholars involves, or so it seems to us, being activists who seek, along with indigenous peoples around the world, to promote human rights and social justice for all.

Notes

1. Note by Samuel Totten: It was a great pleasure and honor to co-edit this volume with Dr. Robert K. Hitchcock, professor of geography at Michigan State University. Dr. Hitchcock is renowned as an expert on southern Africa, and has studied and worked on the behalf of the Basarwa people (Bushmen) for well over thirty years. I was fortunate enough to travel with his team in Botswana in the late 1970s as they conducted interviews with nomadic and sedentary Basarwa throughout the Kalahari Desert. Over the years, I have sought his advice on issues relating to indigenous peoples and human rights, and have solicited contributions from him for inclusion in special journal issues (e.g., "Teaching About International Human Rights" *Social Education*, volume 49, no. 6, September, 1985) and books (*Century of Genocide: Critical Essays and Eyewitness Accounts* co-edited with William S. Parsons, third edition, Routledge, London, 2009) I have edited or co-edited. His many contributions to this volume have added immeasurably to its depth and value.
2. Bernard Neitschmann (1987). "The Third World War." *Cultural Survival Quarterly* 11(3): 1-16.
3. Jean E. Jackson and Kay B. Warren (2005), "Indigenous Movements in Latin America, 1992-2004: Controversies, Ironies, and New Directions." *Annual Review of Anthropology* 34:549-573. See, especially, p. 552.
4. Kari-Oka Declaration and the Indigenous Peoples Earth Charter, World Conference of Indigenous Peoples on Territory, Environment and Development, 25-30 May, 1992.
5. See "Indigenous Peoples and Industrial Corporations: Fact Sheet." New York: United Nations Permanent Forum on Indigenous Issues, 2009.
6. For excellent discussions of apologies, see Elazar Barkan, *The Guilt of Nations: Restitution and Negotiating Historical Injustices* (New York and London: W.W. Norton & Company, 2000) and Mark Gibney, Rhoda E. Howard-Hassman, Jean-Marc Coicaud, and Niklaus Steiner (Eds.) *The Age of Apology: Facing Up to the Past* (Philadelphia: University of Pennsylvania Press, 2009).
7. Distinctions are often drawn between genocide and ethnocide. For purposes of this volume, genocide refers to the physical destruction of a people, the removal of their children, or the depriving of a group of its ability to reproduce, while ethnocide refers to cultural genocide, or the destruction of a society's culture.
8. See, for example, David Hyndman's *Ancestral Rain Forests and the Mountain of Gold: Indigenous Peoples and Mining in New Guinea* (Boulder, CO: Westview Press, 1994); Robert K. Hitchcock's "Indigenous Peoples, Multinational Corporations, and Human Rights." *Indigenous Affairs* 1997, 2: 6-11; Al Gedicks' *Resource Rebels: Native Challenges to Mining and Oil Corporations* (Cambridge, MA: South End Press, 2001); Laura Westra's *Environmental Justice and the Rights of Indigenous Peoples: International and Domestic Legal Perspectives* (London: Earthscan, 2008), pp. 219-222.
9. For an enlightening discussion of this complex issue, see Elazar Barkan's "Genocides of Indigenous Peoples: Rhetoric of Human Rights" in *The Specter of Genocide: Mass Murder in Historical Perspective*, Robert Gellately and Ben Kiernan (Eds.) (Cambridge: Cambridge University Press, 2003), pp. 117-139.
10. See Hitchcock, Flowerday, and Koperski, this volume; Richard Arens (Ed.) *Genocide in Paraguay* (Philadelphia, PA: Temple University Press, 1976); cf. Kim Hill and Ana Magdalena Hurtado's *Ache Life History: The Ecology and Demography of a Foraging People* (New York: Aldine de Gruyter, 1996), pp. 168-169.

1

Genocide of Native Americans: Historical Facts and Historiographic Debates

Brenden Rensink

Introduction

One of the most sobering themes that underlie North American history is the demographic collapse that Euro-American contact initiated among many of the continent's indigenous peoples. As twentieth-century scholars consider the post-contact unfolding of Euro-American and Native American histories and the ways in which they have become inextricably intertwined, their oft-divergent trajectories raise immediate questions of causality. There is no doubt that contact with Euro-Americans served as the catalyst for sea changes in Native America, but the demographic decline apparent in historical retrospect was not an inevitable outcome to be imposed upon historical actors or events. To presume that the tragic fate of many indigenous peoples was unavoidable precludes carrying out any inquiry into the causal relationships between cultures, empires, and individuals.

This chapter explores some prominent issues in the field of Native American studies germane to the field of genocide studies. The primary foci are upon philosophical debates, historiographic trends, and the relative virtues and challenges presented by the current body of scholarship. The accompanying set of annotated entries considers both sides of this spectrum: the praiseworthy and the problematic. Doing so should provide a clearer picture of the state of Native American genocide studies.

Troublesome Trends

While many historical events could be investigated within the framework of comparative genocide studies, recent trends in Native American genocide research have often been deterred from such prolificacy. Worthwhile scholarship has not been altogether arrested, but rather, impeded. Foremost, debates and arguments over the very definition of "genocide," and whether it should be applied to Native American history have overwhelmed the scholastic vigor of aspects of the field of genocide studies. On one hand, historians dedicate energy extolling their reasons for terming events as genocide and on the other critics lambaste such efforts. Israel Charny (1996) feared that "such intense concern with establishing the boundaries of a definition" might ultimately downplay the historical realities of human tragedy or infamy (p. ix). While using genocidal terminology too liberally can prove equally damaging to useful scholarship, excessive definitionalism must not come at the cost of moving scholarship forward. Some Native American scholarship focusing on genocide oscillates between two opposing camps: those that devote energy simply to proving that genocide did occur in Native American history and those that more liberally apply the concept of genocide without sufficient analytical support.

Political Activist Foundations

An emotive a subject as any, the ongoing and intense debate and contrasting opinions in genocide scholarship should be no surprise, but the polemical tone which some of this dialog has incorporated is troubling. The genesis of this trend lies in the political activist foundations that underpin much of the contemporary Native American studies field. In the late 1960s, a new brand of Native American political activity, identity and call for Native self-determination gave birth to a prolific body of literature. Much of this literature pointed to historical narratives for support of their political causes.

Prominent and influential figures such as the late Vine Deloria, Jr., who wrote various treatises critiquing the contemporary state of affairs in the United States and Native America by placing them within a historical context, was joined by others who sought to expose past injustices in order to foment change. As the body of literature and Native American studies as a field have become more established, the political undertones of those early works have persisted. While political bias or agendas do not inherently create poor scholarship, their predominance does complicate matters of von Rankean objectivity in the context of broader comparative history.

Genocide in Native America

It is within the aforementioned context that scholars in the field debate over how to define genocide and ascertain its applicability in Native American history. Two issues claim prominence in this dialogue: numbers and intent. These are not new concepts to the broader field of genocide studies, but the unique impacts they have had in Native American historiography merit comment. First, if genocide is defined by the number of victims killed, Native American history mourns some of the highest. Although the consensus on such estimates has been tenuous, much of the related demographic debate over pre-contact and post-contact population statistics asserts per capita loss percentages unparalleled in human history (Dobyns, 1983, and Stannard, 1992). If taken at face value and as the only criteria for assessing genocide, one might conclude that Native American history should stand as *the* archetype. However, the accepted legal definition of genocide entails a second important factor: the *intent* to destroy a targeted group in whole or in part. This consideration greatly complicates the issue.

The demographic collapse which Euro-American contact precipitated and perpetuated in Native America spans centuries and involves no less than eight colonial or federal governments, and thousands of distinct indigenous empires, cultures, and confederacies. How does one parse out the overall demographic decline of Native America as a whole into the appropriately specific geographic and chronologic terms? Furthermore, in ascertaining the commission of genocide, taking into consideration the issue of intent, how can such monumental numbers be properly assigned to the intent of innumerable separate and distinct Euro-American – Native American relationships? To label North America's indigenous populations in such monolithic terms is more than problematic. To generalize about the actions and reactions of all officials at the federal, regional and local levels vis-à-vis their treatment of all Native American groups is equally problematic. To attempt to extrapolate from one case where there was clear genocidal intent to all other cases – across centuries and historical contexts – is to rely on inherently faulty methodological processes.

One way to avoid unfairly extrapolating hemispheric or continental conclusions from regional histories is to refocus the scope of such research. While it is possible that a large composite of isolated events may speak to the existence of broader general trends, those more narrowly focused regional histories must be better understood before such conclusions can be fully supported. The concept of genocide in Native American history must first be analyzed in the micro, rather than macro scale. Once the sundry remote histories of possible genocide in Native North America are better documented and interpreted, and boast a more exhaustive historiography, broader generalized study of genocide in North America as a whole will be more productive, balanced, and substantive.

Examples of Genocide in Native America

Genocide or Not Genocide?

A key concept in this proposed approach of more particularized study lies within the bounds of scale, both temporal and geographic. While painting Native American and North American history in broad strokes vis-à-vis the issue of genocide is not possible at this juncture in time as a result of the current state of the field's historiography, careful scholarship has been—and can be—undertaken on a variety of what might be considered, for lack of better terminology, genocidal events.

Throughout the centuries of interaction between Euro-Americans and the continent's numerous indigenous peoples, various events appear as if they may constitute cases of genocide. Upon closer examination, though, some lie in the context of campaigns, relationships, and cultural negotiations which do not stand up to the criteria of being termed genocide. The task of careful scholarship is to delineate where broader non-genocidal narratives digress into specific genocidal events. Some argue that such delineation is irrelevant. Rather than viewing them as aberrations in larger histories, they perceive these isolated events as the "normative expression" of broader Euro-American civilization. Regardless of where one falls on this debate, the specific events in question must be better understood individually before collective guilt can be drawn (Jaimes, 1992, pp. 3, 5).

An example of a genocidal event that has featured prominently in the field's historiography is the Sand Creek Massacre of 1864. On the morning of November 29, 1864, the Colorado Third Cavalry, under the command of Colonel John M. Chivington, attacked the sleeping encampment of Chief Black Kettle's Cheyenne and Arapaho at Sand Creek. The resulting scene left a large number of unarmed Native American men, women, and children dead, their bodies mutilated by Chivington's men. This horrific event has received considerable attention from scholars due to certain statements made previous to the attack. In authorizing Chivington's Third Cavalry in their 100-day tour of duty, Colorado Governor John Evans gave instructions to "kill and destroy, as enemies of the country, wherever they may be found, all such hostile Indians" (U.S. Congress, House of Representatives, 1865, p. 47). It was later reported that Chivington echoed this policy by pronouncing his goal to "kill and scalp all, little and big; that nits made lice" (U.S. Congress, Senate, 1865, p. 71).

Taken together, a specific group was singled out for utter destruction, and the actions of the Colorado Third Cavalry on the cold morning of November 29, 1864, indicate that such intent was actualized in the massacre of members of that defined group.

The massacre at Sand Creek is perhaps the most prominent event which has been examined as a genocidal event in North American history, but most certainly does not stand alone. The field's historiography features similar events for which some have suggested the need for consideration. First, in 1851, California Governor Peter Burnett called for a "war of extermination" to continue "until the Indian race becomes extinct" (Madley, 2008, p. 309). Governor Burnett's declaration was aimed broadly at the various Native groups in northern California whose presence was deemed deleterious to the development of the region and its new-found mineral wealth. Governor John McDougal, who followed Burnett as governor, echoed similar sentiments, stating that if negotiations with Natives were unproductive, the Natives would wage war, which would, by necessity, result in the "extermination [of] many of the tribes" (Madley, 2008, p. 310). For years to follow, the Yuki Indians of Northern California's Round Valley (present Humboldt and Mendocino Counties) were severely decimated by this policy, losing tens of thousands of their population (Baumgardner, 2005, p. 34). In this case, the intent to utterly extirpate groups of California Natives was declared, and in the case of the Yuki, actualized. These are the facts that have attracted the interest of certain genocide scholars.

There are also events which have been presented in genocidal terms due to their shocking brutality, but lack the specific declarations of intent that were clearly evident in the cases of the Sand Creek Massacre and Round Valley Wars. One year before the Sand Creek Massacre, a less publicized event in Cache County, Idaho (then southwestern Washington territory), took place that ended up bearing striking similarities to Chivington's attack on Black Kettle's sleeping encampment. As settlers came into increased contact with Shoshoni populations in the region, tensions ran high and U.S. Army detachments were eventually dispatched. The protracted conflict which followed reached a climax on January 29, 1863, on the banks of the Bear River, when Colonel Patrick E. Connor's command attacked Shoshoni Chief Bear Hunter's encampment. The attack left up to 400 Shoshoni dead, some of whom were unarmed, and was followed by the raping of Shoshoni women and killing of Shoshoni children. Unlike the precursory inflammatory language in the Sand Creek case, no such pronouncements of genocidal intent were made in the case of the Bear River Massacre.

Likewise, attention has focused on the Battle of Washita River on November 27, 1868, and the infamous Wounded Knee Massacre of December 28, 1890. Unarmed Cheyenne women and children were counted among the fallen at the Washita River, as were arguably noncombatant Miniconjou and Hunkpapa Lakota women and children at Wounded Knee Creek. With such cases, the horror of the events was unquestionable but the underlying historical context of each was not explicitly genocidal.

In understanding the continental contexts of intercultural conflict, both the events, which may eventually be classified as genocidal and those which may more appropriately be deemed tragedies that fall outside the genocide paradigm, offer historical understanding and insight. It is in these micro-histories, be they of genocide or of other forms of violent altercation, that the groundwork for broad conclusions may be based. All such events, regardless of whether genocidal intent was declared or not, share a role in the overarching narrative of, Euro-American expansion, Native American resistance and cultural misunderstanding.

Other Conceptualizations of Genocide

The production of ongoing scholarship of intertribal conflict is expanding historical understanding of genocide outside the traditional dichotomy of white-Native conflict. For example, the recently published collection of essays, *Indian Conquistadors: Indigenous Allies in the Conquest of Mesoamerica,* points towards such intertribal complexities (Matthew and Oudijk [2007]). The pioneering work of Richard White (1978), which asked scholars to reorient their view of the Western Sioux to that of an expanding empire, and now followed by Pekka Hämäläinen (2008) in his study of the Comanche as empire, suggest a more complicated historical reality of violence in North America. These studies make no claims of intertribal genocide, however the theoretical shift that such studies provide suggest that further investigation of such possibilities is needed. Effectively, they expand our traditional view outside the binary paradigm of white-Native violence to consider more complex relationships.

On a different note, considerable scholarship has been conducted on the various other "-cides" (e.g., linguicide, culturicide, enthnocide), and no doubt some of those "cides" have contributed to the denigration of Native populations (Adams, 1995). Linguistic genocide (linguicide) and cultural genocide (culturicide) have both received significant scholarly attention. The nineteenth- and twentieth-century efforts of the United States government to forcibly assimilate Native peoples into "American" society by discouraging or criminalizing Native culture, language, and religion, are all being examined as forms of one "cide" or another. Finally, the role of sexual violence as a form of genocide adds another facet to the current historiography (Smith, 2005; and Fleisher, 2004, pp. 293-298). Whatever spirited or polemical debates result from these and future studies, the study of the various forms, examples, and conceptualization of genocide in North America can, if properly and fairly executed, add to a broad field of knowledge, ready and ripe for comparative analysis with similar work being done elsewhere.

What are the Critical Challenges Facing the Field Today?

Certainly the impediments of definitionalist debates, political bias and polemical rhetoric must be surmounted. To whatever degree possible, the ever present desire to assign guilt to historical parties, which more often than not does more to satisfy contemporary sensibilities of justice than to move historical understanding forward in any significant way, must be jettisoned. Bias inherent in any scholarship places the proverbial set of blinders on the scope, interpretation, and conclusions of historical study. Scholarship suffering from the latter often adheres more to political activism than the tenets of objective historical methodology.

When embroiled in contemporary political and cultural discord between disparate concerned parties, this will prove difficult. Native American scholars, especially those with close cultural, familial, and personal ties to the historical accounts they investigate, may have fundamentally different aims than those of less personally invested scholars. These personal motives are significant and important. Scholarship which helps Native communities today with their sense of cultural identity, political awareness, and historical foundations are paramount for all involved in the multitudinous facets of Native American studies. The best scholarship, however, will offer understanding and relevance to a much broader demographic.

Perhaps the call for a new kind of Native American genocide scholarship has simply been lost in the mix. Other voices for equally worthy topics have swung the field in various directions in recent decades, but widespread enthusiasm for Native genocide studies has not yet taken that center stage. The growing list of publications in the field, however suggest that momentum is growing.

The Real Probabilities of Progress in the Field

Discerning the why's and how's of genocide, genocidal events, and overall intercultural violence in North America promises to provide something of much broader value: the groundwork for meaningful comparative study. Perhaps it is this angle that may provide Native American genocide studies the momentum and exposure it needs to come to the forefront of broader associated fields. Thankfully, a growing number of scholars are focusing their attention on Native American histories and, in various cases, the comparison of such with other groups across the globe. From comparing the conquest of defiant Sioux and Zulus in the nineteenth century, to the role of women in indigenous child removal and boarding schools of Native Americans and Australian aborigines, the possibilities for comparative scholarship in general are limitless (see, for example, Gump, 1996, and Jacobs, 2005). In terms of comparative genocide studies, those possibilities are invaluable – both to indigenous populations worldwide, to Native American communities and to members of the so-called dominant cultures implicated in these tempestuous histories.

Conclusion

The historiography of genocide studies in North America and Native America is slowly emerging. By avoiding the pitfalls of largely fruitless definitionalist debates over whether or not widespread genocide occurred in North America and polemical work that constitutes unsatisfactory scholarship, scholars are bound to make valuable contributions to the literature. With an expanding foundation of balanced and carefully researched regional or thematically narrow studies, broader applications will likely be forthcoming. That, in turn, will likely result in a deeper and more significant understanding of the events that unfolded in North America in years past.

References

Adams, David Wallace (1995). *Education for Extinction: American Indians and the Boarding School Experience*. Lawrence: University of Kansas Press.

Baumgardner, Frank H. (2005). *Killing for Land in Early California: Indian Blood at Round Valley, 1856-1863*. New York: Algora Publishing.

Charny, Israel W. (1996). "Forward." In Alan S. Rosenbaum (Ed.) *Is the Holocaust Unique? Perspectives on Comparative Genocide*. Boulder, CO: Westview Press.

Congress, House of Representatives (1865). "Massacre of the Cheyenne Indians," *Report on the Conduct of War*, 38th Cong., 2nd Session, 1865, Part III.

Congress, Senate (1865). "The Chivington Massacre," 39th Cong., 2nd Session, 1865, Senate Report 156.

Dobyns, Henry F. (1983). *Their Numbers Become Thinned: Native American Population Dynamics in Eastern North America*. Knoxville: The University of Tennessee Press.

Fleisher, Kass (2004). *The Bear River Massacre and the Making of History*. Albany: State University of New York Press.

Gump, James O. (1996). *The Dust Rose Like Smoke: The Subjugation of the Zulu and the Sioux*. Lincoln: University of Nebraska Press.

Hämäläinen, Pekka (2008). *The Comanche Empire*. New Haven, CT: Yale University Press.

Jacobs, Margaret D. (2005), "Maternal Colonialism: White Women and Indigenous Child Removal in the American West and Australia, 1880-1940." *Western Historical Quarterly* 36(4), 453-476.

Jaimes, M. Annette (Ed.) (1992). *The State of Native America: Genocide, Colonization and Resistance*. Boston, MA: South End Press.

Madley, Benjamin (2008), "California's Yuki Indians: Defining Genocide in Native American History." *Western Historical Quarterly* 39(3):309.

Matthew, Laura and Michel R. Oudijk (Eds.) (2007). *Indian Conquistadors: Indigenous Allies in the Conquest of Mesoamerica*. Norman: University of Oklahoma Press.

Smith, Andrea (2005). *Conquest: Sexual Violence and American Indian Genocide*. Cambridge, MA: South End Press.

Stannard, David E. (1992). *American Holocaust: Columbus and the Conquest of the New World*. New York: Oxford University Press.

Weitz, Eric D. (2005). *A Century of Genocide: Utopias of Race and Nation.* Princeton, NJ: Princeton University Press.

White, R. (1978). "The Winning of the West: The Expansion of the Western Sioux in the Eighteenth and Nineteenth Centuries." *Journal of American History* 62(2): 319-343.

Annotated Bibliography

Adams, David Wallace (1995). *Education for Extinction: American Indians and the Boarding School Experience, 1875-1928.* Lawrence: University of Kansas Press. 396 pp.

An important issue in the concept of cultural genocide is the boarding school program implemented for Native American youth across the country in the late nineteenth to early-twentieth centuries. Adams gives a detailed account of how the boarding school system, geography, curriculum and philosophy sought to systematically dismantle Native children's cultural upbringing. By analyzing the day-by-day occurrences at Indian boarding schools during a fifty-year time period, Adams provides an important context for the statement by Richard Henry Pratt (founder of the Pennsylvania Carlisle Indian School), that his goal was to "Kill the Indian, Save the Man." This is a significant synthesis of primary and secondary research, and an invaluable resource for understanding the United States' attempts to assimilate Native peoples through childhood education.

Baker, Bob (1968). *Americans in Bondage: California's Dark History of Indian Slavery and Extermination and the Continuing Oppression of the Klamath River-Yurok Indians.* Fairfax, CA: Allan Morris. 20 pp.

This early report, written by journalist Bob Baker in the midst of political turmoil on the Northern California Hoopa Valley Indian Reservation, lays out an argument linking past extermination attempts to contemporary socio-political affairs. Though the term genocide is not employed, his short pamphlet presents an intriguing picture into early attempts to address contemporary Native issues with the history of past injustices. Very much in the vein of Vine Deloria, Jr., Helen Hunt Jackson, John Kenneth Turner, and others.

Bradford, William C. (2006). "Acknowledging and Rectifying the Genocide of American Indians: 'Why is it That They Carry their Lives on Their Fingernails?'" *Metaphilosophy* 37 (3-4): 515-543.

Providing commentary on physical extermination, land theft, cultural oppression, termination, relocation and forced sterilization, Bradford (a former law professor) presents a useful overview of many of the key issues facing current political debates of how to redress injustices Native American communities have faced historically. Most interestingly, Bradford's detailed analysis of the various ways in which redress may be enacted leads to his conclusion that the United States should use this as a moment to provide leadership and stand at the forefront of global indigenous issues.

Carranco, Lynwood, and Estle Beard (1981). *Genocide and Vendetta: The Round Valley Wars of Northern California.* Norman: University of Oklahoma Press. 384 pp.

Though the work of Carranco and Beard is narrowly focused, both geographically and chronologically, its potential for comparative application is broad. By detailing the struggle between Northern Californian Indians such as the Yuki and white settlers, miners, and military forces, this study asserts that these various white groups actively sought the extermination of the Round Valley region's indigenous populations. It lacks significant amounts of direct comparative analysis, but provides a detailed case study for such future research to utilize. Furthermore, it presents detail and information that add to earlier works (e.g., Garry Garrett's "The Destruction of the Indian in Mendocino County, 1856–1860," MA Thesis Sacramento State College, 1969). Combined with other more recent scholarship, a full picture of the Round Valley Wars and the genocidal themes in the region's history are well defined.

Churchill, Ward (1994). *Indians are Us? Culture and Genocide in Native North America.* Monroe, ME: Common Courage Press. 382 pp.

Despite the inherent bias and nonacademic tone of Churchill's study, *Indians are Us?* does succeed in presenting ways in which international understanding of genocide and genocide-related legal issues should be applied to events and trends in Native American history. Specifically, he details episodes from twentieth century U.S. history that provide evidence for his case of past and current genocidal intent being exhibited by the United States and its citizenry.

Churchill, Ward (2004). *Kill the Indian, Save the Man: The Genocidal Impact of American Indian Residential Schools.* San Francisco, CA: City Lights Books. 128 pp.

The concept of the United States' Indian Boarding School program in the nineteenth and twentieth centuries contributing to the physical and cultural genocide of Native Americans is not exclusive to this text. Herein, Churchill makes greater strides towards integrating this narrative into more international contexts of comparative genocide studies. Churchill argues that the curriculum, physical infrastructure, and underlying philosophy of boarding school programs were all aimed at erasing Native culture, language, and even life by forced assimilation of children. Churchill provides copious footnotes to support his claims, but the overwhelming bias in both his prose and unbalanced selection of sources undermines some of the text's value. Nevertheless, it does contribute useful information that can be extracted through careful and judicious analysis.

Churchill, Ward (2001). *A Little Matter of Genocide: Holocaust and Denial in the Americas, 1492 to the Present.* San Francisco, CA: City Light Books. 531 pp.

A Little Matter of Genocide represents Churchill's most exhaustive and unbalanced treatise on Native American genocide. The bias and polemics often present in his writings are represented here in their strongest form, but the text is not without merit. Churchill compiles a phenomenal amount of information and presents useful foundations for future scholarship. His source material is extremely useful if careful reading of the sources cited is undertaken. The latter is imperative as close examination of his footnotes reveals that some citations are misleading and that quotations are taken out of context.

Churchill, Ward (2002). *Struggle for the Land: Native North American Resistance to Genocide, Ecocide, and Colonization.* San Francisco, CA: City Lights Books. 460 pp.

Herein, Churchill narrows his focus to how issues of land management and environmental policy have become intertwined with Native genocide and survival. This text adds another important facet to our understanding of an oft-overlooked aspect of the implications of U.S. colonization, and geographic expansion vis-à-vis the environments they encountered. These altered landscapes, ecosystem, and geographies had direct impact on Native populations and cultures.

Costo, Rupert and Jeannette Henry Costo (Eds.) (1987). *The Missions of California: A Legacy of Genocide.* San Francisco, CA: The Indian Historian Press. 246 pp.

California boasts an impressive historiography of its colonial and federal history, but the presence of the dense indigenous populations which Spanish colonizers met is somewhat lacking. This edited volume explores a variety of issues concerning this early history. It contains essays on the Spanish mission system, Native perspectives on the mission era, and a report of a scholar's opinions of the lasting influence of Father Junipero Serra. Together, these resources suggest that the mission to civilize California's Native populations was often enacted through vicious means and, whether intended or not, had genocidal consequences.

Deloria, Vine Jr. (1969). *Custer Died for Your Sins: An Indian Manifesto.* New York: The Macmillan Company. 279 pp.

Nowhere in this text, or elsewhere in his prolific writings, does Vine Deloria directly equate events in Native American history with genocide. However, this seminal text laid the foundational groundwork upon which nearly all such subsequent studies have been built. In *Custer Died for Your Sins*, Deloria made some of the first cohesive arguments along the line that current Native American problems were directly caused by—and thus, should be rectified by—the United States government. He details past and current U.S. government policies that precipitated disastrous consequences for the continent's indigenous peoples. In doing so, Deloria most notably cites the Termination policy of the mid-twentieth century, the preoccupation of anthropologists with "saving" Native culture and the deleterious effects of missionary efforts among Native peoples.

Dobyns, Henry F. (1983). *Their Numbers Become Thinned: Native American Population Dynamics in Eastern North America.* Knoxville: The University of Tennessee Press. 378 pp.

By exploring ways in which demographers can ascertain the pre-Columbian population levels of various North American regions, Dobyns' (an anthropologist) overarching conclusion supports the general idea that regardless of what exact pre-contact population levels were, dealings with Euro-American civilization triggered universal demographic collapse. His estimate regarding pre-contact populations (as high as 18 million) has been critiqued by some as too high.

Fleisher, Kass. (2004). *The Bear River Massacre and the Making of History.* Albany: State University of New York Press. 352 pp.

The Bear River Massacre of 1863 provides a shocking picture of violence and depredation that has perhaps been overshadowed by the more heavily publicized Sand Creek Massacre of 1864. Fleisher examines a broad spectrum of issues that detail not only the history leading up to the massacre and the massacre itself, but its aftermath as well. This text is of particular import in its analysis of the formation of historical memory. Applying theories of historical memory to this Native American history bolsters the overall value of the text.

Freeman, Michael (1995). "Puritans and Pequots: The Question of Genocide." *New England Quarterly* 68 (2): 278-293.

In response to Steven T. Katz's 1991 article questioning the application of the concept of genocide to North American history, Freeman analyzes Katz's take on the 1630s Pequot War ("The Pequot War Reconsidered" in *The New England Quarterly*). In that conflict, colonists from Massachusetts Bay and the Plymouth

Colony allied with Narragansetts and Mohegans to eliminate the Pequot tribe of present day Connecticut. Freeman concludes that calling the Pequot War genocide does not imply any sort of comparison with Nazi Germany, but rather acknowledges the event for what it was: "nation-destruction" as a part of "nation-building." Freeman's arguments, when compared with Katz's original statement provide an essential foundation for understanding much of the political debate amongst scholars over defining genocide and applying it to North American history.

Friedberg, Lilian (2000). "Dare to Compare: Americanizing the Holocaust." *American Indian Quarterly* 24 (3): 353-380.

Artistic director of the Chicago Djembe Project, which promotes cross-cultural understanding through public arts programs, Friedberg applies her expertise in German studies to better understand links between Jewish Holocaust studies and Native American studies as the latter relates to genocide. While some Holocaust historians have borrowed from Native American history in exploring their histories, the same cooption of Holocaust history has not been afforded to Native American scholars. Friedberg presents an interdisciplinary analysis of using the Holocaust in comparative terms with Native American history and shows why doing so has proved so controversial.

Hauptman, Laurence M., and James D. Wherry (Eds.) (1990). *The Pequots in Southern New England: The Fall and Rise of an American Indian Nation*. Norman: University of Oklahoma Press. 288 pp.

As a whole, this edited volume offers a broad and firm foundation for understanding the context in which the Pequot War (which some refer to as a genocide) can be best understood. Of particular import is Laurence M. Hauptman's chapter entitled "The Pequot War and Its Legacies." Therein, he argues that the Pequot War is one of the most important events in early American history because it laid a foundation of white-Native relations that included the possibility and actualization of genocide. In understanding the attempted extirpation of Pequots by allied colonists and Native groups, Hauptman examines the legacy of the latter on modern

Pequots, their self-identity and contemporary struggles for self-determination and tribal recognition.

Jaimes, M. Annette (Ed.) (1992). *The State of Native America: Genocide, Colonization, and Resistance.* Boston, MA: South End Press. 468 pp.

This edited work includes a number of provocative essays. Contributors such as Jaimes (the editor of the book), Ward Churchill, Lenore A. Stiffarm, and Phil Lane, Jr. all comment on the genocide of Native Americans. While some of the text waxes strongly political in its agenda and bias, distracting from objective historical understanding, it is still a valuable resource for understanding the contemporary political climate surrounding Native American studies and genocide.

Katz, Steven T. (1991). "The Pequot War Reconsidered." *New England Quarterly* 64 (2): 206-224.

In this essay, Holocaust historian Steven Katz addresses the history of the 1630s Pequot War and whether it should be discussed in comparative terms with the Jewish Holocaust of World War II. Katz asserts that the demographic collapse of the indigenous New World is without precedent and stands as the "greatest demographic tragedy in history" (p. 223). However, for a variety of reasons, Katz argues that direct comparison with the Holocaust is problematic. In so doing, Katz opened a lively debate in both the fields of Holocaust Studies and Native American Studies.

Katz, Steven T. (1995). "Pequots and the Question of Genocide: A Reply to Michael Freeman." *New England Quarterly* 68 (4), 641-649.

After Katz had published his 1991 article "The Pequot War Reconsidered," Michael Freeman answered in 1995 with "Puritans and Pequots: The Question of Genocide." In publishing Freeman's piece, the *New England Quarterly* offered Katz the opportunity to concurrently reply to Freeman's critique of his work. In his response, Katz does not back down from his previous assertions, but does refine them somewhat, showing how Freeman perhaps misunderstood his original 1991 statements. Taken as a whole with the two other pieces, the Katz-Freeman dialogue is a fascinating study in how and why the opposing sides apply or do not apply the concept of genocide to Native American history as a whole and the Pequot War in particular. This dialogue has broad applicability to both of the fields of Holocaust Studies and Native American Studies.

Lewy, Guenter (2004). "Were American Indians the Victims of Genocide?" *Commentary*, September, 55-63.

In the midst of increasing debate concerning genocide in Native American history, Lewy, a professor emeritus of political science and the author of a number of very controversial works on the Armenian genocide and the fate of the Roma and Sinti during the Holocaust, attempts to synthesize and bring together disparate voices into the debate. Lewy seeks to discuss a few key issues and events that have been predominant in these dialogues. In particular, Lewy discusses the role of disease in decimating Native populations, the complicity of U.S. Army officials in purposefully spreading disease, the early violence between Natives and Puritan settlements, and the much debated Sand Creek Massacre, Round Valley Wars, and the mid- to late-nineteenth-century Indian Wars of the Great Plains. This provides a useful, albeit slanted, introduction to the debate as a whole. Lewy concludes that although extermination was at times implemented, it was never the policy of the U.S. government. Hence, he argues, the history involved was a tragedy, but did not constitute genocide.

Madley, Benjamin (2008). "California's Yuki Indians: Defining Genocide in Native American History." *Western Historical Quarterly* 39(3): 303-332.

Building on past work about the Yuki Indians of Northern California's Round Valley, Madley offers a concise explanation of why Yuki decimation constitutes genocide. Trying to more coherently link on the ground factual history with broader issues of U.S. federal and California state policy, Madley makes a convincing case. His introductory statement concerning the 1948 United

Nations Genocide Convention definition of genocide is useful in framing his subsequent presentation of Yuki history. That said, the UNCG definition could have been better integrated as an analytical anchor to the article before concluding that the "Yuki catastrophe [fits] the two-part legal definition set forth by the United Nations Genocide Convention." Nevertheless, Madley's work stands as an excellent example of a useful case study micro-history.

McDonnell, Michael A., and Moses, Dirk (2005). "Raphael Lemkin as Historian of Genocide in the Americas." *Journal of Genocide Research* 7 (4): 501-529.

This article provides an analysis of Raphael Lemkin's writings prior to that of his 1944 coinage of the term *genocide,* and how they relate to Native American history. This is a significant contribution to the growing scholarship linking genocide studies with Native American studies. McDonnell and Moses illustrate how Lemkin's study of colonial and pre-colonial history were instrumental in his original conception of genocide.

Neu, Dean, and Therrien, Richard (2003). *Accounting for Genocide: Canada's Bureaucratic Assault on Aboriginal People.* Winnipeg, MB: Fernwood Publishing - Zed Books. 192 pp.

The work of Neu and Therrien aims to show the bureaucratic structure of Canadian Indian policy which often led to genocide of Canada's First Nations peoples. The discussion of aboriginal genocide in terms of financial accounting and bureaucratic structuring is chilling. Behind the more public violence of genocide lies a deep and carefully constructed framework of governmental policy. Like work concerning U.S. Indian policy and bureaucracy, direct analysis of Canadian documents concerning the genocidal effects of policy, bureaucracy and finances could prove fruitful.

Rosenbaum, Alan S. (Ed.). *Is the Holocaust Unique? Perspectives on Comparative Genocide.* Boulder, CO: Westview Press. 288 pp.

There are two chapters in this volume of particular import: Steven Katz's "The Uniqueness of the Holocaust: The Historical

Dimension," and David E. Stannard's "Uniqueness as Denial: The Politics of Genocide Scholarship." Both speak to the underlying debate over whether or not comparative genocide studies should be undertaken. Both address issues related to Native American history.

Scheper-Hughes, Nancy (2001). "Ishi's Brain, Ishi's Ashes: Anthropology and Genocide." *Anthropology Today* 17 (1): 12-18.

   This article discusses the controversy over the repatriation of indigenous ancestral remains and the relationship between Native American anthropology and historical genocides, ethnocides and demographic mass destruction. The author uses the example of Alfred Kroeber, an University of California anthropologist in the early twentieth century, and Ishi, the last remaining Yahi of Northern California. Upon "discovering" Ishi, Kroeber employed him as a janitor and studied him as a sort of living specimen. Subsequently, Ishi's preserved brain was forgotten and rediscovered in 1999, opening a new debate about repatriation of ancestral remains. Relatively little direct commentary is made of the extinction of Yahis in California, but the underlying framework of Scheper-Hughes' brief article, which calls into question past and current anthropologic study when underwritten by the realities of past genocides, is intriguing and worth consideration.

Smith, Andrea (2005). *Conquest: Sexual Violence and American Indian Genocide.* Cambridge, MA: South End Press. 250 pp.

   Andrea Smith's study presents a shocking chronicle and analysis of cultural and genetic genocide via sexual violence. Her study is deeply rooted in the gendered history of rape as a tool of genocide. Other significant issues include the sexual violence built into the Indian boarding school system, issues of Native women's reproductive rights, and ways in which Native bodies were used during medical experiments. Smith's deconstruction of the Native body and its role as a battleground for colonization and associated genocidal results is a worthwhile contribution to Native American studies, genocide studies and the burgeoning field of decolonization and gender studies in North America.

Stannard, David (1992). *American Holocaust: The Conquest of the New World.* New York: Oxford University Press. 358 pp.

Stannard's history of the conquest of America by European powers stands at the forefront of a body of literature that came forth around the 500 year anniversary of Columbus' "discovery" of the American continents. As part of an effort to reorient how the public viewed this historic anniversary, Stannard presents colonization in terms of repeated European atrocities and de facto genocide in a variety of forms perpetrated by a variety of groups. The text is informative and useful as a general reference, but plagued and ultimately devalued by the author's overbearing bias.

Thornton, Russell (1990). *American Indian Holocaust and Survival: A Population History since 1492.* Norman: University of Oklahoma Press. 312 pp.

Following in the footsteps of Henry Dobyns' earlier work, Russell Thornton reinvestigates the demographics of Native America from 1492 onward. Finding Dobyn's pre-contact estimate of 18 million too high, Thornton provides a well-supported argument for something in the range of 5 million plus. Others find this estimate too low, and so the debate continues on. When coupled with the work of Dobyns, a still uncertain, but clearer picture can be ascertained of the situation. Analyzing ecosystems and calculating the pre-contact populations they could sustain is no exact science, but these works provide much of the statistical data used by others to make their case for or against the genocide of various indigenous peoples of North and South America.

Tinker, George E. (1993). *Missionary Conquest: The Gospel and Native American Cultural Genocide.* Minneapolis, MN: Fortress Press. 196 pp.

Providing a detailed examination of the role of Christianity and the conversion attempts of various groups, Tinker offers four case studies of prominent missionaries (the Franciscan Junipero Serra, the Puritan John Eliot, the Jesuit Pierre-Jean de Smet, and the Episcopalian Henry B. Whipple) through which broader conclusions can be made. Offering a wide chronological and geographic sampling, Tinker concludes that although intentions may have been pure, the results of these missionizing efforts were often devastating.

2

Genocide in Colonial South-West Africa: The German War against the Herero and Nama, 1904-1907

Dominik J. Schaller

Introduction

The fate of the Namibian Herero and Nama became a highly contested international issue after Germany's defeat in World War I. British politicians and newspapers, in particular, denounced Germany's unparalleled cruelties in its African colonies. The brutal suppression of indigenous resistance in South-West Africa 1904-1907, which resulted in the murder of about 60,000 Herero and 10,000 Nama, served as the prime example of the Germans' inability to develop their colonies for the benefit of the Africans. British efforts to investigate colonial massacres committed more than a decade earlier, though, were not at all inspired by humanitarian reasons; what the British needed was a credible and convincing case for adding German South-West Africa to their colonial holdings.

The 1918 published "Report on the Natives of South-West Africa and their Treatment by Germany" was the basic evidence for the British colonial claims. After the capture of Namibia by South African troops, British authorities ordered Major Thomas Leslie O'Reilly to collect all possible information about German atrocities against the African population. O'Reilly's report concentrated on the German colonial war (1904-1907) against the Herero and Nama, and contained statements by fifty African survivors. Although O'Reilly's report served a political purpose it is still an important and valuable historical source for the reconstruction of the events in Namibia as it provides Western historians with rare written African testimonies.

When Raphael Lemkin (1900-1959) was working on a global history of mass violence spanning from antiquity to the twentieth century he resorted to the British report in order to analyze the consequences of German colonial rule in Africa. Lemkin shared British ideas about Germany's colonial incompetence and had no doubts about the Germans' genocidal intentions in South-West Africa:

> The Germans did not colonize Africa with the intention of ruling the country justly, living in peace with the true owners of the land and developing its resources for the mutual advantage of both races. Their idea was to settle some of the surplus German population in Africa and to turn it into a German white empire.... It was undoubtedly this idea which encouraged the policy of deliberate extermination. (Lemkin, n.d., pp. 49-50)

In his original concept of genocide, Lemkin emphasized that the new term did not exclusively characterize the immediate physical destruction of an ethnic or religious group. He recognized the processual nature of genocide and differentiated between two phases, "one, destruction of the national pattern of the oppressed group; the other, imposition of the national pattern of the oppressor." Furthermore, Lemkin argued this imposition "may be made upon the oppressed population which is allowed to remain or upon the territory alone, after removal of the population and the colonization of the area by the oppressor's own nationals." The idea of colonization was thus crucial in Lemkin's thinking and work. Therefore, his first broad definition of genocide covers the systematic "disintegration of the political and social institutions, of culture, language, national feelings, religion and the economic existence" of a targeted group (Lemkin, 1944, p. 79).

Consequently, Lemkin not only perceived the outcome of the German war against the Herero and Nama as genocidal but saw the *situation coloniale* as such:

In the German colonies no attempt was made to respect native tribal customs or to invest the chiefs with their former dignity and authority.... The natives were denied all rights and were compelled to perform forced labor for officials and colonists so that they lived in a state of enslavement, overworked and undernourished and subjected to degradation and cruelty. The laborers were hunted down like beasts and taken in chains from their villages and forests to work on the plantations and roads, and were unmercifully flogged with rhinoceros hide whips if they made any attempt to escape. (Lemkin, n.d., pp. 18, 50)

Lemkin's approach to the study of colonialism and genocide was innovative because of its emphasis on cultural extermination. Social-anthropologists revitalized this idea in the late 1960s and have referred to the systematic dissolution of indigenous identities and cultural institutions as ethnocide. Unfortunately, Lemkin did not manage to publish his global history of mass violence and his manuscripts on German rule in Africa remained forgotten for decades. The same fate happened to Major O'Reilly's report. When South African and British authorities in Namibia realized that they depended on the cooperation with local German settlers they let the politically explosive report disappear. Copies were removed from public libraries and destroyed. The Foreign Office in London ordered the restoration of all existing copies in the Empire, locked them away and officially consigned the history of the Herero and Nama under German rule to oblivion.

Until recently, most Germans had no idea their country was once a colonial power that "possessed" large parts of Africa. The horrors of World War II had almost totally eclipsed this episode of history. Only a small handful of European experts showed an interest in German colonial history. Among them were some historians from the German Democratic Republic (GDR). Their interest was primarily politically motivated as they perceived the atrocities of German imperialism as a substantial proof of the imperial-fascist foundation of the capitalist German Federal Republic (GFR). Nevertheless, the empirical basis of these works was sound since Eastern German historians had access to the archives of the former colonial office.

Only at the end of the Cold War and Namibia's independence from South Africa in 1990 did the murder of the Herero and Nama attract increased scholarly and public awareness. Then, in autumn

2001, political representatives of the Herero filed a lawsuit against the government in Berlin and three German corporations at the U.S. Federal Court. For the first time an ethnic group demanded reparation for colonial policies that fit the legal definition of genocide. Undoubtedly, the Herero were inspired by the successes of the Holocaust restitution movement. The Herero's demand for historical justice has brought significant pressure upon Germany to come to terms with the dark side of its colonial past. An official apology followed in August 2004. More specifically, the German minister of economic cooperation and development, Heidemarie Wieczorek-Zeul, attended a commemoration ceremony in Namibia and stated the following:

> A century ago, the oppressors – blinded by colonialist fervour – became agents of violence, discrimination, racism and annihilation in Germany's name. The atrocities committed at that time would today be termed genocide — and nowadays a General von Trotha would be prosecuted and convicted. We Germans accept our historical and moral responsibility and the guilt incurred by Germans at that time. And so, in the words of the Lord's Prayer that we share, I ask you to forgive us our trespasses. (Wieczorek-Zeul, 2004, n.p.)

Although Wieczorek-Zeul acknowledged German guilt, the Herero were rather disappointed as the German government rejected the Herero's demand for financial restitution. Politicians in Berlin argued that Namibia is one of the major recipients of German development funds and that preferential treatment shown to one ethnic group could damage political stability in the country.

Today, most scholars of mass violence agree with Wieczorek-Zeul and understand the murder of the Herero and Nama as the first genocide of the twentieth century. However, there is a tendency in scholarly literature to attempt to establish that genocide has to be regarded as an exclusively modern phenomenon and colonial mass violence as a pre-modern occurrence. The proponents of this approach perceive the extermination of the Ottoman Armenians by the Young Turks during World War I and the Holocaust as ideal types of genocide because of the perpetrators' alleged "irrational" motives: nationalism and racism. Colonial atrocities, on the other hand, are often portrayed as "rational" acts of violence that were motivated by greed and the desire for retribution. Such a distinction is artificial and ignores the fact that perpetrators of mass violence never rely on a single motive. As the following discussion of the events in Namibia 1904-1907 shows, the reasons and dynamics of colonial mass violence cannot be understood without considering typically modern concepts and worldviews such as racism and Social Darwinism.

The Historical Background of the German War against the Herero and Nama

The socio-economic and political situation in pre-colonial Namibia can be described as a "raid and tribute economy" that was not inevitably organized along ethnic lines; changing trans-ethnic alliances were rather common. However, in the second half of the nineteenth century the Herero became the dominant force in Central Namibia. A deep social and economic transformation among the Herero had preceded this development: Herero society was originally characterized by social and political decentralization, but as the Herero began to strengthen their position in Central Namibia a gradual process of centralization began. Simultaneously, the Herero managed to build up huge cattle herds and became the leading cattle-breeders in the region. Nama groups in Southern Namibia enjoyed strong economic ties with the Cape Colony and relied on cattle trade. It is estimated that Central and Southern Namibia were inhabited by about 80,000 Herero and 20,000 Nama when Germany claimed South-West Africa as a colony in 1884.

German colonial conquest of Namibia did not follow a well-thought-out master plan. It was rather chaotic and improvised. A major obstacle to the German colonial project in South-West Africa was Berlin's reluctance to provide the colonial administration on the spot with necessary financial and personal resources. These circumstances made German colonial authorities in Namibia dependent on African collaboration. Both the Nama leader Hendrik Witbooi and the Herero paramount chief Samuel Maharero became close allies of the German governor Theodor Leutwein. These two African leaders benefited from the indirect rule practiced by the colonizers because it helped them to secure their contested positions. Political realities on the spot contrasted with the utopian ideas formulated by colonial politicians and propagandists in Berlin: The ultimate goal of the colonization of South-West Africa was the establishment of a white settler colony. Essential requirements of this idea were the abolition of the political institutions of chiefdoms, the seizure of African land, the dissolution of indigenous customs and lifestyles as well as the transformation of the independent African societies into an identity-less proletarian class. Although the available means made the near-term realization of this plan impossible, German colonial authorities agreed with the overall strategic approach and were convinced of the need to eliminate the Africans' political influence and military strength as soon as it was feasible to do so.

It was a natural disaster that helped the German colonizers to shift the balance of power in Central Namibia to their advantage. The *rinderpest* (cattle disease) reached South-West Africa in 1897. Whereas European settlers managed to have their animals vaccinated, the Herero lost almost 90 percent of their herds. Consequently, Herero society went through a deep economic and cultural crisis. Until then the Herero had refused to give their land up to Europeans, but now they had to sell their ancestral lands in order to survive. Many Herero chiefs sold their land at extremely low prices, which caused internal tension and contributed to a profound decline of their legitimacy. Thousands of Herero were forced into European wage labor. This development had far-reaching consequences as it led to a new hierarchy of power between Africans and Europeans and resulted in increasingly brutal behavior of the latter towards the former. Whereas the Africans were gradually losing their influence, the German community prospered. In 1904, South-West Africa's European population was estimated at 5,000. The construction of a railway line from coastal Swakopmund to Windhoek guaranteed further economic expansion and gave reasonable hope to expect the total colonization of Namibia within the foreseeable future.

From Colonial War to Genocide

German settlers had for a long time been waiting for the elimination of the Africans as autonomous actors and their complete subjugation. But they also realized that the colony's military infrastructure was still inadequate for a decisive fight with the Herero and Nama. In such circumstances, a major African uprising could bring the economic and political development in the colony to a standstill. The likelihood of a Herero rebellion became an obsession among European settlers. It was just this paranoid fear in combination with an accumulation of misunderstandings that triggered off the war on 12 January in the Central Namibian town Okahandja.

In the first months of the war, about 8,000 Herero (4,000 armed with rifles) were facing 2,000 German soldiers. The Africans took the initiative; they plundered farms, killed more than 100 settlers and besieged small towns. German reactions were rather helpless at the beginning. But reinforcements from Germany, equipped with machine guns and artillery, brought about a rebound. While the Germans reorganized their troops, the Herero gathered with their families and herds in the Waterberg region because they were hoping to negotiate peace with Governor Leutwein. However, a negotiated solution was no longer an option. Colonial lobbies in Berlin put the government under pressure and insisted on a "final solution" in Namibia. The appointment of a new radical supreme commander for South-West Africa was a concession to these demands.

Lothar von Trotha (1848-1920) was an experienced colonial soldier. He had participated in the war of annihilation against the Wahehe in Tanzania in the 1890s and took part in the suppression of the so-called Boxer Rebellion in China 1900-1901. His worldview was deeply racist and social-Darwinist. The new commander understood the disappearance and extermination of indigenous societies as an inevitable and integral part of the historical process. As the following excerpts from his letters to the German chief of staff reveal, he perceived his duty in South-West Africa as a historical mission consistent with the law of nature:

> From my close knowledge of many Central-African tribes, Bantu and others, I have reached the conviction that the negro does not submit to contracts but only to raw violence.... This uprising [of the Herero] is and remains the beginning of a racial fight.... (von Trotha, 1904, p. 4)

> I know enough tribes in Africa. They all have the same mentality insofar as they yield only to force. It was and remains my policy to apply this force by unmitigated terrorism and even cruelty. I shall destroy the rebellious tribes by shedding rivers of blood and money. Only thus will it be possible to sow the seeds of something new that will endure (quoted in Drechsler, 1980, p. 161).

Lothar von Trotha had no doubts about how to end the war: "My initial plan for the operation, which I always adhered to, was to encircle the masses of Hereros at Waterberg and annihilate these masses at one fell swoop" (cited in Drechsler, 1980, p. 154). As soon as he got a green light from his superiors in Berlin, von Trotha attacked the Herero at Hamakari (Waterberg) on 11 August 1904. German military superiority and von Trotha's will to annihilate the Africans led to a massacre. Although the Herero were militarily defeated, the battle at Hamakari was a failure. The bulk of the Herero escaped from the battle of encirclement and extermination to the neighboring Omaheke desert. The paths to British Bechuanaland followed traditional trade roads. But even though the Herero knew these routes and the most important watering places, the amount of water available was hardly enough to guarantee the survival of the refugees. In order to accomplish his mission, von Trotha ordered his troops to first cordon off the Omaheke and then to kill the survivors. It was the failure of his original plan to exterminate the Herero at Hamakari that made him resort to the systematic and genocidal persecution of the Herero in the Omaheke and the proclamation of the infamous *Schiessbefehl* (shooting order):

> I, the great General of the German troops, send this letter to the Herero people. The Herero are no longer German subjects.… The Herero people must leave the country. If the nation does not do this I will force them with the *Groot Rohr* [cannon]. Within the German borders, every Herero, with or without gun, with or without cattle, will be shot. I will no longer accept women and children, I will drive them back to their people or I will let them be shot at.… (cited in Pool, 1991, p. 251)

The war in South-West Africa did not end with the defeat of the Herero. In October 1904, the Nama chief Witbooi started hostilities against the German colonizers. The Namas' decision to attack the Germans stemmed most probably from their fear of being next in line after the extermination of the Herero. The German war against the Nama lasted three years and differed from their previous fight against the Herero. The Nama avoided open battles and launched systematic guerilla attacks against the German army. The Africans' successful and efficient tactics, the harsh climate, and the inaccessible terrain in Southern Namibia presented the colonialists with considerable problems. Moreover, Lothar von Trotha was under political pressure to end the expensive war and to pacify the colony as quickly as possible, all of which frustrated the Germans and prompted them to engage in scorched earth tactics in which fields and villages were burnt and to deport the civilian population to concentration camps.

Concentration Camps, Forced Labor, Cultural Genocide

Although Emperor Wilhelm II and the German general staff supported Lothar von Trotha's policy of genocide, the civilian government tried to replace him with a more controllable supreme commander once the threat of losing control in the colony was over. German settlers in South-West Africa, in particular, disapproved of von Trotha's determination to exterminate all the Herero and Nama. For them, the defeat of the Africans was the perfect opportunity to obtain control over indigenous manpower.

Ultimately, it was the immense costs of the war that led to increased political pressure. This development strengthened the position of the civilian government regarding colonial policy. Lothar von Trotha received orders to repeal his genocide order and to cooperate with representatives of the Rhenish mission. The missionaries were entrusted with the gathering of African survivors and their transfer to concentration camps in the coastal areas of Central and Southern Namibia.

The refugees who had already been very weak when they arrived in the camps suffered from the harsh and cold climate at the Atlantic coast. Malnutrition and insufficient sanitary equipment contributed to the distress of the detainees.

The concentration camps in South-West Africa served different purposes. First, army personnel who were still in favor of a "final solution" welcomed the deaths of thousands of Africans in the camps. In March 1907, the command of the colonial army reported that 7,682 out of a total of 17,000 inmates in the camps had died within a period of two and a half years (Report of the Schutztruppe, n.d., p. 151). Mortality among African prisoners was thus almost 50 percent. Therefore, the German treatment of the Herero and Nama in the concentration camps can be understood as a continuation of Lothar von Trotha's genocidal practice.

Second, another function of the concentration camps was of an economic nature. They served as work camps, providing public and private entrepreneurs with slave laborers. Thus, the Germans saw the concentration of the surviving Africans as a solution to the chronic shortage of labor that had endangered the economic development of the colony. The construction of the Otavi railroad would not have been possible without the efforts of 2,000 African forced laborers, whose mortality was about 30 percent.

The state of war in Namibia was officially terminated on 31 March 1907. Although the Africans were released from captivity, the demolition of their culture and socio-economic institutions continued incessantly. Already during the war, German colonial authorities had prepared the systematic legal disenfranchisement and expropriation of the Herero and Nama. Moreover, German policy in South-West Africa aimed at the suppression of autonomous indigenous groups. For this purpose, the deputy governor, Tecklenburg, proclaimed that all indigenous tribal organizations ought to come to an end. The so-called native decrees of 1907 restricted the Africans' freedom of movement gravely and forced them to carry a tiny identity badge around the neck. The colonizers' obsession with control over the Herero and Nama grew relentlessly and manifested itself in more radical and totalitarian utopias. Settlers, for example, suggested the tattooing of all African laborers in order to identify them more easily. Although neither the Herero nor the Nama posed a threat to the colonial order after 1904 the Germans were still afraid of indigenous rebellions. In order to contain this danger, colonial authorities in Windhoek and in Berlin considered large-scale deportations of Herero and Nama to the German colony in Papua New Guinea. The realization of these plans of social-engineering, however, was averted by Germany's defeat in World War I and the loss of its overseas possessions.

Conclusion: Challenges to the Study of the German Genocide in South-West Africa and Probabilities of Progress

Germany fought several colonial wars in Africa. The so-called Maji-Maji-War in East Africa 1905-1907 is almost completely forgotten outside Tanzania although it cost even more African lives than the war against the Herero and Nama. Italian atrocities in Libya 1923-1933 and the British suppression of the Mau-Mau movement in Kenya 1952-1957 were equally brutal and devastating as the German campaign in Namibia. However, it is the fate of the Herero and Nama that has gained considerable scholarly and public attention in the last five years and is widely recognized as *the* imperial genocide. What are the reasons for this development?

When the Herero People's Reparation Corporation filed a lawsuit against Germany and three German companies in September 2001, it was clear that the plaintiffs would encounter numerous political and legal obstacles. In order to increase moral pressure and fuel public emotions, the Herero emphasized that the murder of their ancestors had to be seen as an important precursor of the Holocaust: "Foreshadowing with chilling precision the irredeemable horror of the European Holocaust only decades later, the defendants [the three German companies] and Imperial Germany formed a German commercial enterprise which cold-bloodedly employed explicitly-sanctioned extermination, the destruction of tribal culture and social organization, concentration camps, forced labor, medical experimentation and the exploitation of women and children in order to advance their common financial interests" (Superior Court of the District of Columbia Civil Division, 2009, p. 21).

The Hereros' claim motivated many historians to resort to Hannah Arendt's thesis of the colonial roots of totalitarian regimes in Europe and to historicize the Holocaust in a postcolonial way. Indeed, the search for transnational links between these two genocides is an attractive task for historians and scholars of mass violence and has significantly contributed to the incorporation of the German genocide in Africa into global collective memory. However, many of these studies lack a serious empirical foundation and suggest a simplified monocausal connection from the murder of the Herero to the Nazis' persecution of European Jewry. Such a simplified approach cannot do justice to any of the cases. Moreover, it renders the study of German rule in South-West Africa rather Eurocentric and neglects African agency. The historiography of the German genocide in Namibia has for a long time ignored African resistance to the colonial claims and thus contributed to a pathologization of the Herero. The Herero were usually portrayed as helpless victims whose fate was sealed forever. To describe the situation in post-genocidal Namibia historians resorted to the expression of the "silence of the graveyard" (see Drechsler, 1980). Only in recent years have historians analyzed the survival strategies of the Herero and Nama and documented the reconstruction process Herero society went through. Although German colonial ambitions were totalitarian, Africans found ways and means to resist them and to preserve their identities and customs. Furthermore, the Herero undertook sophisticated nation-building after 1904 and developed different coping mechanisms and creative forms of remembrance. Future anthropological and historical studies will have to deal with these aspects and examine the repercussions of the Hereros' and Namas' demands for historical justice and financial restitution for postcolonial nation- and identity-building in present-day Namibia.

References

Drechsler, Horst (1980). *Let Us Die Fighting: The Struggle of the Herero and Nama against German Imperialism*. London: Zed Press, p. 161.

Lemkin, Raphael (1944). *Axis Rule in Occupied Europe: Laws of Occupation – Analysis of Government-Proposals for Redress*. Washington DC: Carnegie Endowment for International Peace, p. 79.

Lemkin, Raphael (n.d.). The Germans in Africa. Unpublished and undated typewritten manuscript. Jacob Rader Marcus Center of the American Jewish Archives, Hebrew Union College, Cincinnati, Raphael Lemkin Papers, Box 6, Folder 12, pp. 49-50.

Pool, Gerhard (1991). *Samuel Maharero*. Windhoek: Gambsberg Macmillan, 251.

Report of the *Schutztruppe* on the Mortality in German Concentration Camps. GFA, R1001: 2140, 151.

Superior Court of the District of Columbia Civil Division (2001). Herero Case. Accessed at: http://www.ipr.uniheidelberg.de/Mitarbeiter/Professoren/Hess/HessForschung/ zwang/herero.pdf (17 October 2009). Quote from p. 21.

Trotha, Lothar von (1904a). Letter to the chief of the German General Staff von Schlieffen, October 1904, German Federal Archive, Berlin Lichterfelde, Reichskolonialamt 1001, 2089, p. 4.

Trotha, Lothar von (1904b). Proclamation. 2 October 1904, German Federal Archive, R1001, 2098, 7f.
Wieczorek-Zeul, Heidemarie (2004). Speech Presented at the commemorations of the 100th Anniversary of the Suppression of the Herero Uprising, Okakarara, Namibia, 14 August 2004. An English version of the speech can be found on the website of the German embassy in Windhoek: http://www.windhuk.diplo.de/Vertretung/windhuk/en/03/Bilaterale__Beziehungen/seite__rede__bmz__engl__okakahandja.html (last accessed 17 October 2009).

Annotated Bibliography

(Compiled by Dominik J. Schaller and Samuel Totten)

Andersson, Rachel (2005). "Redressing Colonial Genocide Under International Law. The Herero's Cause of Action against Germany." *California Law Review*, 93:1155-1189.

Andersson asserts that current scholarship largely overlooks the illegality of specific forms of genocide under nineteenth century international law, and as a result of that wars of annihilation perpetrated by colonial administrations are not generally understood or looked at as violations of international law. She argues that such a stance has incorrectly led to the conclusion in contemporary scholarship to date (2005) that the Herero people of Namibia have no cause for action to claim reparations for the German-Herero War of Annihilation (1904-1907). She goes on to assert that "an analysis of contemporaneous international law reveals that, at the end of the nineteenth century, wars of annihilation were considered violations of international law. More specifically, the 1885 Berlin Convention required the preservation of the African peoples and conferred third-party beneficiary rights to certain indigenous peoples of Africa. The Herero Nation was one of these peoples. This paper attempts to reestablish their formal legal liability as a result of the re-remembering of the actionable rights of the peoples of Africa."

Bley, Helmut (1971). *South-West Africa under German Rule 1894-1914*. London: Heinemann. 303pp.

Bley discusses the socio-economic and political development of German South-West Africa. His nuanced account shows how German colonial policy in Namibia was shaped by different interest groups: settlers and their lobbies, colonial administrators, army, and business men. Bley analyzes Governor Leutwein's system of "divide and rule" and explains why it failed. Another focus of the study is the portrayal German colonial officials' efforts to establish a system of totalitarian control over the Africans after 1904. This classic study is based on archival research.

Bridgman, Jon M. (1981). *The Revolt of the Hereros.* Berkeley and Los Angeles: University of California Press. 184 pp.
    A study of the German destruction of the Herero of German Southwest Africa in the first decade of the twentieth century. A key theme of the work is how racism contributed to the oppression and mass murder of the Herero.

Bridgman, Jon, and Clarke, David E. (Eds.) (1965). *German Africa: A Select Annotated Bibliography.* Stanford, CA: Hoover Institution. 120 pp.
    Contains information on primary and secondary documents on the Herero uprising in southwest African in the early part of the twentieth century and the concomitant reaction of the German colonialist power.

Bridgman, Jon M, and Worley, Leslie (2009). "Genocide of the Hereros, pp. 15-50. In Samuel Totten and William S. Parsons (Eds.) *Century of Genocide: Critical Essays and Eyewitness Testimony.* New York: Routledge.
    This chapter consists of a short essay that provides an overview of the genocide of the Herero and accompanying first-person accounts of the genocide.

Bühler, Andreas Heinrich (2003). *Der Namaaufstand Gegen die Deutsche Kolonialherrschaft in Namibia.* Frankfurt am Main: IKO-Verlag für Interkulturelle Kommunikation. 435 pp.
    The fate of the Nama has often been neglected in the historiography of the German colonial wars in South-West Africa. Bühler's study fills this gap. He discusses the impact of German colonization on the different Nama groups and sheds light on Hendrik Witbooi's motives to wage war against the Germans after the military defeat of the Herero in 1904.

Cooper, Allan D. (2006). "Reparations for the Herero Genocide: Defining the Limits of International Litigation." *African Affairs* 106 (422): 113-126

Cooper analyzes the 2001 legal arguments put forth by the Herero as they became the first ethnic group to seek reparations for colonial policies (in this case, against Germany) that fit the definition of genocide, and the latest plaintiff to use the procedures of the Alien Torts Claim Act of 1789 to seek reparations in a U.S. federal court for war crimes committed overseas. The author also identifies the challenges that lie ahead for this claim, and explores the implications of the Herero claim for other ethnic groups victimized by colonization.

Dedering, Tilman (1999) "'A Certain Rigorous Treatment of All Parts of the Nation': The Annihilation of the Herero in South West Africa, 1904," pp. 205-221. In Mark Levene and Penny Roberts (Eds.) *The Massacare in History*. New York: Berghahn Books.

In this chapter, Dedering discusses the events leading up to and eventuating in Von Trotha's genocidal strategies against the Herero.

Dedering, Tilman (1993). "The German-Herero War of 1904: Revisionism of Genocide or Imaginary Historiography?" *Journal of Southern African Studies*, 19(1):80-88.

The author examines Namibian historiography of the German war against the Herero and asserts it has been dominated by European writers. He encourages post-independence Namibian historians to write the history of their own country.

Drechsler, Horst (1980). *"Let Us Die Fighting": The Struggle of the Herero and Nama against German Imperialism (1884-1915)*. London: Zed Press. 277 pp.

Drechsler published the first major account of the German colonial war in South-West Africa in 1966. He was the first German historian who labeled the suppression of the Herero uprising a genocide. Drechsler's work is empirically based as the author had access to the archives of the former *Reichskolonialamt* (colonial office) in Potsdam. The book is a classic and marked the state of knowledge until the 1990s.

Förster, Larissa (2008). "From 'General Field Marshall' to 'Miss Genocide': The Reworking of Traumatic Experiences among Herero-Speaking Namibians." *Journal of Material Culture*, 13(2): 175-194.

This article examines the ways in which the Herero today commemorate the slaughter of their brethren in Southwest Africa in the early years of the twentieth century. In her abstract, Förster writes as follows: "The colonial war of 1904-8 in Namibia still features prominently in contemporary Namibian memory culture. Above all, Herero-speaking Namibians have created various practices by which the war is commemorated annually. Seminal are commemorative rituals held in different areas of Namibia and organized by a ritual and social network established in the aftermath of the war. These commemorations provide a stage for the continuous reworking of the memory of defeat and flight, of dispersal, displacement and genocide, but also of survival and reorganization. The employment of uniforms in the commemorative practices of Herero-speaking Namibians is but one example for the way such memory work is also embodied in material culture. Historic as well as more recent developments of Herero memory culture are scrutinized in an appraisal of different images and representations of the past."

Gewald, Jan-Bart (1999). *Herero Heroes: A Socio-political History of the Herero of Namibia, 1890-1923.* Athens: Ohio University Press. 310 pp.

This book examines the Herero struggle in South-West Africa to fend off the German colonialist effort to subjugate them. In doing so, it describes and discusses the destruction of the Herero by the German colonialists as well as the reemergence of Herero society around the structures of the German colonial army and Rhenish missionary movement.

Gewald, J.B. (2004). "The Herero and Nama Genocides, 1904 – 1908," n.p. In Dinah Shelton (Ed.) *Encyclopedia of Genocide and Crimes Against Humanity.* New York: Macmillan.

A short but authoritative encyclopedic entry about the history of the genocide of the Herero.

Gewald, J.B. (2004). "Imperial Germany and the Herero of Southern Africa: Genocide and the Quest for Recompense," pp. 59-77. In A. Jones (Ed.) *Genocide, War Crimes and the West: History and Complicity*. London: Zed Books.
A discussion of the genocide of the Herero, and the attempts of Herero today to be granted reparations.

Gerwarth, Robert, and Malinowski, Stefan (2007). "Der Holocaust als "Kolonialer Genozid"? Europäische Kolonialgewalt und Nationalsozialistischer Vernichtungskrieg." *Geschichte und Gesellschaft* 33: 439-466.
The authors critically analyze the current scholarly discussion about links and structural similarities between European colonialism and German National Socialism. Following the recent publication of books on the allegedly genocidal nature of German colonialism and the role of the Herero and Nama wars as a precursor of and model for the German war of extermination in Eastern Europe, Gerwarth and Malinowski examine the allegedly "exceptional" character of the German colonial wars within the broader trans-national context of colonial violence. They argue that German policy in Namibia 1904 was in fact very much in line with common European colonial standards.

Hull, Isabel V. (2005). *Absolute Destruction. Military Culture and the Practices of War in Imperial Germany*. Ithaca, NY: Cornell University Press. 384pp.
The author identifies Prussian military culture as a crucial catalyst for the radicalization and escalation from colonial war to genocide. Hull examines the cumulative internal pressures on the colonial army in Namibia to resort to the use of genocidal violence.

Kössler, Reinhart (2004). "Sjambok or Cane? Reading the *Blue Book*." *Journal of Southern African Studies* 30:3:703-708.
Kössler discusses the value of *The British Blue Book* as a historical source. Although the report served a political purpose it is an important document for the reconstruction of the events in South-West Africa 1904-1908. The affidavits and testimonies collected in the

Blue Book not only shed light on colonial warfare but on everyday oppression in Namibia during the closing decade of German rule. Nevertheless, Kössler argues that the African voices in the *Blue Book* were filtered through a pro-British discourse. This is why the author pleads for a close and critical reading of the "Report on the Natives of South-West Africa and their Treatment by Germany."

Krüger, Gesine (1999). *Kriegsbewältigung und Geschichtsbewusstsein. Realität, Deutung und Verarbeitung des deutschen Kolonialkriegs in Namibia 1904 bis 1907.* Göttingen: Vandenhoeck and Ruprecht. 344 pp.

Krüger deals mainly with the social reorganization of the Herero after 1904. She argues that the funeral of Samuel Maharero in 1923 was a crucial event in the reformulation of Herero identity and describes the emergence of the idea of a Herero nation as an invented tradition. The author analyzes oral testimonies such as Herero praise songs and examines how the Herero remember the war and its devastating consequences. Krüger's important study was the first attempt to portray the experiences of Herero women and children during and after the colonial war.

Krüger, Gesine (2005). "Coming to Terms with the Past." *GHI Bulletin*, Fall, No. 37: 45-49.

The author discusses how Germany is being confronted with its past actions in Southwest Africa, both as a result of the centenary of the Herero rebellion and because the Herero People's Reparation Corporation filed a claim for restitution in 2001.

Lau, Brigitte (1989). "Uncertain Certainties. The Herero-German War of 1904." *Mibagus* 2: 4-8.

The revisionist assumption of the author that the Herero-German war of 1904 cannot be described as genocide caused a heated debate in 1989. Lau rejected the application of the concept of genocide to the events in Namibia, and asserted that applying the concept/term to the war was Eurocentric. However, Lau's plea for an increased awareness of African agency and resistance was innovative at the time.

Melber, Henning (1992). "Kontinuitäten Totaler Herrschaft. Völkermord und Apartheid in 'Deutsch-Südwestafria'. Zur Kolonialen Herrschaftspraxis im Deutschen Kaiserreich." *Jahrbuch für Antisemitismusforschung* 1: 91-114.
This article highlights the continuities between German rule in Namibia and the racial regimes of Apartheid South Africa. Melber identifies Theodor Leutwein, the German governor in Namibia, as one of the inventors of apartheid politics in Africa.

Melber, Henning (Ed.) (2005). *Genozid und Gedenken. Namibisch-deutsche Geschichte und Gegenwart.* Frankfurt am Main: Brandes und Apsel. 204 pp.
The essays in this collection deal with the question how Namibians and Germans deal with their difficult history. The authors show that the German genocide against the Herero and Nama is still a highly contested and politicized issue both in Germany and Namibia. The collection contains articles by Jürgen Zimmerer, Christoph Marx, and Reinhart Kössler.

Pool, Gerhardus (1991). *Samuel Maharero.* Windhoek, Namibia: Gamsberg Macmillian. 359 pp.
A biography of Samuel Maharero, who was the chief of the Herero during their war against the German colonizers in South West Africa at the turn of the century (from the nineteenth to the twentieth).

Sarkin, Jeremy (2008). *Colonial Genocide and Reparations Claims in the 21st Century: The Socio-Legal Context of Claims under International Law by the Herero against Germany for Genocide in Namibia, 1904-1908.* Westport, CT: Praeger Publishers. 320 pp.
Sarkin examines the historical and legal issues surrounding the massacre of the Herero in South West African by German colonialists. In doing so, he examines whether the events constitute legally defined genocide, crimes against humanity, and other international crimes. He does so by evaluating the legal status of indigenous polities in Africa at the time. He also raises key issues regarding issues of current international human rights law, and

draws important conclusions vis-à-vis the development of norms of reparation for indigenous peoples. The book is comprised of the following: "Introduction"; 1. "The Legacy of the Herero Genocide on Namibia Today"; 2. "The Historical and Current Legal Implications of Germany's Conduct"; 3. "The Developing Norm of Reparations and Apologies for Historical Claims: Past, Present and Future"; and "Conclusion."

Schaller, Dominik J. (2004). "Kolonialkrieg, Völkermord und Awangsarbeit in 'Deutsch-Südwestafrika,'" pp. 147-232. In Dominik J. Schaller, e. a. (Eds.). *Enteignet-Vertrieben-Ermordet. Beiträge zur Genozidforschung.* Zürich: Chronos Verlag.

This chapter is based on research in German, Namibian and Finnish archives. It offers an account of Namibia's colonization by Germany and the Herero-German war of 1904 and its consequences for the indigenous societies. The author reconstructs the forced transfer of Nama to Togo and Cameroon and discusses German plans to deport the surviving Herero to Papua New Guinea.

Schaller, Dominik J. (2008). "From Conquest to Genocide: Colonial Rule in German Southwest Africa and German East Africa," pp. 296-234. In A. Dirk Moses (Ed). *Empire, Colony, Genocide. Conquest, Occupation, and Subaltern Resistance in World History.* New York: Berghahn.

Schaller examines the dynamics of violence committed during colonial wars. He argues racism alone cannot sufficiently explain the readiness of German settlers and soldiers in Namibia and Tanzania to resort to genocidal warfare. The reference to racist theories in letters, diaries and published memoirs was more a retrospective justification than a driving factor. The author highlights the importance of a social-psychological approach to colonial violence and shows how German soldiers were in constant fear of ambushes. Rumors about African women committing mutilations were widespread. Schaller concludes the analysis of situational factors such as fear, the course of war, and group dynamics is crucial for an adequate understanding of colonial mass violence.

Schaller, Dominik J. (2009). "Raphael Lemkin's View of European Colonial Rule in Africa: Between Condemnation and Admiration," pp. 87-94. In Dominik J. Schaller and Jürgen Zimmerer (Eds.). *The Origins of Genocide. Raphael Lemkin as a Historian of Mass Violence.* London: Routledge.

The chapter examines Raphael Lemkin's unpublished writings on European colonial rule in Africa. The author shows how Lemkin understood atrocities committed by the Belgians in the Congo and the Germans in Namibia, Tanzania, and Cameroon. Schaller argues Lemkin's perception of colonialism as such was ambivalent. Although Lemkin condemned colonial violence he believed in the ameliorative effect of the European *mission civilisatrice.* The author highlights some problematic aspects of Lemkin's historical scholarship on mass violence in colonial Africa, that is, Lemkin's perception of Africans was racist as he portrays them as them as either weak-willed or helpless victims or as bloodthirsty cannibals. Schaller concludes that Lemkin's lack of adequate ethnographic knowledge made him misunderstand Africa as the "heart of darkness."

Silvester, Jeremy, and Gewald, Jan-Bart (Eds.) (2003). *Words Cannot Be Found: German Colonial Rule in Namibia: An Annotated Reprint of the 1918 Blue Book.* Leiden: Brill Academic Publishers. 312 pp.

The statements in the reprint of the official *British Blue Book* which was originally published in 1918 provides a powerful and disturbing report of the clash between African societies residing in South-West Africa in the early part of the twentieth century and Germany. Tellingly, in 1926, the "Blue Book" was withdrawn from the public domain and marked for destruction. "It is the intention of the authors that this annotated re-publication of the *Blue Book* will, in some measure, be a memorial to those that died."

Steinmetz, George (2007). *The Devil's Handwriting. Precoloniality and the German Colonial State in Qingdao, Samoa, and Southwest Africa.* Chicago, IL: University of Chicago Press. 640 pp.

Steinmetz asserts that Germany practiced different forms of rule in its colonies: they spanned from indirect rule and cultural exchange to genocide. The author seeks to uncover different colonial behaviors and practices by analyzing the impact of pre-colonial European ethnographies.

Stone, Dan (2001). "White Men with Low Moral Standards: German Anthropology and the Herero Genocide." *Patterns of Prejudice*, 35(2):33-45.
 In this article, Stone "argues that although German anthropologists were relatively liberal thinkers before 1900, they nevertheless advocated an understanding of race that encouraged hierarchical thinking. Such thinking saw colonized peoples as primitive and culturally inferior. When, around 1900, anthropologists became increasingly reactionary and drawn to social Darwinist and racist ideas, their work served as a scientific legitimation for colonial atrocity, as the case of the Herero genocide in German South West Africa (1904-1905) demonstrates. At this point anthropologists, along with the colonial military, were more sanguine about the disappearance of 'backward races.'"

Whitaker, Benjamin (1985*). Revised and Updated Report on the Question of the Prevention and Punishment of the Crime of Genocide* (E/CN.4/Sub.2/416/1985/6, 2 July 1985). New York: United Nations. 62 pp.
 Whitaker refers to the atrocities visited on the Herero by the Germans in 1904 as genocide.

Zimmerer, Jürgen (2001). *Deutsche Herrschaft über Afrikaner: Staatlicher Machtanspruch und Koloniale Wirklichkeit im Kolonialen Namibia.* Hamburg: LIT. 329pp.
 The author deconstructs the widespread assumption that Governor Leutwein can be seen as the positive antithesis of Lothar von Trotha. Zimmerer shows that Leutwein's pre-war plans for the development of South-West Africa were thoroughly proto-genocidal.

Zimmerer, Jürgen (2005). "The Birth of the 'Ostland' Out of the Spirit of Colonialism. A Postcolonial Perspective on Nazi policy of Conquest and Extermination." *Patterns of Prejudice*, 39(2): 197-219.

Zimmerer asserts historical analysis of the German conquest of Eastern Europe in World War II has neglected an important tradition that could contribute to a better understanding of the Nazis' policy of extermination: colonial rule. The author argues both colonial rule and Nazi occupation policies in Eastern Europe are structurally similar as they both are based on the same concepts of "race" and "space." The colonial war against the Herero and the corresponding incarceration of Africans in concentration camps are identified as precursors of the Holocaust. Zimmerer concludes that massacres and the destruction of all essentials for life were common practices in both colonial wars and the German war in the East.

Zimmerer, Jürgen (2008). "Colonial Genocide: The Herero and Nama War (1904-9) in German South West Africa and Its Significance," pp. 323-343. In Dan Stone (Ed.) *The Historiography of Genocide*. New York: Palgrave Macmillan.

This chapter offers a valuable overview of the historiography of the German colonial war against the Herero and Nama. Zimmerer notes that many popular memoirs and accounts on the war by contemporaries, which glorify German rule in South-West Africa, are still used by non-historians of German descent in Namibia to dismiss the genocide charge.

Zimmerer, Jürgen, and Zeller, Joachim (Eds.) (2008). *Genocide in German South-West Africa. The Colonial War of 1904-1908 and Its Aftermath*. Monmouth, UK: Merlin Press.

This collection of essays considers the most important aspects of the colonial war in Namibia: the political and socio-economic situation in pre-colonial Namibia, a critical and empirically well-founded discussion of the events, the histories of the concentration camps in Swakopmund and on Shark Island, the organization of forced labor, the fate of women during the colonial war, the reorganization of the Herero after 1904, forms of remembrance in Germany and Namibia, and the representation of the genocide in contemporary German popular literature. Among the authors are: Andreas Eckert, Jan-Bart Gewald, Gesine Krüger, Henning Melber, and Dominik J. Schaller.

3

Genocide of Canadian First Nations

Andrew Woolford and Jasmine Thomas

Introduction

There is little academic and even less public discussion of genocide in relation to Aboriginal experiences of the colonization and settlement of Canada. This is likely a byproduct of the automatic association of the term genocide with mass killing events such as the Holocaust and the Rwandan genocide. In comparison to these cases, the destructive onslaught experienced by Canadian Aboriginal peoples appears on first glance of a different type. Although Canadian Aboriginal persons were at various times subject to massacre and deadly negligence, the most concerted effort to destroy them as groups came through policies of forced assimilation. For this and other reasons, in much historical, sociological, anthropological, and other work on Canadian Aboriginal peoples, the term genocide is either studiously avoided, or qualified as "cultural" genocide.

Some authors, however, do draw on the Holocaust to make claims for a Canadian genocide. In so doing, they seek to show that the Canadian colonial state was engaged in a project to some degree similar to that undertaken by the Nazis (Neu and Therrien, 2002; Annett, 2001). To further supplement these claims, these authors also turn to the United Nations Convention on the Prevention and Punishment of Genocide (1948, hereafter UNGC) for authoritative support in an attempt to demonstrate how the various criteria spelled out in Article 2 of the UNGC are applicable to Canadian colonialism. These writings tend to hold a somewhat marginal status in discussions of Aboriginal/non-Aboriginal relations in Canada, since their arguments are dismissed for being too polemical and/or historically unfounded.

What is woefully absent within the Canadian academic and public spheres is sustained discussion of the question of genocide informed by a "genocide studies" perspective that moves beyond the confines of Holocaust research. Within the still emerging field of genocide scholarship there is intense debate over matters of genocide definition, cultural destruction, and colonial genocide that would have great bearing on the question of genocide(s) in Canada. Yet, to date, few scholars have drawn upon this literature. An exception can be found in the work of Katherine Bischoping and Natalie Fingerhut (1996), who offer an examination of the ways in which genocide studies frameworks limit our understanding of Aboriginal experiences of destruction and the ways in which these frameworks could benefit through engagement with Canadian case studies. More recently, David MacDonald (2007) and Blanca Tovias (2008) have made useful contributions. (For a description of the latter's work, see the accompanying annotated bibliography.) However, there is need for a wider conversation, since Canadian scholarship on genocide is still far behind that in Australia, where the "History Wars" has produced an impressive literature and sophisticated discussion of settler genocide (e.g., Moses, 2008; Van Krieken, 2004). This chapter attempts to advance the Canadian genocide debate by elucidating some of the primary issues for debate and by offering some arguments for consideration.

In particular, we draw upon Aboriginal experiences of colonial destruction to unsettle some of the taken-for-granted assumptions of the Canadian genocide debate. This involves an effort to interrogate notions about what it means to *destroy* a *group* with *intent*, and to demonstrate how these terms are often premised on Eurocentric and modernist assumptions about the nature of collective life.

The State of Affairs Today

Settler colonialism in Canada involved multi-layered and net-worked actions that stretched over several hundred years and a broad geographic expanse. These actions included forms of physical destruction, such as mass killings through settler and state-led massacres and extreme negligence in the form of the unchecked and facilitated spread of disease, as well as the large-scale loss of life within residential schools caused by factors such as poor nutrition and inadequate shelter. But they also involved those collectivity-destroying interventions that are often relegated to the terrain of "cultural genocide," such as the legislation of a uniform and calculable "Indian" identity that could be targeted and policed through state policy, the prohibition of socially constitutive spiritual ceremonies such as the Potlatch and Sun Dance, the imposition of non-indigenous modes of governance, the expropriation of Aboriginal lands, and forced assimilation through schooling and other means.

The destructive impact of these intertwined assaults is undeniable. But the challenge remains of trying to understand them both in their historical and local specificity as well as through the universal lens of "genocide." But this is a difficult balance to maintain. All too frequently destructive events are simply removed from their local conditions and read through a narrowing interpretive gird, such as the UNGC. For example, in the preamble to Article 2 of the UNGC it is stated, "In the present Convention, genocide means any of the following acts committed with intent to destroy, in whole or in part, a national, ethnical, racial or religious group as such." This statement highlights specific factors that need to be addressed within any genocide claim – namely, that a *group* has been subject to an *intentional* act of *destruction*. However, each criterion raises a number of questions and debates that require attention to local understandings of what it means to be a group and how such a group might be destroyed. Thus, the task is one of opening the UNGC so that it can better respond to indigenous interpretations of colonial destruction.

The Target Group

To begin, one cannot speak of an overarching Canadian genocide since there was not a united Aboriginal *people* targeted by *a*

Canadian genocidal campaign. Instead, the landmass that is now Canada is home to a broad diversity of Aboriginal *peoples*. In the early days of European exploration these groups were often perceived to be related tribes that all belonged to the same "Indian race." Subsequently, following settlement and the creation of the Dominion of Canada, legislation such as the Indian Act (1876) formally entrenched this imagined understanding of the Canadian "Indian." Such efforts to homogenize Aboriginal peoples and to make them more governable are part of a destructive process of denying groups their own powers of collective identity formation. Therefore, they should be subject to critical scrutiny within any discussion of genocide rather than facilely taken as the basis for defining the targeted group.

A related issue is the long temporal period over which colonization took place and its regional variations. If we accept that there are diverse and separate groups of Aboriginal peoples in Canada, then we need to examine their particular experiences of colonialism, allowing for the possibility that some Aboriginal peoples may have experienced genocidal destruction, or, "genocidal moments" (Moses, 2000), while others did not. Simply put, the diverse Aboriginal peoples of Canada experienced colonialism in different ways and at different times. Some groups in the North remained relatively cushioned from the initial brunt of colonial land competition (up until the mid- to late-twentieth century, although they would later feel its impact), while Eastern communities felt this pressure much earlier. The driving force behind colonization also differed according to region, with, for example, settlement a more common motivation in parts of Southern Ontario and the Prairies, while resource exploitation was the original primary concern in British Columbia. These significant differences require any discussion of genocide to be based upon local investigations of Aboriginal/non-Aboriginal relations over multiple historical periods.

To take another example, the residential schooling system that was initiated in the late nineteenth century, and made mandatory for all Aboriginal children in 1920, was not equally enforced across the country, and some Aboriginal communities, such as those on the West Coast and in the Prairie provinces, were far more likely to have their children removed than those in Maritime provinces, where few schools were located (MacDonald, 2007). Similarly, there are several destructive experiences that are particular to specific groups and regions, such as food poisoning and massacres of East Coast Mi'kmaq in the eighteenth century and the violence against Aboriginal peoples associated with the gold rush in mid-nineteenth-century British Columbia. In the latter case, tens of thousands of miners entered the mouth of the Fraser River, bringing with them a sense of frontier justice influenced by American-style manifest destiny.

Of course, the question of the group targeted entails more than just identifying the appropriate collectivity and period for analysis. The UNGC flags specific types of groups for protection – national, ethnic, racial, and religious – while ignoring others (e.g., political and class-based groups). In recent years international tribunals have backed away from an overly rigid categorization of potential target groups, but still usually require an "objective" definition that requires the group's socio-historical persistence. Aboriginal groups in Canada arguably would fit these evolving legal interpretations. However, when we seek to force Aboriginal groups into such categories we risk reifying them in a manner that ignores their cultural specificity; in particular, such binding categories fail to capture the negotiated and processual nature of many forms of Aboriginal group life. The genocide literature, stretching back to Raphael Lemkin, has too often essentialized groups, treating these collectivities as though they possess unchanging characteristics and a single set of interests (Powell, 2007). Such an approach fails to capture the adaptability and fluidity of group life, blanketing sameness over what are, in fact, more complex entities.

Thus, the restrictions placed upon group identity by the UNGC are inappropriate and potentially encourage a "totalization" of community life that is itself a danger to Aboriginal group identities. Put differently, by seeking to impose clear community parameters upon Canadian Aboriginal groups, interpreters of the UNGC may mis-categorize these communities in ways that preclude their status as communities engaged in an ongoing and daily process of self-definition and re-definition in a manner that does not result in community closure. Indeed, some Aboriginal peoples consider the experience of enforced closure, through mechanisms like the Canadian reserve system and the "self-governance" arrangements offered by the Canadian government, as part of an ongoing process of attempted colonial destruction.

Eurocentric understandings of Aboriginal peoples have too often portrayed Aboriginal peoples as anachronistic and "frozen in time," ignoring the agency of these cultures and the ways in which they adapt to new challenges. However, many Canadian Aboriginal cultures show a remarkable comfort with collective fluidity, allowing greater opportunity for individuals to shift communal allegiances, welcoming strangers to join their communities, and "sharing" territories with neighboring groups rather than establishing absolute boundaries. Under such circumstances, any attempt to impose categories of ethnicity, nationality, or even "persistence" on such groups represents a potentially destructive limitation on their social ontologies.

What this discussion suggests is that we need to better understand both the particular historical and current patterns of Aboriginal groups before we enter into discussion about their experiences of genocide. For, how can one claim that a group has or has not experienced genocide if little is known about the lived reality of that group's existence?

Group Destruction

This brings us to the question of what it means to "destroy" a group. According to Article 2 of the UNGC there are five ways by which a group might be destroyed: "a) Killing members of the group; b) Causing serious bodily or mental harm to members of the group; c) Deliberately inflicting on the group conditions of life calculated to bring about its physical destruction in whole or in part; d) Imposing measures intended to prevent births within the group; and e) Forcibly transferring children of the group to another group." As noted earlier, some have sought to prove the Canadian colonial government guilty on all five counts. Kevin Annett (2001), for example, in his "truth commission" on residential schooling, suggests that the schools met all five criteria: (1) Large numbers of Aboriginal students lost their lives due to homicide and exposure to disease; (2) Aboriginal students suffered physical, sexual, mental and other forms of abuse at the hands of their instructors; (3) Clothing, nutrition, health care, and housing were so inadequate in some schools that they led to excessive physical destruction; (4) Some students were forced to have abortions or were sterilized; and, of course; (5) students were removed from their communities and required to attend residential schools, or later sent to live with non-Aboriginal families in the "Sixties Scoop."

None of these claims are unfounded, and, yet, such efforts to fit Aboriginal experiences to the criteria of the UNGC tend to feel overly selective. Any sense of the historical trajectory of these developments, including their unintended and elliptical dimensions, is lost within this "cut-and-paste" approach. Residential schools were undoubtedly destructive for many Canadian Aboriginal communities, and few communities were entirely spared from their assimilative reach; however, this does not enable one to make sweeping claims that residential schools were a form of genocide for all Canadian Aboriginal peoples. These schools were part of a broader plan that was genocidal in its intent to, in the words of Duncan Campbell Scott, Superintendent of Indian Affairs from 1913-1932, "get rid of the Indian problem [and]...to continue until there is not a single Indian in Canada that has not been absorbed" (quoted in Titley, 1986, 50). But the project was carried out in an uneven fashion that affected some Aboriginal communities, from which a majority of the children were removed, more than others, from which only a few, if any, children were taken.

Problems also arise when scholars attempt to force comparisons between Canadian colonialism and the Holocaust (MacDonald, 2007). This is apparent when the subject of the spread of disease is broached. Rather than guns or death camps, European diseases such as small pox caused the greatest population loss for North American Aboriginal peoples. In some cases, evidence suggests the purposive spread of diseases (Fenn, 2000), but in many instances these diseases preceded European entry into regions, following along existing indigenous trade routes. However, scholars such as

Stannard (1996) argue that if disease-caused fatalities are included in the death tolls for the Holocaust, so too should they be counted for the "American holocaust." In opposition to this view, critics of Aboriginal genocide claims suggest that the massive loss of life through infection was unintended and largely accidental rather than a structural component of the colonial order. Both sides are perhaps too hasty in their conclusions. While Stannard overstates his claim and seeks to inflate the numbers of lives lost through the genocidal push of colonization, critics ignore that the spread of disease often followed social networks and was subject to political decision-making. Such was the case when it was noticed that Aboriginal persons gathered around Fort Victoria in 1862 were exhibiting signs of small pox infection. Quickly a public uproar arose and called upon the government to evict them. So, rather than quarantine or treat the infected, a gunboat was ordered to escort these Aboriginal persons back to their home communities, ensuring the transmission of small pox up and down the Northwest Coast and into the Interior (see Gough, 1984). Thus, a deadly decision was made based upon a perception that Aboriginal persons, themselves infected with European diseases, represented a threat to European settler society.

In such instances, European diseases provided a form of "biological power" (Mann, 2005) that allowed European colonizers to gain control over previously resistant regions. At least half of the Aboriginal population of between 200,000 and 300,000 people were killed by disease between the beginning of the seventeenth century and the end of the nineteenth century (Miller, 1989). This devastating toll opened vast areas of land to European settlement and allowed for economic exploitation in regions where, in healthier circumstances, the indigenous inhabitants may have been able to repel colonial incursions.

The spread of disease represents a braiding of social and natural processes. However, the UNGC is often read within a modernist framework that assumes a stark nature/culture divide. For example, the five forms of destruction highlighted in Article 2 all presume a decidedly social strategy of elimination. The problem with this presumption for understanding the attempted destruction of Canadian Aboriginal peoples is that it allows the colonizer to avoid responsibility for hybridic assaults on Aboriginal peoples. Disease is conveniently removed as relevant evidence because it is relegated to a natural process. But diseases such as small pox, tuberculosis, and industrial ailments like mercury poisoning were experienced by Aboriginal peoples as consequences of enforced contact with non-Aboriginal peoples, and as part of a structured set of destructive relations, that cannot simply be categorized as "natural." To adequately contend with these experiences we must not preclude certain forms of destruction from consideration; instead, genocide scholars must be ready to interrogate the modernist oppositions that shape our ways of knowing and being in the world.

Overemphasis on the spread of disease, however, can lead one into the trap of calculating comparative death tolls, as though the number of fatalities were the sole standard by which a genocide claim can obtain legitimacy. A deeper engagement with genocide studies, in contrast, allows one to interrogate the claim that genocide is only possible through physical forms of destruction. Recent scholarship has brought to light Raphael Lemkin's notes on colonial genocides, demonstrating that he viewed the multiple and interlinked assaults on indigenous group life to be genocidal (MacDonnell and Moses, 2005). Given the priority Lemkin placed upon the survival of "national" and cultural groups, it is also clear that "physical" genocide is not for him simply a matter of individual killings in the aggregate; rather, it refers to the manner in which the mass loss of life debilitates the continuation of a "group." Given this, it must also be acknowledged that extermination is not the only means available to achieve group destruction, although it is certainly a potent and primary means.

In addition, continuing debates regarding genocide definition have resulted in impressive sociological and anthropological efforts to more clearly define what constitutes the destruction of a group (Powell, 2007; Hinton, 2002), thereby allowing one to more closely examine culturally-specific modalities of destruction. In the Canadian context, such an approach would focus attention on the processes through which particular Aboriginal communities came to be perceived as threats and the various, and even sometimes inconsistent, strategies the colonial or Canadian governments employed to address these perceived threats.

It should be noted, however, that to take the stance that killing is not essential to genocide does not mean that one discounts physical force altogether, since it is difficult to imagine the perpetration of cultural or biological destruction without at least the threat of physical violence. Forced assimilation and land dispossession can only occur if the state possesses a monopoly over the legitimate use of violence, to paraphrase Max Weber (1946). Therefore, so-called cultural genocide remains to some degree a *violent* crime.

Despite the backdrop of a potential for violence, the argument persists that genocide, just like homicide, requires a direct act of violence. But the suggestion that genocide is analogous to homicide is problematic to the extent that groups and individuals are not *killed* in precisely the same manner. While the most direct and obvious path toward group destruction may be through the physical extermination of its members, there are other means to bring an end to this group, and this is why we feel there must be room for consideration of forced assimilation in discussions of genocide. Forced assimilation targets those qualities of a group that make it a source of identity for its members. By denying group members their languages, spiritual practices, cultural traditions, familial and political structures, and other core elements of their social lives, a surgical strike at the capacity of group members to constitute themselves as a group can be achieved. This capacity is a prominent characteristic of many Canadian Aboriginal peoples, and colonial efforts to destabilize these processes of collective identity formation were experienced as an assault on group life.

In sum, the question of group destruction must take into consideration the interlinked and overlapping forces of physical destruction and cultural devastation.

Intention and the Ethos of Colonial Destruction

It is with respect to the question of intent that Canadian Aboriginal genocide claims come under greatest scrutiny. Some would argue that the project of colonial settlement was not guided by an ideological hatred of Aboriginal persons. Instead, Aboriginal individuals were viewed as fully redeemable within settler society—so long as they consented to cultural assimilation. In fact, this was considered an enlightened and liberal perspective in the period of initial settlement since it contrasted with those who viewed Aboriginal peoples as a "dying race" that should be allowed to disappear once and for all. For these reasons, some scholars would suggest that there is no Canadian case of genocide since there is no Canadian colonial intent.

But, despite its progressive claims, this so-called enlightened view of Aboriginality was still built upon a sense that Aboriginal peoples represented a "threat" to colonial society. Whether they were perceived as a potential military danger, an obstacle to economic development, or an impure and abject blight upon the settler's world, at root was a way of seeing and understanding Aboriginal peoples that denied their full humanity. Indeed, underlying all of these sentiments, one can point to an overarching genocidal ethos that shaped colonial viewpoints on Aboriginal peoples.

Colonialism has operated in accordance with an ethos that allows it to present actions that are designed to replace indigenous lifeworlds with the cultural patterns of the colonizers and to do so in a way that makes these actions appear benign and even well intentioned. As van Krieken (2004) states with respect to the experiences of the "stolen generation" of Australian Aboriginal peoples, the source of destruction may lie less in an "unambiguous 'intent to destroy' a human group, than in the presumption that there was not much *to* destroy" (p. 141). In these terms, the assumptive universe of the colonial ethos, although it does not spell out a clear plan of destruction, provides ideational sponsorship for genocidal actions.

The Canadian discussion of genocide would be better advanced through investigation of how Aboriginal experiences of destruction were made thinkable and therefore possible. To do this, one must move beyond a legalistic notion of intent that seeks to locate specific calculations of destruction within the "mind" and mechanisms of a particular "regime." Instead, an understanding of intent is needed that is not predicated on maliciousness, but which also acknowledges the destructive potential of catastrophic forms of misrecognition that emanate from an ethos that devalues populations to the point that assimilation is assumed to be a matter of their general welfare. It was the fact that dominant European imaginings of Aboriginal peoples allowed the latter to be viewed as destitute, backward, uncivilized and savage groups that stood in the path of development and which possessed a notion of "land" irreconcilable with European concepts of "property" (see Bischoping and Fingerhut, 1996). These perceptions fed a "liberal humanism" that refused to acknowledge the specificity of Aboriginal ways of being and furthermore sought to make them disappear.

Occasionally, this destructive ethos found clear expression, such as in the already quoted words of Duncan Campbell Scott. In the U.S. context, a similar sentiment was articulated in terms of the need to "kill the Indian in him and save the man" (Carlisle boarding school for Indian youth founder, Captain Richard Pratt, quoted in Wolfe, 2006, p. 397). At root in these statements, but also in the routine and mundane operations of the colonial world, is a guiding rationality that interprets indigenous forms of group life as both threatening and disposable.

Aboriginal Agency and Adaptation

One of the most powerful criticisms of the claim of genocide(s) in Canada comes not from scholars reluctant to admit any Canadian colonial guilt, but rather from those whose work is intended to increase Canadian understanding of and tolerance toward Aboriginal peoples. The concern held by many in fields such as Native Studies, Aboriginal History, Anthropology, and Aboriginal Politics, is that the term genocide signals the passivity and primordial status of Aboriginal peoples. In other words, when one suggests that Aboriginal peoples were, in some cases, subject to an attempted genocide, this could be taken as a statement that Aboriginal communities existed within a determinate and fixed cultural state and colonial powers simply forced their ways upon them. Such a view would, of course, ignore the capacity of Aboriginal cultures to adapt to and develop through new interactions. Certainly Aboriginal communities did not hesitate to borrow European technologies, norms, or methods when they felt these to be to their advantage.

This is an understandable reaction to the aforementioned essentializing tendency of the genocide studies literature, whereby categories of "race, ethnicity, religion and nation" have too often been taken to be permanent and clearly bounded. However, this view also comes as a result of the continuing influence of the Holocaust on the Canadian genocide debate. In part, it is the residue of descriptions of European Jews going passively to their doom like sheep to the slaughter, evident in the work of Arendt (1992) and Hilberg (1985). This was never a fair description of European Jews, who resisted genocide in both everyday and sustained ways. Indeed, complete passivity in the face of genocide is also not empirically identifiable in any case of which we know. Although genocide studies in its focus on criminally inclined states has tended to emphasize the near absolute power of the perpetrators of genocide, resistance continues even in the most abject of circumstances (such as the cultural, artistic and intellectual life that thrived within the ghetto Theresienstadt and allowed the inmates a sense of empowerment in dehumanizing circumstances). Thus, to speak of genocide in Canada is not to suggest that Aboriginal peoples neither resisted nor adapted to colonization.

Critical Challenges Facing the Field Today

The plight of Aboriginal peoples in Canada, with respect to the question of genocide, faces at least three challenges. First, as has been argued throughout this chapter, the discussion of genocide needs to grow beyond narrow and polarizing questions of whether or not Canadian colonization shares similarities with the Holocaust. Although the Holocaust remains the most infamous example of genocide, it is not paradigmatic of the category. To advance recognition of genocide in Canada scholars need to probe more deeply existent and competing definitions of genocide and to check their applicability to instances of attempted Aboriginal group destruction. In particular, investigation is needed into how particular Aboriginal cultural-linguistic groups experienced the matrix of destructive forces: e.g., violence, disease, legal domination, land appropriation, and forced assimilation. Moreover, this research must extend past academic circles and strive to foster broader public deliberation.

Second, for this discussion to promote meaningful change, critical attention is required to identify the ways in which existing genocide studies' theoretical and methodological frameworks are often situated within a Eurocentric universe that excludes Aboriginal realities. As an illustration, the UNGC addresses environmental destruction only in terms of the effect such destruction has on the survival of the group (e.g., "deliberately inflicting on the group conditions of life calculated to bring about its physical destruction in whole or in part"). However, this does not allow us to address Aboriginal cosmologies in which land and environment are *part of* the group rather than simply their habitat. Peter Kulchyski (2005) describes this sense of territory as an "embodied inscription" that is central to the group's understanding of itself as a collectivity. But prevalent Eurocentric standards in genocidal studies lead us to treat the group and land as linked only in a utilitarian sense. It is a disservice to force Aboriginal experiences of ecological destruction into a framework that only acknowledges the subsistence value of land to a group, even if this move might appear to initially advance their justice claims by clearly locating land and wildlife destruction within the terms of the UNGC. To fully acknowledge the Aboriginal experience of attempted destruction we need to understand land and environment not simply as means for sustaining group life, but as key components of group life.

Oversights such as these can be partially addressed by fostering dialogue with Aboriginal scholars, leaders, elders, and community members. It is not uncommon to hear Aboriginal people speak of genocide when discussing Canadian history, although they are often ignored or dismissed for allegedly using the term for political purposes. However, seldom is effort made to inquire what they *mean* when they use this term. This results in a lost opportunity for improved understanding, which is especially troublesome since we cannot ignore the self-definition and culturally-informed interpretations of any group we claim to want to help protect. In addition, failure to engage with Aboriginal persons on these issues risks continuing the Canadian pattern of paternalism toward Aboriginal peoples by dismissing their claims before even attempting to understand them.

Finally, although the genocide debate may help Canadians better come to grips with their collective history, it cannot become a distraction from contending with ongoing challenges within Aboriginal communities. On most indicators of societal wellbeing, Aboriginal persons measure well below their fellow Canadians. They are more likely to be arrested, have lower incomes, be more susceptible to ill health, have poorer living conditions, and receive less education than their non-Aboriginal counterparts. Conditions are the worst on the poorest reserves, where Aboriginal persons struggle in tragic conditions, still recovering from the societal assault of residential schooling, and witnessing all too frequently physical, mental, and sexual abuse, suicide, and addiction. In these circumstances, we expect they feel that the genocide has not yet ended and will not end until they decolonize their communities and reclaim self-determination.

The Real Probabilities of Progress in the Field

In September 2007, the Canadian courts approved a plan to redress the long-standing injustice of residential schooling. Previous attempts to resolve this issue, such as the federal government's 1996 "statement of reconciliation," which was delivered on Parliament Hill in response to the Royal Commission on Aboriginal Peoples, failed because they did not fully recognize the harms of residential schooling, nor did they provide satisfactory compensation. In the aftermath of the 1996 statement, for example, residential school survivors pressed forward with their civil lawsuits against the government, and a subsequent government effort to create an "alternative dispute resolution" process only resulted in heightened frustrations. Finally, the government consented to a strategy that had been recommended all along—a full apology, compensation payments akin to those provided to World War II-era Japanese Canadian internment camp victims, and a South Africa-influenced Truth and Reconciliation Commission. The apology issued by Conservative Prime Minister Stephen Harper on 11 June

2008 captured more honestly than ever before the damages done to Aboriginal communities through residential schooling, but it stopped short of using the term genocide. For example, Harper stated, "The government now recognizes that the consequences of the Indian residential schools policy were profoundly negative and that this policy has had a lasting and damaging impact on aboriginal culture, heritage and language."

Compensation payments provide an average of $28,000 to residential school survivors—an amount that may vary depending on the number of years spent within a particular institution and any physical or sexual abuses experienced by the claimant. These payments have been welcomed by many members of Aboriginal communities, although the bureaucratic application process has been seen as too cumbersome by some, and has also been criticized for excluding those whose names do not appear on the (not wholly reliable) residential school ledgers. Finally, the Canadian Truth and Reconciliation Commission got off to a rocky start when its first chief commissioner resigned because of a conflict with the other commissioners over control of the vision of the commission and the role it might play in "reconciliation." However, if this commission can recover and spark a national discussion of reconciliation, this will be a welcome accomplishment. In particular, if it allows for broadening Canadian knowledge of the destructive consequences of colonialism for Aboriginal peoples, it will have served at least an initial purpose.

Conclusion

Conditions for Aboriginal people in many parts of Canada are dire. Despite strong networks of Aboriginal activism, mainstream Canada remains largely indifferent to the destructive acts upon which the nation was formed and inattentive to their lingering effects. We contend that a more intensive public understanding of these matters could place the national dialogue more firmly upon a path toward the end of the colonial project. In addition, we suggest that this dialogue will prove more productive if an attempt is made to understand the basic terms of the debate – what it means to be a group, what it means to destroy a group, and what constitutes intent—through a lens sensitive to the various Canadian Aboriginal ways of seeing the world.

References

Annett, Kevin (2001). *Hidden from History: The Canadian Holocaust*. Vancouver: Truth Commission into Genocide in Canada.

Arendt, Hannah (1992). *Eichmann in Jerusalem: A Report on the Banality of Evil*. New York: Penguin Classics.

Bischoping, Katherine, and Fingerhut, Natalie (1996). "Border Lines: Indigenous Peoples in Genocide Studies." *Canadian Review of Sociology and Anthropology*, 33 (4): 481-506.

Fenn, Elizabeth A. (2000). "Biological Warfare in Eighteenth-century North America: Beyond Jeffrey Amherst." *Journal of American History*, 86 (4):1552-80.

Gough, Barry M. (1984). *Gunboat Frontier: British Maritime Authority and Northwest Coast Indians, 1846-90*. Vancouver: University of British Columbia Press.

Hilberg, Raul. (1985). *The Destruction of European Jewry*. Teaneck, NJ: Holmes & Meier.

Hinton, Alexander Laben (2002). "The Dark Side of Modernity: Toward an Anthropology of Genocide," pp. 1-40. In A. L. Hinton (Ed.) *Annihilating Difference: The Anthropology of Genocide*. Berkeley: University of California Press.

Kulchyski, Peter (2005). *Like the Sound of a Drum: Aboriginal Cultural Politics in Denendeh and Nunavut*. Winnipeg, MB: University of Manitoba Press.

MacDonald, David (2007). "First Nations, Residential Schools, and the Americanization of the Holocaust: Rewriting Indigenous History in the United States and Canada." *Canadian Journal of Political Science* 40 (4): 995-1015.

Mann, Michael (2005). *The Dark Side of Democracy: Explaining Ethnic Cleansing*. Cambridge, UK: Cambridge University Press.

McDonnell, Michael A., and Moses, A. Dirk (2005). "Raphael Lemkin as Historian of Genocide in the Americas." *Journal of Genocide Research*, 7 (4): 501-529.

Miller, J.R. (1989). *Skyscrapers Hide the Heavens: A History of Indian-White Relations in Canada*, Revised Edition. Toronto: University of Toronto Press.

Moses. A. Dirk (2008). "Moving the Genocide Debate Beyond the History Wars." *Australian Journal of Politics and history*, 54 (2): 248-270.

Moses, A. Dirk (2000). "An Antipodean Genocide? The Origins of the Genocidal Moment in the Colonization of Australia." *Journal of Genocide Research*, 2 (1): 89-106.

Neu, Dean, and Therrien, Richard (2002). *Accounting for Genocide: Canada's Bureaucratic Assault on Aboriginal People*. Black Point, NS: Fernwood.

Powell, Christopher (2007). "What Do Genocides Kill? A Relational Conception of Genocide." *Journal of Genocide Research*, 9 (4): 527-47.

Stannard, David (1992). *American Holocaust: Columbus and the Conquest of the New World*. New York: Oxford University Press.

Titley, E. Brian (1986). *A Narrow Vision: Duncan Campbell Scott and the Administration of Indian Affairs in Canada*. Vancouver: University of British Columbia Press.

van Krieken, Robert (2004). "Rethinking Cultural Genocide: Aboriginal Child Removal and Settler-colonial State Formation." *Oceania*, 75 (22): 125-150.

Weber, Max (1946). *From Max Weber: Essays in Sociology* (Edited by H.H. Gerth and C. Wright Mills). New York: Oxford University Press.

Wolfe, Patrick (2006). "Settler Colonialism and the Elimination of the Native." *Journal of Genocide Research*, 8 (4): 387-409.

Annotated Bibliography

Annett, Kevin (2001). *Hidden from History: The Canadian Holocaust*. Vancouver: Truth Commission into Genocide in Canada. 113 pp.

This is the report of an informal truth commission chaired by Kevin Annett, a former United Church minister. In the report, Annett takes pains to draw comparisons between Aboriginal residential schooling experiences and the Holocaust, in addition to matching the criteria of the UNGC to the crimes of residential schooling. The report also features testimony from residential school survivors in which they tell of the horrors they faced during their school years, as well as the hardship experienced afterward.

Bischoping, K., and Fingerhut, N. (1996). "Border Lines: Indigenous Peoples in Genocide studies." *Canadian Review of Sociology and Anthropology*, 33(4): 481-506.

In this article, Bischoping and Fingerhut explore the absence of attention to indigenous experiences of destruction within the field of genocide studies. This oversight is, according to the authors, the result of dominant tendencies within genocide studies, such as common emphases on perpetrator motivation and ideology. The authors suggest, in contrast, an approach to indigenous genocides that takes into account culturally-specific experiences of destruction, processes of healing, and interpretations of justice. They conclude that a comparative approach to genocide studies is essential, but that it should include indigenous perspectives on colonial destruction. In particular, Bischoping and Fingerhut argue that genocide studies needs to overcome its Eurocentric biases in order to advance the comparative study of genocide.

Churchill, Ward (2003). *Perversions of Justice: Indigenous Peoples and Angloamerican Law*. San Francisco: City Lights Books. 465 pp.

Although Churchill discusses Canadian Aboriginal peoples in his other books on genocide, such as *A Little Matter of Genocide: Holocaust Denial in The Americas, 1492 to Present* (San Francisco, CA: City Lights Books, 2001), he does so more directly in this volume in a chapter entitled "Forbidding the 'G-word': Holocaust Denial as Judicial Doctrine in Canada." Through a brief overview of Raphael Lemkin's initial framing of the term, and the subsequent drawing of the UNGC, Churchill contends that genocide quite clearly applies to the Canadian context. But he also notes that the government of Canada has been selective in its adoption of the UNGC by accepting only physical killing as constitutive of its judicial understanding of genocide. Having established this broader context, Churchill turns his attention to the struggles of the Lubicon Cree in Northern Alberta, who have long been in contention with the resource exploitation efforts of the Alberta and Canadian governments. Churchill's particular focus is on a Daishawa lawsuit against the Friends of the Lubicon for, among other things, defamation by way of accusing the company of "genocide." The judge argued in Daishawa's favor that the use of the term was inappropriate—a judgment Churchill views as unreflective of the full meaning of genocide and thus as another chapter in colonial holocaust denial.

Davis, R., and Zannis, M. (1973). *The Genocide Machine in Canada: The Pacification of the North*. Montreal: Black Rose Books. 198 pp.

This book outlines how military, economic and social controls are utilized as mechanisms for genocide. The authors assert that the colonial project is inherently violent and that colonization cannot occur without some level of cultural destruction and group displacement. They further suggest that scholars must examine the subject of genocide in their studies of Canadian colonial history so as not to be complicit in genocide suppression. However, Davis and Zannis also repeat the genocide studies truism that both physical and emotional distance contribute to processes of dehumanization. For example, the rush for minerals and oil in the Northern wilderness played a major role in dehumanization, with the language of development and the multi-national corporations taking precedence over the needs and survival of indigenous peoples. Indeed, through the push for capitalist development traditional indigenous ways of life based on living in harmony with the natural environment were eroded in the name of hydro-electricity, forestry, mining, and tourism. This loss led to a decline in the physical and psychological health of these once vibrant and healthy communities, which was compounded by factors such as loss of hunting rights, poor housing, and inadequate sanitation. According to Davis and Zannis, the Genocide Machine ruins the sustainable economies of Aboriginal communities, settles people into permanent reserves that are poorly maintained and do not fit their traditional ways of life, and attacks the value of local cultural traditions. The authors argue that the UNGC must be elaborated in order to deal with these complex issues arising from colonialist projects such as Canada.

Hall, Anthony (2003). *The American Empire and the Fourth World.* Montreal, QC and Kingston, ON: McGill-Queen's University Press. 736 pp.

Hall examines interactions between the Aboriginal peoples of North America and Europeans during the 500 years of colonial conquest and global ideological expansion. He also identifies the philosophical, legal, cultural and social changes that arrived in North America through the logic of possessive individualism and were further exacerbated through economic globalization. Of particular interest to genocide studies scholars are the ways in which Hall illustrates the catastrophic impacts of global multinational corporations on indigenous lands and cultures. Indeed, Hall goes to great efforts to illustrate the physical, cultural, and ecological assault on indigenous peoples. But he also suggests that an intercultural encounter of this scale did not need to end in such destruction. In general, Hall discerns two opposing paradigms as the driving forces of world history. The first seeks to harmonize the diverse cultures and languages of the world into a single system. The second flows from the struggle and resistance of the world's peoples against an aggressive assimilation that is omnipresent in the current geopolitical climate. This second tendency moves toward tolerance, mutual understanding, and respect for self-determination between groups rather than a monocultural, state-dominated social world.

MacDonald, David (2007). "First Nations, Residential Schools, and the Americanization of the Holocaust: Rewriting Indigenous History in the United States and Canada." *Canadian Journal of Political Science*, 40 (4): 995-1015.

This article briefly summarizes the history of Aboriginal peoples in Canada with a focus on the residential school system. The author targets for criticism those scholars who claim an indigenous "holocaust" through reference to the Jewish Holocaust. In contrast, MacDonald argues that academics and activists should focus upon the traumatic experiences of individuals and families for a more accurate reflection and balanced interpretation of Canadian history. In this manner, MacDonald hopes to move the debate beyond sweeping claims that the entire history of interactions between Aboriginal Peoples and Europeans was genocidal. He acknowledges that the residential school system has had a damaging cultural, psycho-social, and economic intergenerational impact on Aboriginal peoples in Canada, but stresses that the severe cultural harm caused by the schools does not necessarily amount to genocide since, in his view, there are substantial differences between physical and cultural genocide. Furthermore, he contends that the crucial endeavor should be to analyze the psychological legacies of the atrocities committed against Indigenous peoples in the residential schools and that such studies would be more fruitful than drawing comparisons between the Holocaust and the colonization of Canada.

Miller, J. R. (1996). *Shingwauk's Vision: A History of Native Residential Schools*. Toronto: University of Toronto Press. 582 pp.

In this large volume, the esteemed Canadian historian, J. R. Miller, offers a comprehensive overview of the Canadian residential school system. He begins with the formation of the system, taking the reader through both the ideational roots of Aboriginal education and the dual roles of religion and government in establishing residential institutions. He follows with a discussion of various dimensions (e.g., class, race, gender, work and play, abuse, and resistance) of everyday life within the schools. Finally, Miller reviews the end of the schools and their continuing legacy. This wide-ranging discussion is framed around the dream of Chief Shingwauk (Ojibwa), who wanted a "teaching wigwam" that would allow his people to learn from and adapt to European ways. Shingwauk's vision of an education based upon principles of cultural tolerance and exchange was not realized, though, and instead his people were subjected to what Miller refers to as "attempted cultural genocide" (p. 10).

Milloy, John S. (1999). *A National Crime: The Canadian Government and the Residential School System, 1879 to 1986.* Winnipeg: University of Manitoba Press. 462 pp.

Milloy does not name the crime cited in his title as genocide, but his book, alongside J.R. Miller's *Shingwauk's Vision*, offers much needed historical insight into the residential school system. Milloy completed research for this book as part of his investigation for the Royal Commission on Aboriginal Peoples, which provided him access to some Department of Indian Affairs documents that had been left unstudied. Although the book suffers from a noticeable lack of Aboriginal voices describing their experiences of residential schooling, and also does not include much in terms of the perspectives of various teachers and administrators, Milloy nonetheless offers a detailed picture of the vision that inspired the Canadian government to implement assimilative schools, the failure of the churches to administer them in an adequate fashion, and the physical and cultural destruction wrought as a consequence of both of these actions.

Neu, D., and Therrien, R. (2003). *Accounting for Genocide: Canada's Bureaucratic Assault on Aboriginal People.* Black Point, NS: Fernwood Publishing. 194 pp.

This book proposes that the assault on Aboriginal cultures in Canada was not an inevitable process, but rather the result of a deliberate enactment of policies and practices that destructively targeted Aboriginal peoples. Neu and Therrien focus on the struggle for Aboriginal cultural survival against a bureaucratic onslaught that, in their view, can only be characterized as genocide. Although the Canadian policy of forced assimilation may not have been as overt as the Holocaust, Neu and Therrien argue it was still violent, and reached toward ends similar to those that animated the Nazis.

A more interesting component of their argument comes through their examination of the facilitative role played by accounting in the process of quantifying, defining and manipulating the targeted population. Accounting, Neu and Therrien suggest, was fundamental to the Canadian government's efforts to solve the "Indian problem." Actuarial methods and rationalities had a role to play in diverse policies, such as restrictions on Aboriginal hunting rights and forced residential schooling. Neu and Therrien view this calculative destruction as a form of aggressive social engineering comprised of multiple techniques for uprooting Aboriginal cultures. Furthermore, accounting techniques contributed to the degradation and commodification of the natural environment, and therefore also played a role in disrupting Aboriginal subsistence lifestyles. This resulted in a high degree of dependence upon the federal government for Aboriginal survival. In sum, Neu and Therrien suggest that the evolution of colonialism relied upon accounting practices that created distance between the Indigenous populations and the government. This disconnection resulted in brutal practices of forced assimilation and cost-saving measures that played a role in the physical, cultural, and ecological destruction of Aboriginal ways of life.

Shkilnyk, Anastasia M. (1985). *A Poison Stronger than Love: The Destruction of an Ojibwa Community*. New Haven, CT: Yale University Press. 275 pp.

Shkilnyk offers an intensive and gripping account of a complicated process of community destruction. Through her in-depth portrayal of life and death in the community of Grassy Narrows in Northwestern Ontario, she illustrates how governments, bogged down within their bureaucratic rationalities and paternalistic attitudes, too often failed to listen to community members when they spoke of their specific survival needs. This governing ethos, in the case of Grassy Narrows, resulted in catastrophic decisions, such as the one made in 1964 to relocate the community closer to the city of Kenora. Although motivated primarily by a modernist sensibility that saw greater potential for housing and services to the community if they lived in a less remote location, the move resulted in social dislocation, cultural disruption and a deadly exposure to mercury poisoning. Thus, Shkilnyk provides a striking case study of destruction wrought not by malevolent intent but rather a Eurocentric disregard for Aboriginal perspectives.

Stannard, David E. (1992). *American Holocaust: The Conquest of the New World*. New York: Oxford University Press. 358 pp.
    Stannard's book does not focus squarely on Canadian Aboriginal peoples. Instead, it offers a broad overview of deadly colonial encounters between European nations and the indigenous peoples of the Americas. It is, however, a useful entry point into discussions of Canadian genocide, in particular because Stannard makes the provocative argument that the disease and destruction experienced by the indigenous peoples of the Americas through their encounter with colonial powers was part of a larger genocidal campaign, which, at its base, was supported by an ideological dehumanization of indigenous peoples and their, contrary to colonial mythology, advanced and complex societies.

Tovias, Blanca (2008). "Navigating the Cultural Encounter. Blackfoot Religious Resistance in Canada (c. 1870-1930)," pp. 271-295. In Dirk A. Moses (Ed.) *Empire, Colony, Genocide: Conquest, Occupation and Subaltern Resistance in World History*. New York: Berghahn Books, pp. 271-95.
    This chapter focuses upon the question of whether or not cultural genocide was committed against the Blackfoot people during European colonization. With the destruction of Aboriginal food sources and subsequent reliance of Aboriginal peoples on government support, the Canadian government gained greater control over many Aboriginal peoples. This enabled the government to prohibit traditional spiritual practices such as the Potlatch and the Sun Dance, which were considered obstacles to the process of "civilizing" indigenous persons. The Sun Dance provided a space of cultural ritual that offered participants opportunities to obtain

social prestige, find a marriage partner, engage in the transmission of cultural values to the younger generations, and ensure Blackfoot social cohesion. There were attempts by some missionaries and government agents to stop the Sun Dance because they viewed it as "barbaric" and as a potential threat insofar as it was a chance for multiple tribes to gather and organize in a movement against the federal government. But the project of spiritual suppression and potential cultural destruction was not straightforward. Although laws were enacted to prevent such religious ceremonies, it was difficult for agents and police to implement the prohibition. Some agents tried to enforce the legislation against the Sun Dance, but others did not, and this resulted in a lack of uniform compliance. This fact must be acknowledged as an example of how the colonized can resist the dominant discourse and manipulate it to their needs. It also leads to the conclusion that the prohibition of the Sun Dance was not in and of itself clearly genocidal since there was no sustained and "surgical" effort to ensure its application.

Woolford, Andrew (2009). "Ontological Destruction: Genocide and Aboriginal Peoples in Canada." *Genocide Studies and Prevention: An International Journal,* Spring, 4(1):81-97.

In this article, the author argues that the designation of "cultural genocide" is too qualified and imprecise for understanding Canadian Aboriginal experiences of colonialism, since it fails to contend with Aboriginal experiences and understandings of group destruction. The author further proposes that a re-reading and opening of certain components of the UNGC through an engagement with Canadian Aboriginal notions of group identity, destruction, and intent provides a clearer path to discerning the nature of genocide in Canada.

4

The Destruction of Aboriginal Society in Australia

Colin Tatz

Introduction

Assimilation has always been a powerful social force in Australia. Despite efforts at cultural diversity, Australians still need to feel and be seen as one people, and in such oneness there is little room for disparate views about a country considered 220 years old by the white mainstream and 60,000 years old by the native peoples.

The "history wars"—waged particularly between 1996 and 2007—juxtaposed two visions. One is of a transported convict people who overcame their origins in Britain and blossomed Down Under into a generous, egalitarian society, decent democrats, and good colonists in the "land of the fair go." The other is of some 750,000 indigenous people who from 1788 onward were systematically hunted down because of who they were; shot or poisoned; "indentured" as a form of slave labor; abducted and abused as sexual chattels; and institutionalized as wards—yet who now have a sense of cultural pride and a land-based identity from both an earlier independence and an oppressive past (and present). The prevalent conservative view is that the pendulum has swung too sympathetically in the Aboriginal direction—in school curricula, museums, media depictions—resulting in a "black armband view of history."

Genocide is now in the political lexicon, resulting in anger, dismay, and, inevitably, denialism. Breaches of human rights are strongly denied on the ground that "Australianness" is an inherent prophylactic against, or an antidote to, such behavior. A recent foreign minister, Alexander Downer, has argued that Australia can't possibly breach international treaties on child, sex, and race discrimination *because* we are Australians.

Parliamentarians blanched at the notion of genocide when Australia ratified the UN Convention on the Prevention and Punishment of the Crime of Genocide (UNCG) in June 1949. Archie Cameron, Liberal member for Barker, stated that "no one in his right senses believes that the Commonwealth of Australia will be called before the bar of public opinion" (Hansard, 1949, p. 1871). Leslie Haylen, Labor member for Parkes, declared that "the horrible crime of genocide is unthinkable in Australia.… That we detest all forms of genocide…arises from the fact that we are a moral people" (same Parliamentary session).

Nonetheless, research, several official inquiries, a small number of judicial cases and Aboriginal voices *have brought* Australia before the bar of public and, on occasion, legal opinion. The Australian case diverges from the "classic" genocides of last century, but the uncommon aspects do not invalidate the case for the crime. Rather, they broaden our narrower Eurocentric templates of what constitutes genocide.

Little on this issue was written before the 1970s, the decade in which "Aboriginal history" began to emerge as a discrete facet of the nation's story. While a few early historians and memoirists wrote about massacres, the Aboriginal genocide literature can be said to have begun in 1985.

Unique Aspects

Australia's genocidal history is perhaps unique. First, the case rests essentially on the UNCG's Article II(a) physical killing and II(e) the forcible transfer of children. Most scholars have not addressed II(b) causing serious bodily or mental harm and II(c) inflicting conditions that bring about their physical destruction or destroy their essential foundations. Be that as it may, these aspects do impact on, and help explain, the destruction of Aboriginal society, as discussed below. Second, these acts of genocide have occurred over at least two hundred years, quite unlike Europe's forty-five frenetic months between December 1941 and May 1945, or Rwanda's one hundred days in 1994. Third, the killing was done in twos and threes, sometimes dozens at a time, usually during weekend "hunting" parties—images foreign to scholars "accustomed" to short-term mega-death. Fourth, much of the killing phase was a private genocide, committed by released convicts and settlers, unhindered by the colonial authorities who later used the homicidal Native Police forces to "disperse kangaroos," a euphemism of the time. Fifth, eugenicist programs of child removal occurred in different periods of time and only became relatively uniform policy and practice from 1937 forward. Sixth, while child removal to eliminate Aboriginality is now generally acknowledged, the defense has been that "benevolence" and "good intent" precluded any possibility of genocide in Australia. Seventh, apart from the occasional memoir, white–Aboriginal relations were largely ignored in history texts until the 1970s. Eighth, denialism of the killing and of child removal has not been propelled as much by academics or politicians as by a dozen media people. Lastly, while there is now a politics of apology, there is, apart from Tasmania, a steadfast refusal to discuss reparations.

Disease as Genocide?

The disease-as-genocide theme is common in texts and needs but brief comment. A noted economic historian, Noel Butlin (1983) was the chief proponent: "it is possible and, in 1789, likely, that infection [smallpox] of the Aborigines was a deliberate exterminating act" (p. 175). Be that as it may, it is not feasible that the first fleet of soldiers and settlers, arriving in 1788, who themselves were suffering from a disease they didn't understand, who were ignorant of germ theory that would finally explain such diseases a hundred years later, could conceive of extermination by deliberately inflicting "variolous matter" on the native people. There was no text, pretext, or context for genocide one year after first white settlement. Smallpox, whooping cough, measles, and influenza certainly caused havoc among the Aborigines, but while this byproduct of colonialism was catastrophic, it was not deliberate and it was not genocide.

Physical Killing, With Intent

The organized massacres of the nineteenth century were essentially by settlers, with the state authorities usually in the role of bystanders. (Only rarely did the state prosecute white killers.) Settlers killed some 10,000 Aborigines in the colony of Queensland between 1824 and 1908. Perceived as wild animals, vermin, scarcely human, *ferae naturâ*, hideous scandals to humanity, loathsome, and a nuisance (to use the dehumanizing language of the time), they were treated as fair game. As one settler wrote, "and the more they are shot at, the sooner they will learn what gunpowder means" (Evans, 1988, p. 77). In 1883, the British High Commissioner in Queensland, Arthur Hamilton Gordon, wrote to his friend William Gladstone, then prime minister of England: "The habit of regarding the natives as vermin, to be cleared off the face of the earth, has given the average Queenslander a tone of brutality and cruelty in dealing with 'blacks' … I have heard men of culture and refinement…. talk, not only of the *wholesale* butchery…but of the *individual* murder of natives, exactly as they would talk of a day's sport, or having to kill some troublesome animal" (Evans, 1988, p. 78).

In 1896, the Queensland Colonial Secretary appointed Archibald Meston as special commissioner to investigate the Aboriginal condition. What he discovered was that "men and women [were] hunted like wild beasts"; "kidnapping of women and nameless outrages were reported"; in twenty-five years, one tribe of 3,000 "was down to 100 survivors" as a result of "the old style of 'dispersal'"; "boys and girls were frequently taken from their parents…with no chance of returning"; and "the Mosman [district] blacks had been exterminated." All of which, he wrote, was "a reproach to our common humanity" (Meston, 1896, pp. 723-736). In a letter to the colonial secretary that year, he described the Aboriginal reaction to his visit: "their manifest joy at assurances of safety and protection is pathetic beyond expression...God knows they were in need of it" (Evans, 1988, p. 86). The "only way to arrest their destruction," to "save any part of the race from extinction," was to abolish the Native Police force, ban opium, and ensure the "absolute isolation" from the whites who—'colored by prejudice, distorted by ignorance'—committed "shameful deeds" (Meston, 1896, pp. 733-734).

Massive population loss occurred in Central Australia, then administered by South Australia, between 1860 and 1895. Possibly 20 percent of Aborigines may have died from diseases not previously encountered, but some 1,750 people, or 40 percent of the Aboriginal population in the Alice Springs region, were mostly shot in what was called "dispersal" (Kimber, 1997, p. 61). Native Police, the white-officered black brigades, were now the perpetrators. Giving evidence in 1861, a lieutenant was asked what he meant by "dispersing." "Firing at them" was his reply, but "I gave strict orders not to shoot any gins [Aboriginal women]" (Kimber, 1997, p. 43).

The history of Aborigines in Western Australia was little different. There were numerous massacres between the period of settlement and the 1920s, with the last of them, the Forrest River killings, in 1926. This was the only episode to result in a Royal Commission inquiry, but the latter was yet another inquiry which resulted in the acquittal (and the promotion) of the two police officers allegedly involved in the shooting and burning of people. Across the continent, and across a century, names like Bathurst (New South Wales, 1824), Fremantle (Western Australia, 1830), Portland (Victoria, 1833–34), Pinjarra (Western Australia, 1834), Myall Creek (New South Wales, 1838), Waterloo Creek (New South Wales, 1838), Gippsland (Victoria, 1840–50), Butchers Creek (Victoria, 1841), Rufus River (South Australia, 1841), Wonnerup (Western Australia, 1841), Barrow Creek (Northern Territory, 1874), Battle Mountain (Queensland, 1884), Bedford Downs (Western Australia, 1924) and Forrest River (Western Australia, 1926) evoke and memorialize these events.

The Tasmanian story is legendary, though not always accurate. Most texts regard Truganini (or Trugernanner), who died in 1876, as the last Tasmanian. She was the daughter of Mangana, the chief of the Bruny Island tribe; her mother was killed and one of her sisters was abducted by seal-hunters who, together with the whaler men, were the major perpetrators of massacres. That there was genocidal intent, which sometimes failed to come to fruition, and that there was genocidal massacre is not in scholarly dispute, except by Keith Windschuttle (2000, 2002) and Reynolds (2006). There was conspiracy, complicity and an attempt to exterminate: "fruition" or "completion" is not the issue, as some historians have contended. There was some rescue, there were survivors and today there are 17,000 descendants of that era.

Protection–Segregation and Articles II(B) And II(C)

Two fences—one legal, one geographic—were erected to protect Aborigines from genocide. Elementary protection began in most colonies in the nineteenth century: in New South Wales as early as 1814, Victoria in 1837, South Australia in 1850, and in Western Australia in 1844 and again in 1886. One of the world's first specific anti-genocide statutes was Queensland's *Aboriginals Protection and Restriction of the Sale of Opium Act 1897*, based essentially on Meston's sympathetic yet paternalistic report. So began the era of protection by segregation, with Western Australia (1886 and 1905), New South Wales (1909), South Australia and the Northern Territory (1911), and Tasmania (1912) following soon after. When legal cocoons were insufficient, Aborigines were located on remote reservations, incarcerated in government-run settlements and church-run mission stations. These centers were rarely Aboriginal choices or places of natural habitation but almost unreachable domains that were, to use one mission society's phrase, "splendidly secluded" or, as Meston noted, "foolishly selected situations" (Meston, 1896, p. 734).

Following the federation of Australia in 1901, Aborigines were essentially a state matter, and policies and practices were not uniform. Queensland began rigid control in 1897 and ended that much condemned regime in 1985. The Northern Territory, the only specifically federal jurisdiction, introduced special laws in 1911 and repealed most of them in 1964. In common, Aborigines, as defined, were under legal guardianship, minors in law, specifically denied civil rights and many benefits of the rule of law.

Protection-segregation generally embodied contradictions from the start. To keep predators out, "inmates" had to be kept in. Hunter-gatherers were made both sedentary and stationary. They couldn't leave without permission, or sell their labor in free markets. They couldn't work for the minimum wage prescribed by the wage arbitration system. Labor groups were organized by officials and "sold" to neighboring crop-growers or cattlemen for seasonal work. Rations were given in lieu of payment, and where actual remuneration was paid, these monies went into state-run trust funds, much of which "disappeared." (Queensland now has a "Stolen Wages" mechanism following clamor for some restitution.) Nor could they join the (racist) trade unions.

Concomitantly, Aborigines couldn't marry non-Aborigines without permission; nor could they have sex across the "color line." Pubescent girls were locked in dormitories to circumvent the traditional bride-promissory system. The power of elders to engage in conflict-resolution or administer tribal punishments was either limited or prohibited. Officials sent "trouble-makers" to even more remote penal settlements, like Palm Island in Queensland, most often without wives and children, with no rights of appeal and no time limits on their exile (Tatz, 1963, pp. 33-49).

Material culture, rituals and rites were often proscribed. In the Northern Territory, Aboriginal art was forbidden in many institutions or, where allowed, had to be sold to the administering authorities or to the public at prices determined by officials or by missionaries in their urban outlet shops.

Aborigines couldn't vote in federal elections until 1962 or in some state elections (for example, Queensland) until 1965. They couldn't drink or have access to alcohol. In Queensland, they could be imprisoned—for up to three weeks at a time—on settlements and missions for crimes no other Australian could commit, such as playing cards, being cheeky, committing adultery or refusing to give fecal samples. In Western Australia, people were punished for being untidy, chopping down trees or wasting water. There were no appeals and there was no outside scrutiny. Eligible in theory,

Aborigines were not paid their social welfare entitlements, such monies going to state treasuries or to cattlemen who "maintained" them on their properties.

Remote populations had no access to, and no involvement with, the normal civic institutions. Generally, administrators were under-educated and untrained people who could obtain employment and status only where the clients were Aboriginal. Missionaries were prepared to work in locations where governments would not and so they became agencies of government. In most states they were delegated the same draconian powers as government officials, and were given the authority to act as civic authorities normally do, providing food, education, housing, health services, roads, buildings, sewage, garbage disposal facilities, safe water, electricity—and justice. They were, to put it mildly, out of their pastoral depths.

For over a century in some domains, a genuine attempt at protection from predators turned into incarceration, in what Canadian sociologist Erving Goffman (1968) called "asylums"—total institutions where "a large number of like-situated individuals, cut off from the wider society for an appreciable period...together lead an enclosed, formally administered round of life" (p. 11). Prisons, Goffman wrote, were a good example but what is prison-like about prisons is to be found in institutions where the residents have broken no laws. Here, indeed, was another universe for inmates who had committed no crimes: a separated, inferior legal class of people, perpetual wards of the state (and church), geographically remote, under special laws that prescribed codes of conduct, administered by officials, priests and police in secrecy, with visitors unwelcome and required to have both written permission and recent chest x-rays for entry. This system of secretive (and often paranoid) Aboriginal administration saved people from murder, but it did not stop the removal of their "mixed-race" children. Ironically, the segregationary protection system became its opposite, causing Aborigines serious mental and bodily harm and destroying many of their cultural and social institutions.

Child Removal, With Intent

Despite the profound difference between killing people and forcibly transferring children to another cultural domain, the UNCG brackets Article II(a) with II(e) as coequal—and so child removal *is* an act of genocide. Victoria began programs of forced assimilation and child "retention" and separation as early as the 1830s, at Yarra Government "Mission" (1837-1839), Buntingdale Mission (1838-1848) and Merri Creek Baptist School (1845-1851); Western Australia closed its major "assimilation home," Sister Kate's Orphanage, in 1987 and New South Wales closed the last such mission institution in Bomaderry in 1988. For over a century, across the continent, between 35,000 and 55,000 children—progeny of Aboriginal women and white cattle station workers, crop-growers, miners and adventurers —were "taken away." In northern Australia, "yellafellas," the common derogatory term, were embarrassments to white society and were quickly taken to institutions to be weaned of their Aboriginality. Private shame became a cornerstone of state and federal administrators. Australians always assumed that their culture and color genes were the stronger and that any degree of "white blood" made Aboriginal children more likely to survive biologically and more "salvageable" for cleanliness, Christianity, and civilization. In southern Australia, children of "part-Aboriginal" parents were removed.

In 1909, the Chief Protector in Western Australia, C.F. Gale, quoted one of his travelling Protectors: "I would not hesitate for one moment to separate any half-caste from its Aboriginal mother, no matter how frantic her momentary grief might be at the time. They soon forget their offspring" (p. 9).

Several of the key bureaucrats—C. F. Gale and A. O. Neville in the West, Dr. W. E. Roth and J. W. Bleakley in Queensland, and Dr. Cecil Cook in the Northern Territory—were educated men and were doubtless aware of the eugenicist principles that were then prevalent and prominent in Europe and the United States. Ultimately, they consummated their ideas at a national summit in Canberra in 1937: "The destiny of the natives of Aboriginal origin, but not of full blood, lies in their ultimate absorption by the people of the Commonwealth and it is therefore recommended that all efforts shall be directed to this end" (Tatz, 2003, pp. 88-94).

Neville presented a three-point plan (Beresford and Omaji, 1998, pp. 30-34, 47-52). First, keep "full-bloods" in inviolable reserves where they were destined to die out. Second, take all "half-castes" away from their mothers. Third, control marriages so that "pleasant, placid, complacent, strikingly attractive, auburn-haired and rosy-freckled" quarter- and half-blood Aboriginal maidens would marry into the white community. In doing so, it would be possible to "eventually forget that there were ever any Aborigines in Australia." "The native," Neville concluded, "must be helped in spite of himself!...Even if a measure of discipline is necessary it must be applied, but it can be applied in such a way as to appear to be gentle persuasion...the end in view will justify the means employed" (quoted in Haebich, 1988, p. 156).

Such notions became official practices. After 1937, dozens of reserves were established and older ones reinforced by tougher regulations. Coaxed (or even coerced) Christian marriages were never going to succeed and thus child removal by policemen became the order of the day. Run by government staff and by mission agencies, "assimilation homes"—in the form of residential schools, dormitories, hostels, welfare institutions—flourished. Several were in urban domains, some in settled rural areas, but most were in remote Australia.

Good and Bad Intent

Whatever justifications were offered before 1949, there can be no exoneration of child removal after Australia ratified the UNCG in mid-1949. Ultimately, the saga of the "stolen generations" came to public light in the 1980s. That "dissociating the children from [native] camp life must eventually solve the Aboriginal problem" was official New South Wales practice. To leave them where they were, "in comparative idleness in the midst of more or less vicious surroundings," the government claimed, would be "an injustice to the children themselves, and a positive menace to the State" (Read, 1981, p.7). Historian Peter Read (1981) ascertained that there were 5,625 removals in that jurisdiction between 1883 and 1969. Until 1939 there was never any investigation of individual children or families, only wholesale generalization. In the columns headed "Reasons for [Aborigines Welfare] Board Taking Control of the Child," the great majority carried this standard, handwritten entry: "For being Aboriginal" (Read, 1981, p. 6). After 1939, removals required a hearing before a magistrate.

The Aboriginal "Link-Up" movement to locate lost children, siblings and parents began in 1981. By then, locating and reuniting with removed family members had become the single-most important issue in Aboriginal life. Strident Aboriginal voices persuaded the federal Labor government to initiate an inquiry into "the separation by compulsion" of Aboriginal children from their families. The word "separation" in the terms of reference seemed to infer that some re-uniting was once envisaged. That was never the intention of the "removers": children were to be separated forever from their Aboriginality.

Bringing Them Home (HREOC, 1997), a major report on the plight of the Aborigines, was something of a bestseller: "A finding of genocide was presented: the essence of the crime was acting with the intention of destroying the group, not the extent to which that intention was achieved" (p. 270). The removals were intended to "absorb," "merge," and "assimilate" the children "so that Aborigines as a distinct group would disappear" (HREOC, pp. 270-275).

Several former officials responded that while the practices were based on the notion of the "rescuability" of "half-caste" children, the removals were "for their own good" and "not done heartlessly" (Macleod, 1997, p. 166). (A widespread fallacy, even among scholars, is that *motive* is synonymous with *intent*.) "Destroy" in the UNCG resonates with some 50 million dead worldwide as a result of Hitler's war against the Jews. Given the proximity of the Holocaust to the UNCG, "with intent to destroy" is assumed as meaning intent with *male fides*, bad faith, with evil intent. But nowhere does the UNCG distinguish or define the kind of intent needed to commit acts of genocide. There are some strong legal argument in Australia that the reasons for the crime are irrelevant (Tatz, 2003, p. 99). One legal view is that "it can be (misguidedly) committed 'in the interests' of a protected population" (Storey, 1997, 11-14). Or, as the philosopher Raimond Gaita (1997) contends, "the concept of good intention cannot be relativised indefinitely to an agent's perception of it as good" (p. 21). If we could, he writes, then we must say that Nazi murderers had good, but radically benighted intentions, because most of them believed they had a sacred duty to the world to rid the world of the race that polluted it.

The Current State of Affairs

Denialism

Australian denialism is a curious case. From time to time, one or another specific massacre—such as at Forrest River—is sometimes denied. One urban politics specialist, Keith Windschuttle (2000, 2002), for example, has written extensively (in his privately published volume) about "the fabrication of Aboriginal history" in Tasmania, concentrating his efforts on the lack of integrity and the mistaken or dubious footnotes of several historians to sustain his case. If genocide occurred, he argues, it was somehow warranted by the behavior of the natives in attacking settlers or killing livestock for food.

Denialism tends to focus more commonly, though, on child removal. The most ardent attackers of the case of the "stolen generations" are a coterie of senior newspaper journalists and commercial radio talkback comperes: contentions vary from "it was good for them" to "it was just like boarding school" and from "look how many Aborigines from that kind of background are successful" to "it is and was all a case of false memory syndrome and it never happened in the first place."

Australian political scientist Robert Manne (2001) has made an astute observation about the reasons underlying what he calls a denialist "campaign": [There is] "a right-wing and populist resistance to discussions of historical injustice and the Aborigines" (p.134). [Separation of mother and child] "deeply captured the national imagination"—that [stolen generations] story had the power to change forever the way they saw their country's history —hence the imperative to destroy that story (Manne, 2001, p. 134). It is also about an affirmation of Australian decency and morality in the face of the judicial injustices that transported them from Britain in the first instance.

The Politics of Apology

The Australian public accepted *Bringing Them Home*. Hundreds of thousands signed "sorry books" located in public places; thousands stood in lines to listen to "removed children" telling their stories; many more thousands planted small wooden hands on lawns and beaches signifying hands held up in guilt or sorrow; and thousands more marched in solidarity across city bridges. Between 1997 and 2000, state and territory governments, numerous police departments, churches, mission societies, city and shire councils proclaimed both sorrow and apology. The outstanding exception was the federal Coalition (conservative) government. The then deputy prime minister argued that his generation should not have to accept the guilt of the previous one. The then prime minister, John Howard, was adamant that for the nation to say sorry was to open the way for costly compensation claims. Nor, he said, could he apologize on behalf of migrant groups who had had nothing to do with these events.

During Howard's rule, from 1996 to 2007, Canada and New Zealand made signal changes to their politics of apology and to their financial reparation and land restoration programs. As for Australia, it shrank from all such notions. Howard declared that he wanted Australians to "feel relaxed and comfortable about their past," that he didn't wish to wake up each day to hear that Australia has had "a racist, bigoted past," and, accordingly, he would attempt a national school history program that accentuated "positive achievements." Despite his offer of a personal apology, his government was steadfast in not offering an official acknowledgment of these events.

The Australian Labor Party won the November 2007 election and Prime Minister Kevin Rudd set about issuing a national apology. On 13 February 2008, the nation came close to a standstill as the national apology was televised from federal Parliament for several hours. The event was dramatic, grand theater, made much more so by the intransigence of the former government. When state and local governments apologized years earlier, the press notices were there, recognized, but somewhat muted. The delayed and therefore much-awaited national apology was climactic and, in a real sense, a *tremendum* in the national psyche.

Critical Challenges

Reparations

Several stolen generation groups have resorted to civil law in search of recognition of their experience and compensation for their [usually] troubled lives. Two dozen cases have been heard in various jurisdictions. Most have focused on sexual assaults while incarcerated, or on breaches of fiduciary care, arguing that state or territory administrations had, by removing them, not cared for them appropriately. Most have lost on technicalities and several have cost enormous sums (Cunneen 2004). Not one case has sought to establish *directly* that child transfer is the essence of Article II(e).

The federal government spent at least $A6 million defending the cases brought by Lorna Cubillo and Peter Gunner. In 2007, South Australia's Supreme Court awarded Bruce Trevorrow $A525,000 for being treated unlawfully and falsely imprisoned when he was removed, at thirteen months of age, from his mother and handed to a white family in 1957.

Tellingly, Howard's refusal to apologize lest it open such legal doors was in vain. There has been no shortage of complainants and the Trevorrow case has opened more legal avenues of restitution than can be accommodated by a limited and (doubtless tokenistic) reparations program.

Early in 2008, a minority party senator introduced a Stolen Generations Compensation Bill. It was referred to a legal and constitutional Senate committee which reported in June 2008. Not surprisingly, the Senate committee recommended that the Bill not proceed, that there be greater consultation with such bodies as the National Sorry Day Committee and the Stolen Generations Alliance, and that there be a National Healing Fund "to provide health, housing, aging, funding for funerals and other family support services for members of the stolen generation as a matter of priority." This kind of recommendation is consistent with Howard's concept of "reconciliation" as "practical reconciliation" in the form of housing, education, health and employment—which, of course, ought to be standard provisions in a "civilized and conscionable society" but which are always proffered as an especial "gift" to Aborigines. Reparations, as normally understood, are not open for discussion. The alternative is a succession of lawsuits which may well prove more painful and costly.

Ironic, perhaps, but it is the state of Tasmania alone that has initiated financial restitution. In January 2008, Premier Paul Lennon declared that the lives of 106 claimants had been "deeply affected by this flawed policy of separation." Of the 106, eighty-four were paid approximately $A55,000 each and each family of deceased claimants received approximately $A4,700.

Recovery

Forty years after the abolition of most restrictive laws, there has been a notable recovery of Aboriginal cultural, economic and legal rights. The pluses—in land acquisition, tertiary education numbers, in the artistic, musical, literary and sporting domains, small-scale entrepreneurship, negotiating mining agreements on their land, in commanding respect for Aboriginality as a civilization—have been offset by some serious minuses. Cardiac, renal, respiratory, and metabolic disease is rampant, as is the youth suicide rate. Life expectation is "officially" seventeen years below the norm (seventy-nine for non-Aboriginal males, sixty-two for Aboriginal males) but in actual terms few men live beyond fifty.

Today there is a resurgence and resurfacing of old policy mantras and shibboleths that not only failed but left incurable wounds. "Wean them from their families," "remove them from their environments of poverty," "send them away to boarding schools," "give them food coupons rather than welfare benefits which they spend on alcohol," "send in more police," and "get rid of the poisonous welfare dependency" are now common parlance.

In 2007, the Howard government launched an "emergency intervention" in the Northern Territory, sending in civilian task forces (largely untrained in this work), and the military (even less qualified) "to save the children" from reported child abuse, sexual molestation and neglect. Amid growing criticism, Kevin Rudd's Labor government has continued the program, which has involved the suspension (and therefore the protections) of the federal *Racial Discrimination Act* and the Northern Territory's anti-discrimination legislation; the suspension of the permit system which allowed Aborigines to decide who could enter their domains; the search for sexual predators, but with not one charge or one arrest in a year's operation; the quarantining of all social welfare payments; the physical medical examination of children; and the banning of alcohol. One immediate precursor to this carrot-and-stick philosophy was a "Shared Responsibility Agreement" (one of about a hundred such mutual "pacts") in remote Mulan, Western Australia in 2005; that is, that community would continue to be denied a gasoline pump unless it could be shown that litter was being tidied and that children were washing their hands and brushing their teeth.

There is a Meston-like quality about this "save-the-children" intervention. There are some positive outcomes to date, notably the reduction of alcohol-fueled pressures on women to hand over their food money, but it must be said that not very much has changed since Meston pushed for such protections 112 years ago: there is still a governmental philosophy of blanket ascription—that is, any instance of deviant behavior by an individual, a group or a community is considered the behavior of *all* Aborigines, and *all* must surrender to a national or state "remedy."

The removal of children, no matter the motive, has remained a constant for over a century. Children are incarcerated, one way or another, often at enormous distances from homelands, in disproportionate numbers to White children. As of 2008, just over 500,000 Aborigines formed 2.4 percent of the total 20.1 million population. Yet in most jurisdictions they form between 25 and 35 percent of prison and juvenile facility populations, proportions that grow daily. The reality is that Aboriginal children—to the extent of one in four, possibly even one in three—are separated in this way from their parents and spend undue portions of their short lives in custodial institutions.

Conclusion

The very idea of genocide in Australia has come a long way in a remarkably short time. In 1970, the historian Charles Rowley discussed the way in which Aborigines and their physical killing had been ignored by practically every historian to date. Rowley was always polite. Australian historians "tended to play down" the history, consigning "the moral and social issues to the past" (Rowley, 1970, p. 1). Rowley (1970) noted that "The mental block had by no means disappeared…. There was a majority sentiment that raking up the misdeeds of the past served no good purpose" (vol. 1, pp. 1-9). He was encouraged by seeing that "a few young historians are beginning to work in the field" (Rowley, 1970).

Work they did. *Aboriginal History*, born in 1977, was both a new journal and a new sub-discipline in schools and universities. The doyen historians published new editions, quickly adding Aboriginal and gender chapters. The Tasmanian and north Australian frontier stories began to be told. Some removed Aboriginal children became prominent as activists and public servants and a strong articulation began for a national inquiry "to determine how many of our children were taken away and how this occurred…. We also want to consider whether these policies fall within the definition of genocide in Article II(e) of the United Nations Convention" (Tatz, 2003, p. 96).

The National Museum in Canberra, which opened in 2001, immediately fell foul of conservative critics: it was too historical, too Aboriginal, not celebratory enough of [white] Australian triumphs. But by 2001, and certainly by this time of writing, the "racist, bigoted past" is in the open. Aboriginal Studies, including the "misdeeds" of the past, are embedded in school curricula and university courses. Furthermore, *Aboriginal History* produced a seminal volume on Australian genocide in 2001 and the "unthinkable" word is now relatively commonplace. Concomitantly, the 2008 Senate committee, discussed above, used the phrase stolen generation (without the quote marks) throughout its report.

Several scholarly arguments need resolution. Historians writing in the 1970s and 1980s talked of pacifying, killing, cleansing, exterminating, starving, poisoning, shooting, beheading, sterilizing, exiling—but avoided talking about and using the term *genocide*. There is no need for synonyms. Some insist on "complete outcome" to warrant the "g" label; some split hairs between cultural and biological absorption of children; some, however much in vain, chase after non-UNCG definitions of the crime and seek "more appropriate nomenclature" for the Aboriginal experience; some make awkward and difficult-to-sustain analogies or parallels between Aboriginal and Holocaust victims; and a few insist that only the striped *musselmanner* hanging on the wire in Auschwitz represent "the true meaning of genocide." None seem to take into account that the UNCG's Article III on conspiracy, incitement and complicity treats those actions as seriously as the physical crime itself.

There is a national catchcry in a country that has been so dismissive of its past yet so overwhelmingly dedicated to World War One memories: "it's time to move on." There is no inherent problem in "moving on"—provided one knows what it is that one is moving on *from*. Australia now has a glimmer of fromness.

References

Beresford, Quentin and Omaji, Paul (1998). *Our State of Mind: Racial Planning and the Stolen Generations*. Fremantle: Fremantle Arts Centre Press.

Butlin, Noel (1983). *Our Original Aggression: Aboriginal Populations of Southeastern Australia 1788–1850*. Sydney: Allen & Unwin.

Cunneen, Chris and Grix, Julia (2004). *The Limitations of Litigation in Stolen Generations Cases*. Research Discussion Paper No. 15. Canberra: Aboriginal Studies Press.

Evans, Raymond; Saunders, Kay; and Cronin, Kathryn (1988). *Race Relations in Colonial Queensland: A History of Exclusion, Exploitation and Extermination*. St Lucia: University of Queensland Press.

Gaita, Raymond (1997). "Genocide: the Holocaust and the Aborigines." *Quadrant*, November, No. 341, Vol. XLI (11): 17-22.

Gaita, Raymond (1997). "The Genocide and Pedantry." *Quadrant*, July -August, No. 338, Vol. XLI (7-8): 41-45.

Gale, C.F. (1909). *Report of the Chief Protector*. Western Australia Parliament: Votes and Proceedings, Volume 2, p. 9.

Goffman, Erving (1968). *Asylums: Essays in the Social Situation of Mental Patients and Other Inmates*. Harmondsworth UK: Penguin.

Haebich, Anna (1988). *For Their Own Good: Aborigines and Government in the South West of Western Australia 1900-1940*. Perth: University of Western Australia Press.

Hansard, House of Representatives (1949), *Volume 203*, 30 June, p.1871.

HREOC (Human Rights and Equal Opportunity Commission)(1997). *Bringing Them Home: Report of the National Inquiry into the Separation of Aboriginal and Torres*

Strait Islander Children from Their Families. Sydney: Commonwealth of Australia.

Kimber, Richard (1997). "Genocide or Not? The Situation in Central Australia, 1860-1895," pp. 33-65. In Colin Tatz, Peter Arnold, and Sandra Tatz (Eds.), *Genocide Perspectives I: Essays in Comparative Genocide*. Sydney: Centre for Comparative Genocide Studies.

Manne, Robert (2001). *Quarterly Essay: In Denial—the Stolen Generations and the Right*. Volume 1. Melbourne: Morry Schwartz, Black Inc.

Read, Peter (1981). *The Stolen Generations: The Removal of Aboriginal Children in New South Wales 1883 to 1969*. Sydney: NSW Ministry of Aboriginal Affairs, Occasional Paper (No. 1).

Macleod, Colin (1997). *Patrol in the Dreamtime*. Sydney: Random House.

Meston, Archibald (1896). *Report on the Aboriginals of Queensland*, Queensland Parliament, Votes and Proceedings, IV (85): 723-740.

Rowley, Charles (1970). *The Destruction of Aboriginal Society: Aboriginal Policy and Practice, Vol 1*. Canberra: Australian National University Press.

Storey, Matthew (1997). "Kruger v the Commonwealth: Does Genocide Require Malice?" *University of New South Wales Law Journal Forum*, December, 4(1):11-14.

Tatz, Colin (1963). "Queensland's Aborigines: Natural Justice and the Rule of Law." *Australian Quarterly*, XXXV(3), 33-49.

Tatz, Colin (2003). *With Intent to Destroy: Reflecting on Genocide*. London: Verso.

Windschuttle, Keith (2000). "The Myths of Frontier Massacres, Part II. The Fabrication of the Aboriginal Death Toll." *Quadrant*, November, 341, XLIV (11):17-24.

Windschuttle, Keith (2000). "The Myths of Frontier Massacres." *Quadrant*, October, October, No. 370, Vol. XLIV (10), 8-21.

Annotated Bibliography

The Idea of Genocide

Aboriginal History (2001). Special section: "Genocide?" Australian Aboriginal History in International Perspective, 25, 1-172.

Despite the title's question mark, this volume endorses the use of the term genocide. Scholarly arguments and evidence are provided by eleven historians.

Barta, Tony (1985). "After the Holocaust: Consciousness of Genocide in Australia." *Australian Journal of Politics and History*, 31(1): 154-161.

This conference paper, treated initially with skepticism, opened the way for discussion of genocide as part of the Aboriginal experience.

Curthoys, Ann (2008). "Genocide in Tasmania: The History of an Idea," pp. 229-252. In Dirk A. Moses (Ed.) *Empire Colony Geno-*

cide: Conquest, Occupation and Subaltern Resistance in World History. New York: Berghann Books.

This essay is one of many challenges to the customary focus on twentieth-century mass crimes and shows that genocide and "ethnic cleansing" have been intrinsic to imperial expansion for some 500 years.

Curthoys, Ann; Genovese, Ann; and Reilly, Alexander (2008). *Rights and Redemption: History, Law and Indigenous People*. Sydney: University of NSW Press. 278 pp.

An important examination of the role of historians in Aboriginal litigation on land rights, native title, the stolen generations and the question of genocide. The significant *Nulyarimma* and *Buzzacott* court cases (1998 and 1999) are analyzed.

Moses, A. Dirk (Ed.) (2004*). Genocide and Settler Society: Frontier Violence and Stolen Aboriginal Children in Australian History*. New York: Berghann Books. 325 pp.

Thirteen essays address the conceptual and historical determinants of genocide, the massacres, and the removal of children. Topics range widely, from considerations of the white Australia policy to "clearing" the land of specific tribes.

Reynolds, Henry (2001). *An Indelible Stain? The Question of Genocide in Australian History*. Ringwood, Victoria, Australia: Penguin. 209 pp.

The doyen of historians of the Aboriginal experience confronts the issue as to whether genocide has ever been perpetrated in Australia. The title, the question mark and the text indicate his ambivalence about the appropriateness of the term genocide; the author tends not to see conspiracy, incitement, complicity, or attempts as elements of the crime.

Tatz, Colin (2003). *With Intent to Destroy: Reflecting on Genocide*. London: Verso. 222 pp.

A consolidation and re-thinking of several of his papers on genocide in Australia, Tatz explores the unexamined issues of causing serious bodily and mental harm and the "group conditions of life" that have destroyed much of Aboriginal society.

Killings, Massacres

Cannon, Michael (1990). *Who Killed the Koories?* Melbourne: William Heinemann. 295 pp.

A critical review of Victoria's race relations, violent clashes and government policy during the gold rush era. The roles of Aboriginal Protectors and the Native Police Corps are discussed. The author is one of few historians to confront the acts that constitute the crime of genocide, and to use that term.

Clark, Ian (1995). *Scars in the Landscape: A Register of Massacre Sites in Western Victoria 1803–1859.* Canberra: Aboriginal Studies Press. 199 pp.

A register and documentation of massacre sites in ten language groups; each language group includes details of clans, history of white occupation and government policy.

Elder, Bruce (2003). *Blood on the Wattle: Massacres and Mal-treatment of Aboriginal Australians Since 1788.* French's Forest: New Holland. 309 pp.

In examining massacres—including those along the Darling River in Tasmania, Gippsland in Victoria, Western Australia and Coniston in the Northern Territory in 1928—the author rebuts Keith Windschuttle's arguments over the veracity of these events.

Evans, Raymond; Saunders, Kay; and Cronin, Kathryn (1988). *Race Relations in Colonial Queensland: A History of Exclusion, Exploitation and Extermination.* St Lucia: University of Queensland Press. 456 pp.

A key work on murderous violence by settlers towards Aborigines in the nineteenth century, the role of the Native Police and the massacres they perpetrated, the development of racial stereotypes, alcoholism, and the spread of opium to Aborigines.

Green, Neville (1995). *The Forrest River Massacres*. Fremantle, Western Australia: Fremantle Arts Centre Press. 253 pp.

An account of the events that led to the massacre of 1926, the Royal Commission that followed, and the frontier violence and earlier massacres in the region.

Kimber, Richard (1997). "Genocide or Not? The Situation in Central Australia, 1860-1895," pp. 33-65. In Colin Tatz, Peter Arnold, and Sandra Tatz (Eds.). *Genocide Perspectives I: Essays in Comparative Genocide* (1997). Sydney: Centre for Comparative Genocide Studies, Macquarie University.

A meticulous essay on events in Central Australia and on the euphemisms that bedevil Australian history. Official and unofficial "acknowledgements" of the shootings attest to "dispersals" as acts of genocide.

Loos, Noel (1982). *Invasion and Resistance: Aboriginal – European Relations on the North Queensland Frontier 1861-1897*. Canberra: Australian National University Press. 325 pp.

A pioneering work on the first white settlement and the Aboriginal contacts with gold mining, timber-cutting, farming and pearl-shell collecting. An essential background to Queensland's Aboriginal policies, it includes a chapter on "The Decent Disposal of the Native Inhabitants."

Palmer, Alison (2000). *Colonial Genocide*. Adelaide: Crawford House Publishing. 248 pp.

In one of the very few comparative studies, Palmer compares and assesses the plights of Aboriginal people in colonial Queensland with the Herero of South West Africa. Differences between the two indicate a distinction between state and civilian genocide but not between colonial and modern genocide.

Reece, Robert (1974). *Aborigines and Colonists: Aborigines and Colonial Society in New South Wales in the 1830s and 1840s*. Sydney, New South Wales, Australia: Sydney University Press. 254 pp.

Discusses the governmental efforts to protect Aborigines during a period of intense conflict with settlers, including the infamous Myall Creek massacre in 1838 and its aftermath. The bibliography is valuable for early writings on squatter/settler relations with Aborigines.

Richards, Jonathon (2008). *The Secret War: A True History of Queensland's Native Police.* St Lucia: University of Queensland Press. 308 pp.

A system once imported into Victoria from South Africa in 1837, the Native Police consisted of Aboriginal mounted troops under White army officer command who "dispersed" Aborigines. These forces spread to all but Western Australia, and became so out of control that all colonies abandoned it, with Queensland the last to do so in 1900.

Ryan, Lyndall (1996). *The Aboriginal Tasmanians*, second edition. St Leonards, New South Wales, Australia: Allen & Unwin. 380 pp.

A comprehensive history of social conditions in Tasmania and Bass Strait islands from 1642 to the present. It includes prehistory, reconstruction of tribal territories and economies, and cultural survival.

Turnbull, Clive (1966). *Black War: The Extermination of the Tasmanian Aborigines.* London: Cheshire-Landsdown. 274 pp.

A crucial account of the Tasmanian "Black War" and the "Black Line," an action in 1830 to capture all Aborigines, to remove them but to treat them "with the utmost tenderness." Some 3,000 settlers, soldiers and police killed two Aborigines and captured two others.

Serious Harm and Conditions of Life

Broome, Richard (2001). *Aboriginal Australians: Black Responses to White Dominance, 1788–2001*, third edition. Sydney: Allen & Unwin. 336 pp.

An introduction to the treatment of Aboriginal confrontations by a host of actors: the British, violent conflicts with settlers, native police, attacks on Aboriginal initiatives in Victoria, racial legislation and missionary attitudes, relations with industries, the growth of Aboriginal rights movements, the history of land rights, the stolen generations, apologies and reconciliation issues.

Horton, David (1994) (General Ed.). *The Encyclopaedia of Aboriginal Australia: Aboriginal and Torres Strait Islander History, Society and Culture.* Canberra: Aboriginal Studies Press, 2 volumes. 1,340 pp.

Despite some omissions, this massive work is among the very best of reference works on any indigenous people. The authoritative entries range from short notes to major essays, many commissioned from recognized specialists. The illustrations, appendices and extensive bibliography are first rate.

Johnston, Elliott (1991). *Royal Commission into Aboriginal Deaths in Custody: National Report,* Vol. 2. Canberra: Australian Government Publishing Service. 569 pp.

A concise overview of historical, social, legal and cultural factors which have contributed to Aboriginal over-representation in custody: Aboriginal relationships with the criminal justice system, welfare dependency and poverty, housing, ill-health, land, self-determination, and self-management.

McCorquodale, John (1987). *Aborigines and the Law: A Digest.* Canberra: Aboriginal Studies Press. 512 pp.

Laws relating to Aborigines were not uniform in the colonies/ states. This essential reference work lists and excerpts all Imperial, federal, state and territory legislation to that date. It also annotates and quotes from major court judgments.

Rowley, Charles (1970). *The Destruction of Aboriginal Society: Aboriginal Policy and Practice.* Canberra: Australian National University Press. Volume 1. 430 pp.

Rowley, Charles (1971). *Outcasts in White Australia: Aboriginal Policy and Practice*. Volume 2. 472 pp.

Rowley, Charles (1971) *The Remote Aborigines: Aboriginal Policy and Practice*. Volume 3. 379 pp.
   This trilogy is the broadest and most detailed history of the Aboriginal experience to that date. It remains the quintessential analysis of Australia's racist history, written with both elegance and calmness by a man of sharp insight into race relations.

The Stolen Generations

Beresford, Quentin, and Omaji, Paul (1998). *Our State of Mind: Racial Planning and the Stolen Generations*. Fremantle, Western Australia: Fremantle Arts Centre Press. 295 pp.
   Examines why governments introduced the child removal and assimilation policies; what was decided at the 1937 conference of state and Commonwealth officials on Aboriginal affairs policy, and the influence of the assimilationst A.O. Neville.

Bleakley, J.W. (1929). *The Aboriginals and Half-Castes of Central and North Australia*. Melbourne, Victoria, Australia: Government Printer. 65 pp.
   The director of Aboriginal affairs in Queensland was invited to provide the federal government with a report on the Northern Territory. The eugenicist ideas of the time come though clearly.

Chisholm, Richard (1985). *Black Children: White Welfare? Aboriginal Child Welfare Law and Policy in New South Wales. SWRC Reports and Proceedings*, 52. Kensington: Social Welfare Research Centre, University of New South Wales. 144 pp.
   In tandem with Peter Read's work, Chisholm raised the issues of Aboriginal child welfare and placements in New South Wales.

Cummings, Barbara (1990). *Take This Child... From Kahlin Compound to the Retta Dixon Children's Home*. Canberra: Aboriginal Studies Press. 139 pp.

An Aboriginal view of the impact of institutionalization on part-Aboriginal people in the Northern Territory. The author grew up under the "dormitory system," which began with the Kahlin Compound, and was later transferred to Bagot Reserve and the Retta Dixon Home, which was administered by the Aborigines Inland Mission.

Cuneen, Chris, and Grix, Julia (2004). *The Limitations of Litigation in Stolen Generations Cases. Research Discussion Paper #15.* Canberra: Aboriginal Studies Press. 48 pp.

The pursuit of court action by Joy Williams, Alex Kruger, George Bray, Lorna Cubillo, Peter Gunner, Valerie Linow and Christopher Johnson. The limitations of the legal system are carefully analyzed. The authors argue for a reparations-style tribunal in place of existing legal processes.

Haebich, Anna (2000). *Broken Circles: Fragmenting Indigenous Families 1800-2000.* Fremantle, Western Australia: Fremantle Arts Centre Press. 725 pp.

The most comprehensive and seminal account of forcible child transfer in the various states and territories: official policies and practices, the Aboriginal reaction to these interventions, and the resultant fragmentation of Aboriginal families. The author documents political campaigns by Aborigines from the 1970s to the 1990s to regain control of their children.

Human Rights and Equal Opportunity Commission (1997). *Bringing Them Home: Report of the National Inquiry into the Separation of Aboriginal and Torres Strait Islander Children from their Families.* Sydney: Human Rights and Equal Opportunity Commission. 689 pp.

This major report traces the history of laws, policies and practices in each state and territory which led to the removal of children; describes the consequences of removal on children, families and communities, including inter-generational effects; and recommends reparation and compensation principles, and services for those affected by removal. The report justifies its use of the term genocide.

Read, Peter (1983). *The Stolen Generations: The Removal of Aboriginal Children in New South Wales 1883 to 1969. Occasional Paper (No. 1)*. Sydney: New South Wales Ministry of Aboriginal Affairs, 20 pp.
    This short account introduced the public to the concept and the reality of forcibly removed children, the stolen rather than the separated children. Read uses the word genocide to describe the child removal.

Van Krieken, Robert (2004). "Rethinking Cultural Genocide: Aboriginal Child Removal and Settler–colonial State Formation." *Oceania*, 75(2), December. 125-151.
    Discusses genocide and the removal of Aboriginal children, and the legislative and administrative bases as well as welfare and genocide involved in Australian child removal.

Denialism

Brunton, Ronald (1998). "Genocide, the 'Stolen Generations' and the 'Unconceived Generations.'" *Quadrant*, May, 5(346): 19-24.
    A controversial anthropologist contends that the *Bringing Them Home* report is both politically and morally irresponsible, and that perhaps only 12,000 children were removed, more so by parental consent than by coercion.

Evans, Raymond, and Thorpe, Bill (2001). "Indigenocide and the Massacre of Aboriginal History." *Overland*, Winter, 163: 21-39.
    A critique of the denialist material appearing regularly in *Quadrant Magazine*, especially the articles by Keith Windschuttle and P. P. (Paddy) McGuiness. They propose "Indigenocide" as a more appropriate term for Australia's empirical realities.

Gaita, Raymond (1997). "Genocide: the Holocaust and the Aborigines." *Quadrant*, November, No. 341, Vol. XLI (11): 17-22.
    The author endorses the definition of genocide as defined in the *Bringing Them Home* report and contends that "absorption policies intended to hasten the end of a race."

Manne, Robert (2001). *Quarterly Essay: In Denial: the Stolen Generations and the Right*, Volume 1. Melbourne: Black Inc. 113 pp

A critical account of the right-wing campaign against the *Bringing Them Home* report. Manne analyzes the nature and motives of those who deny the historical mistreatment of the Australian Aborigines, particularly the conservative newspaper columnists and the *Quadrant* editor, the late Paddy McGuinness.

Windschuttle, Keith (2002). *The Fabrication of Aboriginal History, Volume 1, Van Dieman's Land 1808-1847*. Sydney: Macleay Press. 472 pp.

Essentially a castigation of historical scholarship for the "invention" of massacre stories in Tasmania in the 1815–1830 era. The author argues that Lyndall Ryan and Henry Reynolds deliberately fabricated evidence about conflict in Tasmania, and that claims about frontier violence and death tolls have been exaggerated.

Reparations, Recovery, and Intervention

Commonwealth of Australia, Senate Committee on Legal and Constitutional Issues (2008). *Stolen Generation Compensation Bill 2008*, 16 June 2008.

A useful summary of the issues arising from the *Bringing Them Home* report: acknowledgement and apology, guarantees against repetition, measures of restitution and rehabilitation and monetary compensation.

Tatz, Colin (2005). "From Welfare to Treaty: Reviewing Fifty years of Aboriginal Policy and Practice," pp. 5-24. In Graeme Ward and Andrew Muckle, (Eds.) *The Power of Knowledge, the Resonance of Tradition*. Canberra: Australian Institute of Aboriginal and Torres Strait Islander Studies. Electronic access http://www.aiatsis.gov.au

A critical review of the pluses and minuses in Aboriginal political, legal, economic, social security, land, health, education, housing, cultural, sporting and identity rights from 1955 to 2005.

Toohey, Paul (2008). *Quarterly Essay: Last Drinks: The Impact of the Northern Territory Intervention, Volume 30.* Melbourne, Victoria, Australia: Black Inc. 97 pp. A sharp, critical account of the emergency intervention by the federal government to "save the children" in the Northern Territory. This short-term action suspended the protection of the *Racial Discrimination Act* and the rule of law for a people uniquely "singled out for failing to nurture its children."

5

Genocide in the Chittagong Hill Tracts, Bangladesh

Jenneke Arens

Introduction

There are some two million indigenous people in Bangladesh, less than 1.5 percent of the total population. They belong to forty-nine ethnic groups. Some groups are on the verge of extinction. The largest concentration of indigenous people is in the Chittagong Hill Tracts (CHT) in the southeast of Bangladesh. The CHT covers about one-tenth of the country and borders Burma and the northeastern Indian states of Mizoram and Tripura. The area is rich in oil, gas, uranium, and other mineral resources and used to be covered with thick forest. The twelve indigenous peoples in the CHT, originally comprising 98 percent of the population in the hilly area, differ distinctly from the majority Bengali population in the fertile plains. Each group has its distinct culture, language, and religion. They practice a mixed farming of plough cultivation in the fertile river valleys and swidden (*jum*) cultivation on the hill slopes. Because of their *jum* cultivation they call themselves collectively Jumma.

Bangladesh has ratified International Labor Organization (ILO) Convention 107 concerning the rights of indigenous peoples, but did not ratify ILO Convention 169 (1989). In October 1998 Ban-

117

gladesh acceded to the 1948 UN Convention on the Prevention and Punishment of the Crime of Genocide UNCG). When acceding, Bangladesh entered provisos granting immunity from prosecution for genocide without its consent.

A Short History

The British colonizers annexed the Chittagong Hill Tracts (CHT) in 1860 and confirmed its special status in 1900, thus acknowledging the distinct identity of the indigenous population. Bengalis were not allowed to buy land or settle in the area without special permission from the authorities. Although the British motivation to grant the area special status was to ensure the cooperation of the indigenous rulers in the frontier region with the colonial regime and to secure the border of the empire to the East, the indigenous people still see the so-called Regulation of 1900 as a protective measure against Bengali settlers.

After independence from British rule in 1947, which divided British India into a Hindu-dominated independent India and a Muslim-dominated Pakistan, the Chittagong Hill Tracts became part of (East) Pakistan, against all expectations of the indigenous peoples. The Chittagong Hill Tracts had much more resemblance with the Indian states in the North-East, both physically and population wise. Several Indian politicians had repeatedly assured indigenous leaders of the CHT that it would become part of independent India. However, in a last minute reshuffle, the Radcliffe Boundary Commission added part of Punjab in the west to the Indian territory and in exchange the CHT in the east was ceded to Pakistan.

Right from the beginning, the government of Pakistan failed to acknowledge the distinct identity of the indigenous peoples in the Chittagong Hill Tracts. The first major "development" program in the CHT, the construction of the hydroelectric dam at Kaptai, funded by USAID (United States Agency for International Development), was a major disaster for the indigenous people. Upon completion in the early 1960s, the lake formed by the dam displaced more than 100,000 hill people, about one-fifth of the indigenous population, and inundated 40 percent of the arable land. The displaced people did not receive proper compensation and

40,000 of them fled to neighboring India. Having plans for further "development" of the area, the Pakistani government abolished the special status of the CHT in 1964. Hardly any of the indigenous people were given jobs generated by the construction of the dam, or in the Karnaphuli paper mills, nor were their villages included in the electrification programs.

The 1971 Genocide of Bengalis and After

Not only were the indigenous people discriminated against by the Pakistani government, but the Bengali population was as well. West Pakistani rulers and administrators dominated the Bengali majority in East Pakistan and although most of the economic profits were generated in East Pakistan, especially through the export of jute, most of the development budget was spent in West Pakistan. In 1952, Urdu was declared the national language of Pakistan, completely ignoring the large Bengali-speaking part of the population. This triggered a huge discontent among the Bengali and marked the beginning of the resistance movement against the domination of West Pakistan. Being denied their Bengali identity, Sheikh Mujibur Rahman of the Awami League declared the independence of Bangladesh on 26 March 1971. The Pakistani government responded with brutal force, which resulted in a bloody civil war between the Pakistani army and the Mukhti Bahini (Liberation Forces) in East Pakistan. Three million Bengali were killed and more than 200,000 women were raped by the Pakistani army during the course of the nine-month war. Pakistan was accused of genocide because of the mass killings and rapes. East Pakistan gained independence in December 1971 and became Bangladesh. Sheikh Mujibur Rahman became the first prime minister of the independent Bangladesh.

Many indigenous people played an active role in the liberation war, hoping that their position would also be better in an independent Bangladesh. However, both Chakma Raja Tridiv Roy, a member of the national parliament, and the brother of the Bohmong Raja, sided with Pakistan. As a result, the indigenous people in the CHT were unjustly regarded as traitors.

Cynically, in 1972 Sheikh Mujibur Rahman, who had led the struggle to retain the Bengali identity, denied the same to a delegation of the indigenous peoples, led by Manobendra Larma, an MP from the CHT. The delegation requested regional autonomy and constitutional recognition of their indigenous identity. The demand for an autonomous region for the indigenous people was wrongly interpreted as secessionist and Sheikh Mujib told the delegation: "No, we are all Bengalis, we cannot have two systems of government. Forget your ethnic identity and be Bengalis" (CHT Commission, 1991, p. 14).

Manobendra Larma and his brother Shantu Larma then established their own indigenous political party, the Parbataya Chottogram Jana Samhati Samiti (PCJSS) to bring forward their demands more effectively and defend their existence.

Although Sheikh Mujibur Rahman had threatened to flood the area with the army and Bengali settlers, it was General Ziaur Rahman who fully militarized the Chittagong Hill Tracts after he came to power in 1975 through a military coup. From 1976 onward, the area was under full military occupation. The major part of the Bangladesh army was deployed in the CHT. Next to the three already existing garrisons in Rangamati, Ruma, and Alikadam, three more were constructed in Khagrachari, Dighinala, and Bandarban. Apart from these six garrisons, there are more than 400 camps and check-posts of the security forces (army, border security force, and police) now situated throughout the CHT. According to a conservative estimate, there is one member of the security forces for every ten hill people (CHT Commission, 1991, p. 42). The Shanti Bahini (SB, Peace Force), the armed wing of the PCJSS, carried out its first armed attack on a military camp in 1976.

"We Want the Land and Not the People"

Simultaneous with the militarization of the area, secret transmigration programs, initiated by General Zia, were carried out. Bengali from the plains were encouraged by local government officials to move to the CHT by promising them five acres of land there. The approximately 500,000 Bengali from the plains who were settled in the CHT between 1978 and 1985 were mostly landless peasants. But among them were also Bengali who had sold their land in their native area, lured by the promises of five acres

of land, which was much more than they had. Bengali business-
men also took advantage of lucrative land leases for plantations.
Settlers occupied the indigenous people's lands on a massive scale.
This put heavy pressure on the already scarce land in the area and
led to further depletion of the soil as the cycle of shifting cultivation became shorter and shorter. The Shanti Bahini stepped up
its armed actions and also started carrying out attacks on Bengali
settlements and killing settlers in an attempt to drive them out and
prevent more settlers from settling in the CHT.

The transmigration programs were officially stopped in 1985.
By then the composition of the population had been changed
fundamentally. The percentage of Bengali in the CHT rose from
19 percent in 1974 to 41 percent in 1981. At present, the population balance between indigenous and Bengali is around 50/50.
Even after 1985, the influx of settlers and occupation of land of
the indigenous peoples, with the backing of the army, continued
and is still continuing. Even those settlers who wanted to move
out of the area were prevented from doing so by the army. Settlers have occupied all seven fertile river valleys and many parts
of the hilly *jum* lands. Essentially, the Jumma have been robbed
of their livelihood.

When these transmigration programs became known to the outside world and the Bangladesh government was questioned about
it, the official argument was that the hills were "thinly populated"
in contrast to the overpopulated plains. This argument totally ignored the different character and quality of the land in the hills and
its reduced carrying capacity. In reality, the secret transmigration
programs were part of the army's counter-insurgency program.
By "Bengalizing" the hills, the indigenous peoples, numbering
less than 600,000 at that time, would soon be outnumbered and
could be kept under control more easily. The underlying motive
was the exploitation of the rich resources, especially oil and gas,
in the hills. Chakma Rajguru Aggavansa Mahathero reported in
1981 that on 26 December 1977, a day after the army had set fire to
Jumma houses and temples in Panchari in the northern Khagrachari
District and Bengalis had looted their properties, Jumma people
were forced at gunpoint to attend a public meeting organized by

the army. General Manzoor spoke at the meeting and stressed that the Bengali settlers were poor and landless and should be given shelter. At the end of the speech he shouted: "We don't want you. You can go wherever you like but we want your land. The Muslims should be settled there for the propagation of Islam" (Mey, 1984, p. 150). Deputy Commissioner of the Chittagong Hill Tracts (CHT) Ali Haider Khan and former commissioner of Chittagong Division Abdul Awal warned the indigenous leaders several times that they could be extinct in the next five years (Survival International, 1984, p. 21).

Development as Counter Insurgency

The Bangladesh army also controlled the administration and what they called "development" programs. With financial assistance from the Asian Development Bank, General Zia established the Chittagong Hill Tracts Development Board (CHTDB) in 1976. The CHTDB was headed by the GOC in Chittagong, the military commander in charge of the CHT. The main programs were road construction, telecommunication (both served the security forces) and relocation of the indigenous population. In the name of "upliftment" of the indigenous people who were said to be still living in the stone age, and eradication of swidden (*jum*) cultivation, allegedly to counter environmental degradation, thousands of Jumma people were relocated in cluster villages. Thus they were kept under control of the military and the rebellious Shanti Bahini were isolated from their popular support base. The livelihood of the indigenous peoples was destroyed and they were forced to work as cheap day-laborers on rubber plantations and so-called afforestation projects on the lands they once owned. These "development" programs were clearly an instrument of counter-insurgency (Arens 1997). Additional repressive measures restricted the freedom of movement and the selling and buying of essentials to prevent supplies to the Shanti Bahini, in several cases leading to starvation. People who were caught violating the restrictions were arrested, tortured, raped, and imprisoned.

All these policies resulted in an escalation of the conflict between the Bangladesh government and the Jumma people. Jumma people were uprooted on a large scale from the places where they had lived for centuries, and their livelihoods were destroyed. They were forcefully relocated, killed, detained, tortured, and raped, their villages burnt and temples destroyed. Many Jumma fled into the forest and to India. Bengali settlers who could not be accommodated on the land, which the fleeing and relocated indigenous people had left behind, were settled in "cluster villages," usually next to a military camp "for their own safety." In fact, they served as a protective shield for the military. The Shanti Bahini also stepped up its actions against the security forces and settlers. Their actions were often followed by massive reprisal attacks by the army on the civilian population.

Because the CHT was sealed off from the outside world only sporadic news about what was happening seeped out. From the late 1970s forward, reports of massive human rights violations perpetrated by the Bangladesh security forces started trickling out. In the 1980's a picture of systematic human rights violations started forming. Massacres of Jumma people, burning of their villages, disappearances, detention without trial, rape, torture, forced relocation, and religious persecution occurred on a massive scale and showed a systematic pattern. The influx of large numbers of Jumma refugees into India internationalized the conflict. The systematic human rights violations perpetrated by the security forces in collaboration with Bengali settlers took genocidal forms and from the early 1980s forward allegations of genocide of the indigenous peoples in the CHT were voiced nationally and internationally. As a result of this, the Swedish government development agency SIDA pulled out of an afforestation program and the Australian government pulled out of a road construction program. Oil giant Shell, which was exploring for oil in the CHT on a lucrative contract, pulled out in 1984 after five of its foreign workers were kidnapped by the Shanti Bahini and a large ransom was paid. The ILO, the UN Human Rights Commission, and the UN Sub-Commission on Prevention of Discrimination and Protection of Minorities all repeatedly questioned and criticized the Bangladesh government. Despite the rising international criticism, the British military continued its counter-insurgency training program for the Bangladesh army, and the World Bank, Asian Development Bank, WHO, and UNICEF continued supporting "development" programs in the CHT.

One of the issues in the definition of genocide is the perpetrators' intentionality of extermination. Chalk (1989) has argued that: "…a genocidal society exists when a government and its citizens pursue policies which they know will lead to annihilation of the aboriginal inhabitants of their country. Intentionality is demonstrated by persistence in such policies, whether or not the intent to destroy the aboriginal groups [was/is] verbalized" (p. 154). This is clearly the case in Bangladesh. Not only did the Bangladesh government persist in its genocidal policies, several government officials even alluded to the intention of extermination of the indigenous people.

Does History Repeat Itself?

Since the 1970s, massacres of Jumma people have taken place. These massacres were clearly meant to drive out the Jumma people and make place for the settlers. The massacres followed the same pattern: attacking a village, rounding up the people, burning their houses, killing men, abducting and raping women, and evicting the rest of the population. The massacre in Kaukhali, Kalampati Union, on 25 March 1980, was the first massacre that got wide publicity. Indigenous leaders who had been assembled by the local army commander for a meeting and local Jumma who had been ordered to restore the nearby Buddhist temple were suddenly showered with a rain of bullets from the army. According to varying reports, between fifty and 300 indigenous people were killed. Young women were held and raped for days by the military. Following the shooting, Bengali settlers looted and burned down the houses of the villagers. Following the visit of a parliamentary delegation of three opposition members, including Upendra Lal Chakma, an MP from the CHT, they concluded the following at a press conference in Dhaka: "It is obvious to us that the incident of Kalampati is not an isolated event. It has been perpetrated systematically and with a definite plan."

In turn, they demanded a judicial enquiry, proper security for the indigenous people, compensation and a withdrawal of the settlers from the CHT. The enquiry committee, subsequently established by the government and headed by the home minister, never issued a report. The same year, the home minister introduced the Disturbed Areas Bill which gave the security forces the power to arrest without warrant or to shoot anyone suspected of anti-state activities. Upendra Lal Chakma stated that "the government is looking for a genocidal solution to the problem of ethnic minorities" (Anti Slavery Society, 1984, p. 61). The highly controversial Disturbed Areas Bill was never endorsed in the Parliament, but the publicity given to the Kaukhali massacre and accusations of genocide did not stop the Bangladesh military government from continuing their genocidal policies and from committing more massacres. The Kaukhali massacre is only one in a long list of massacres perpetrated by the army in collusion with settlers. In fact, since 1979 eleven major massacres have taken place in which several thousand Jumma people have been killed. The full figure of those slain will never be known. Massacres took place, among others, at Banraibari, June 1981; Tabalchari, September 1981; Tarabanchari, June-August 1983; Bhusanchara, May 1984; Panchari, May 1986; Matiranga, May 1986; Comillatilla, Taindong, May 1986; Langadu, May 1989; Khagrachari, Pablakhali, August, 1988; Logang, April 1992; and Naniachar, November 1993.

General Ershad, who came to power in 1982 through yet another military coup, continued the same policies and even stepped up the "Jhumia rehabilitation" programs in the name of "development" and "environmental protection." After PCJSS leader Manobendra Larma had been killed in an internal party feud in 1983, General Ershad declared a general amnesty. The government figure of 5,000 Shanti Bahini members who surrendered as a result is highly disputed. The surrendered members were mostly from the dissident faction of the PCJSS, which had killed Manobendra Larma.

Some of the worst series of massacres took place in the Barkal area of Rangamati District in 1984 and in the Panchari, Matiranga, and Comillatilla-Taindong areas in Khagrachari District in 1986. Some of the massacres were in retaliation for Shanti Bahini attacks on army camps and killing of Bengali settlers. In the massacres, hundreds of Jumma people were killed and more than 40,000 people were made homeless. Many Jumma fled into the forest and to India. From mid-1980 forward, approximately 70,000 Jumma refugees, more than one-tenth of the total indigenous population of the CHT, were living in refugee camps in India. Over the years between 50,000 and 100,000 Jummas were internally displaced (Guhathakurta, 2004. p. 197).

During the Ershad government, several rounds of negotiations with the PCJSS took place, but after the initial meeting in December 1985 no other meeting took place until two years later. These negotiations ended in 1989 when the Ershad government unilaterally introduced the Hill District Council Acts for the three districts. These acts were passed in the parliament and in June 1989 sham Council elections were held in the three districts. With these Acts, Ershad claimed to have given autonomy to the hills. The PCJSS rejected them outright as it legitimized the settlers, gave them voting rights and provided no provisions for returning all the occupied lands to the Jumma people. (For more details on the negotiations during the Ershad period, see: http://www.cwis. org/fwdp/Eurasia/upendra.txt.)

After the end of military rule in 1990, the army and settlers continued to perpetrate gross human rights violations, such as the massacres in Malya (1992), Langadu (1992) and Naniarchar (1993). These largely followed the same pattern of burning villages, killing people and Bengalis occupying the land. Even after the Peace Accord between the PCJSS and the Awami League government was signed on 2 December 1997, eviction of Jumma people and occupation of their land by settlers continued in a similar pattern. Major incidents took place in in Mahalchari (2003, see Amnesty International 2004, ASA 13/003/2004) and in Sajek (2008).

Genocidal Process

Levene (1999) argues that a "creeping" genocide of the Jumma peoples in the CHT was taking place. Comparing the struggle of the Jumma with that of the Maya Indians of Guatemala, the Kurd, the Tibetan and the peoples of East Timor and Irian Jaya, Levene (1999) argues as follows:

In none of these instances, we may note, did the state set out to exterminate these people simply on the grounds of their ethnic difference or "otherness." That they have increasingly done so, in part bears witness to these communities' obdurate refusal to be coerced into the national mainstream on terms determined by the state, combined with their coherent political and political-military resistance to deny it hegemonic control over the land and resources which they consider to be theirs. It is this state-community dynamic which has led, in each instance, through a series of state strategies characterized here as a "genocidal process," to their culmination, at some stage, in the actuality of genocide. In the case of the Jummas, the only distinction lies in the fact that this actuality is difficult to isolate to a single sequence of events. This is why I have called it a case of "creeping genocide." In all other respects, the critical preconditions and characteristics of genocide are evident. (346)

As for the refusal of the Jumma to be passive victims, Levene (1999) comments:

> The roots of genocide in the CHT do rest *in part* in the refusal of the Jumma either to lie down and die quietly, or alternatively, to accept a place within the Bangladeshi scheme of things, for instance as colourful but otherwise harmless exotica, weaving carpets and dancing for the tourists, in some ethnographic zoo. Instead, their tenacious and bloody fight-back against state and settler encroachment alike, and their articulation of their political right to self-determination, has challenged the very notion of a religiously and culturally unified Bangladesh. (363)

When all is said and done, the military occupation with the resulting massacres and other systematic human rights violations, and the government policies that completely uprooted the Jumma peoples from their land, and destroyed their livelihood, culture and religious practices, *are nothing less than genocide.*

The Gender Dimension of Genocide

Women have been particularly targeted by the security forces and rape has been used systematically as a weapon. Only recently, on 19 June 2008, the United Nations Security Council adopted Resolution 1820 and noted, "rape and other forms of sexual violence can constitute a war crime, a crime against humanity, or a constitutive act with respect to genocide" and urged the UN to impose sanctions on violators. (Gang) rape is a recurring characteristic of attacks on Jumma villages and women are often (gang) raped in front of their husbands, children and other family members. Women live in continuous fear of rape. Information from one of the refugee camps in Tripura, India, indicated that one in every ten women of the total female population had been raped (Guhathakurta, 1994,

p. 198). One woman in the refugee camps in Tripura told the CHT Commission in 1990:

> About 50 army personnel came in the night and rounded up the whole village and gathered us in one place. In the morning all the men were arrested. I was tied up hands and legs, naked. They raped me. There were three women there. They raped me in front of my father-in-law. After that we were tied up together, naked, facing each other. Then they left. Three other girls were raped in front of me. This happened in the month of Ashat (June/July) of 1985 (CHT Commission, 1991, p. 86).

Many women never admit that they were raped for fear of being ostracized by their families. In Bangladesh women represent the honor of the group. A woman who has been raped is often rejected by her husband and family, or may not be able to get married. If a child is born to a woman as a result of rape, the community will not accept her and she is ostracized.

In 1986, Amnesty International published eye-witness accounts of several of the massacres. A villager from Het Baria gave the following statement about the massacre in 1984 in the Barkal area in which allegedly 200 Jumma people were killed:

> My village falls in the Barkal rehabilitation zone where large numbers of Muslims have settled over the years. There is thus continuous tension between the two communities....The army came on May 31, accompanied by a large group of Muslims some of whom were armed. They destroyed our village, raped women and killed people. I saw two women getting raped and then killed by bayonets. One Aroti, who is my distant cousin, was also raped by several soldiers and her body was disfigured with bayonets. Several people, including children, were thrown into burning huts. I was among the people singled out for torture in public. Five or six of us were hung upside down on a tree and beaten. Perhaps I was given up for dead and thus survived. The memories of that day are still a nightmare for me. Even now I sometimes wake up in a cold sweat remembering the sight of the soldiers thrusting bayonets into private parts of our women. They were all screaming "No Chakmas will be born in Bangladesh." (Amnesty International, 1986, p. 14)

Targeting women's reproductive organs is evidence of the deliberate intent to extinguish the whole ethnic group and its future generations. Women are seen as the procreators of the group. Gang-raping women and then bayoneting them in their genital areas recurs in many of the witness accounts. This is exactly the same method used by the Pakistani army who raped over 200,000 Bengali women during the Bangladesh liberation war: "...soldiers killed babies by throwing them in the air and catching them on their bayonets, and murdered women by raping them and then spearing them through the genitals. *Newsweek* concluded that...the West Pakistani army was 'carrying out a calculated policy of terror amounting to genocide'"(quoted in Sharlach, 2000, pp. 94-95).

The exclamation of a West Pakistani soldier: "We are going. But we are leaving our Seed behind" (also quoted in Sharlach, 2000, p. 95), is strikingly similar to that of the Bengali soldiers asserting that "No Chakmas will be born in Bangladesh."

Another statement of a survivor of the massacres in the CHT in 1986 also indicates clearly that women were specifically targeted:

> ...He [the army officer, J.A.] separated us youngsters from the rest and asked his soldiers to beat us up and kill us if we did not say where the Shanti Bahini people were hiding. One of the soldiers also heated a knife in one of the huts and branded my back with it. I screamed and fell unconscious. By that time a group of Muslim settlers had also joined in with the army. The officer ordered them to start killing men but to take away women so that at least the next generation of Chakmas will behave like good Bangladeshis. (Amnesty International, 1986, n.p.)

The indigenous Hill Women Federation stated in 1995 that over 94 percent of the rape cases of Jumma women in the CHT between 1991 and 1993 were by security forces and over 40 percent of the victims were women under eighteen years of age (CHT Commission, 1997, p. 12). Women who protest against gross human violations are not safe. For example, Kalpana Chakma, Organizing Secretary of the Hill Women's Federation, was kidnapped from her house on the night of 11 to 12 June 1996 by one Lieutenant Ferdous. No sign of Kalapana Chakma has been seen or heard since. Kalpana Chakma had repeatedly protested against attacks on Jumma villages under the command of the army lieutenant.

The Peace Accord and After

After the Awami League headed by Sheikh Hasina came to power through elections in 1996, negotiations between the government and the PCJSS were resumed and on 2 December 1997 a Peace Accord was signed. The main points of Peace Accord are:

- modification of the Hill District Council Acts of 1989 and an indirectly elected Regional Council to coordinate and supervise the District Councils;

- withdrawal of the security forces to the six cantonments;
- land to be placed under the jurisdiction of the Hill District Councils and installation of a Land Commission to resolve all land disputes;
- rehabilitation of surrendered PCJSS and SB members;
- repatriation and rehabilitation of all the refugees.

Until now, more than ten years later, the Peace Accord is yet to be largely implemented and peace in the area is still at large. The Land Commission that is to resolve the thousands of land disputes is yet to start its work. Illegal settlement and serious human rights violations continue. As recent as 20 April 2008, in an attack on villages in Sajek, Rangamati District, settlers, backed by the army, burnt down seventy-seven Jumma houses and then occupied the place.

Indigenous leaders are still not safe and many are in hiding from the security forces. Ranglai Mro, an indigenous leader in Bandarban district who had protested eviction of hundreds of Mro to give way to an army training centre, was arrested in February 2007 and sentenced to seventeen years in jail on false charges of possessing a pistol without a license. He was severely tortured and is suffering from a serious heart condition since. He is denied proper medical treatment (Amnesty International, 12/003/2008). Satyabir Dewan, general secretary of the PCJSS, was sentenced to seventeen years on false charges as well. Also, indigenous leaders from the plains who are resisting the continuous encroachment by outsiders and annexation by the government of their lands are not safe. Cholesh Richil, a Garo leader who had been very vocal in protesting the government annexation of their ancestral land for a tourist "Eco Park," was tortured and brutally murdered in military custody in March 2007.

The Peace Accord also led to a division among the Jumma people themselves. A group of Jumma activists rejected the accord because it failed to give regional autonomy and constitutional recognition. They formed their own political party, the UPDF (United People's Democratic Front), to continue the struggle. This led to a bloody feud between the PCJSS and UPDF. Several mediation attempts by Jumma elders could not bring reconciliation between the two parties so far.

No perpetrators of any of the massacres and other human rights violations have been arrested, let alone tried in court. Nor has the government published any investigation reports. It may be significant that Bangladesh ratified the UN Genocide Convention only in 1998 and entered provisos granting immunity from prosecution for genocide without its consent. During her visit to Bangladesh in January 2008, Secretary General of Amnesty International, Irene Khan, in a press release, commented as follows on such immunity:

> The human rights history of Bangladesh is bound by a red thread of impunity and denial of human rights abuses. It goes all the way back to the war crimes and crimes against humanity during 1971.... The culture of impunity and non-accountability that has persisted for decades must end. This requires institutional reform (Amnesty International, 2008, n.p.).

The crux of the problem is that this requires the political will of the government to redress historical injustices in the first place.

Critical Challenges Facing the Field Today

Three issues are crucial for a resolution of the conflict: demilitarization, land, and official recognition of the identity and rights (to their own livelihood, language, culture, religion) of the indigenous peoples (not only in the CHT, but the entire country). Hardly any of the 400 military camps and check posts have been dismantled. As long as the CHT is a militarized zone, gross human rights violations will continue. Implementation of the withdrawal of the army to its six cantonments in the CHT, as provided for in the Peace Accord, will be a first step in this direction. The voters lists, which include members of the security forces and non-permanent Bengali residents as voters in the CHT, remains a critical issue. The latter is bound to seriously influence the balance of votes in upcoming elections (IWGIA, 2007, p. 386).

As for land, it will be an immense, if not impossible, task to resolve all the land disputes. Acknowledgement that population transfer and relocation programs in the past have been largely responsible for these land conflicts would open the door for voluntary rehabilitation of Bengali settlers outside the CHT. Landless Bengalis have been used as a tool in the CHT conflict by the government, army, and more recently by Bengali leaders (backed by the army) demanding "equal rights" for Bengalis. Poor settlers have repeatedly expressed their willingness to settle anywhere else if they would be given the means to live (Chittagong Hill Tracts Commission, 1992, 1994, 1997, 2000). Foreign governments have since long expressed their willingness to fund such programs. This would reduce the pressure on the land. Given the presence of communal forces that will undoubtedly try to sabotage resettlement programs, this will need a strong united platform to counter opposition to this possibility. Bangladesh civil society—both indigenous and Bengali organizations, in concert—can play a critical role in creating a broad debate to promote an attitude of acknowledgement of past gross injustices and the political will to repair such. The progressive media could play a role here as well. The support of international human rights and other organizations and donor governments in raising the critical issues and pushing the government into action can also strengthen initiatives along those lines.

Official recognition of the status of the indigenous peoples is long overdue. Granting recognition would safeguard their identities, way of living, and livelihood. As a signatory to ILO Convention 107, the Bangladesh government has moral obligations in this respect.

The above measures would probably also reduce the tensions between the PCJSS and UPDF and create a basis for reconciliation.

Probabilities of Progress in the Field

Some recent developments are a positive sign. In December 2007, the Council of Advisers of the Caretaker Government approved the National Human Rights Commission Ordinance 2007. The chief advisor has agreed with Amnesty International that the mandate of the National Human Rights Commission must also include investigation of abuses by the security forces (http://www.amnesty.org/en/for-media/press-releases/one-year-human-rights-bangladesh-under-state-emergency-20080110). The National Human Rights Commission is yet to be formed.

Another development is that Bangladesh applied to the UN for lifting impunity for human rights violations during the liberation war (http://www.amnesty.org/en/for-media/press-releases/bangla-desh-request-un-involvement-ending-impunity-1971-violations-welcom). This could be used to press forward the need for a future step to lift impunity for human rights violations of the indigenous peoples since independence.

Much will depend on the political will of the government to redress historical and recent gross injustices. The Awami League has reiterated its stand that it will implement the Peace Accord, but previous experience suggests that it will have to be pushed to put its words into action. If the BNP/Jamaat-e-Islami alliance gains power then the prospects will be more uncertain as both parties support the forces that have been contributing to communal tensions in the CHT and have taken positions against the Peace Accord.

An extensive debate about the rights of indigenous peoples in Bangladesh, injustices done to them and the urgency to repair these will arouse further support for the cause of the indigenous peoples in civil society. In this respect, the re-established International CHT Commission could contribute all the more as four of its members are widely respected Bangladeshis with strong roots in the field of human rights. The renewed concern of the international donor community regarding the CHT issue could add weight as well.

Conclusion

Militarization of the CHT, population transfer programs settling hundreds of thousands of Bengali in the CHT, and relocation programs of Jumma people in strategic cluster villages have resulted in massacres and other massive human rights violations of the indigenous peoples since independence of Bangladesh. The goal is to root out the Jumma peoples' existence, especially their women.

Women have been systematically raped, abducted and killed with the explicit intent to prevent the births of a new generation of people fighting for their identity and rights. All these violations have repeatedly led to allegations of genocide.

The indigenous peoples have been systematically robbed of their lives, livelihood, culture, and religious freedom on a mass scale. Bengalis who have been victims of genocide themselves during the liberation war in 1971 have turned into perpetrators, inflicting deep traumas on the indigenous population. The culture of impunity continues. Unless historical injustices are repaired, impunity is lifted and perpetrators brought to justice, both of the liberation war and of the armed conflict with the indigenous Jumma, a deep trauma on both sides will result in the continuance of this genocidal process.

References

Anti-Slavery Society (1984). *The Chittagong Hill Tracts: Militarization, Oppression, and the Hill Tribes*. London: Anti-Slavery Society.

Amnesty International (1986). *Unlawful Killings and Torture in the Chittagong Hill Tracts*. London: Amnesty International Publications. 38 pp.

Arens, Jenneke (1997). "Winning Hearts and Minds: Foreign Aid and Militarization in the Chittagong Hill Tracts." *Economic and Political Weekly* , July 19, pp. 1811-1819.

Bhaumik, Subir; Guhathakurta, Meghna; and Chaudhury, Sabyasachi Basu Ray (Eds.) (1997). *Living on the Edge: Essays on the Chittagong Hill Tracts*. Katmandu, Nepal: South Asia Forum for Human Rights.

Chalk, Frank (1989). "Definitions of Genocide and Their Implications for Prediction and Prevention." *Holocaust and Genocide Studies*, 4(2): 149-160.

Chittagong Hill Tracts Commission (1991). *Life is Not Ours': Land and Human Rights in the Chittagong Hill Tracts, Bangladesh*. Amsterdam, Netherlands/Copenhagen, Denmark: Organizing Committee CHT Campaign/International Work Group for Indigenous Affairs.

Chittagong Hill Tracts Commission (1992, 1994, 1997, 2000). *Life is Not Ours': Land and Human Rights in the Chittagong Hill Tracts, Bangladesh. Update 1, 2, 3, 4*. Amsterdam, Netherlands/Copenhagen, Denmark: Organizing Committee CHT Campaign/International Work Group for Indigenous Affairs.

Guhathakurta, Meghna (2004). "Women Negotiating Change: The Structure and Transformation of Gendered Violence in Bangladesh." *Cultural Dynamics*, 16(2/3): 193-211.

International Work Group for Indigenous Affairs (2007). *The Indigenous World 2007*. Copenhagen, Denmark: Author.

Levene, Mark (1999). "The Chittagong Hill Tracts: A Case Study in the Political Economy of 'Creeping' Genocide." *Third World Quarterly*, 20(2): 339-369.

Mey, Wolfgang (Ed.) (1984). *Genocide in the Chittagong Hill Tracts, Bangladesh, Document 51*. Copenhagen, Denmark: IWGIA.

Sharlach, Lisa (2000). "Rape as Genocide: Bangladesh, the Former Yugoslavia, and Rwanda." *New Political Science*, 22(1): 89-102.

Survival International (1984). "Genocide in Bangladesh; Indians and Government in Peru; Indians and the World Bank and Other Articles." *Survival International Annual Review No.43*. London: Survival International, pp. 7-28.

Annotated Bibliography

Adnan, Shapan (2004). *Migration, Land Alienation and Ethnic Conflict: Causes of Poverty in the Chittagong Hill Tracts of Bangladesh*. Dhaka: Research & Advisory Services. 252 pp.

Land is the most contentious issue in the CHT. Herein, Adnan documents and analyzes the land use practices of the indigenous peoples and the changes in the CHT economy as a result of government policies. The latter are the main cause of the processes of impoverishment of the indigenous peoples who were once well off due to the timber, bamboo and surplus of paddy and cotton. The last chapter (50 pp.) provides extensive recommendations on economic and other developmental issues. The book ends with ninety-six pages of photographs that highlight the land, the people and their social and economic life in the CHT.

Amnesty International (1986). *Unlawful Killings and Torture in the Chittagong Hill Tracts*. London: Amnesty International Publications. 38 pp.

Apart from a short history of the CHT and Amnesty's concerns with the CHT, the main part of the document describes a series of massacres and incidents of torture by the military and includes many eyewitness accounts.

Anti-Slavery Society (1984). *The Chittagong Hill Tracts: Militarization, Oppression, and the Hill Tribes*. London: Anti-Slavery Society. 93 pp.

A short and good overview of the history of colonization and resistance, development policies and militarization leading up to the genocide of the indigenous peoples.

Arens, Jenneke (1997). "Winning Hearts and Minds: Foreign Aid and Militarization in the Chittagong Hill Tracts." *Economic and Political Weekly*, July 19-25, XXXII (29): 1811-1819.

Providing numerous details, Arens argues that development aid to Bangladesh has, both directly and indirectly, not only added to continuing militarization of the CHT and human rights violations, but also to a systematic destruction of the mode of production, way of life, and culture of the Jumma peoples.

Arens, Jenneke, and Nishan Chakma, Kirti (2002). "Bangladesh: Indigenous Struggle in the Chittagong Hill Tracts," pp. 304-323.

In Monique Mekenkamp, Paul van Tongeren and Hans van de Veen (Eds.) *Searching for Peace in Central and South Asia: An Overview of Conflict Prevention and Peacebuilding Activities.* Boulder, CO: Lynne Rienner.

An overview of the dynamics of the conflict, official conflict management, role of civil society and NGO initiatives, and prospects for resolution of the conflict. It concludes with a set of recommendations.

Bhaumik, Subir (1996). *Insurgent Crossfire: North-East India.* New Delhi and London: Lancer Publishers. 360 pp.

Bhaumik, a BBC correspondent for East India Subir, examines the origins of how South Asian nations have sponsored, trained and armed guerrilla armies fighting their rivals and presents detailed case studies of the major guerrilla campaigns in North-East India. Chapter 8 deals with the insurgency in the CHT—the various armed groups, the emergence of the PCJSS and its predecessors, and the Indian support to the insurgents (e.g., providing military training and safe havens after the assassination of Sheikh Mujib). Bhaumik includes many interesting inside details not available in other studies, including, material from unpublished diaries of M. N. Larma, and personal interviews with several indigenous leaders and an official of India's intelligence agency RAW.

Bhaumik, Subir; Guhathakurta, Meghna; and Chaudhury, Sabya-sachi Basu Ray (Eds.) (1997). *Living on the Edge: Essays on the Chittagong Hill Tracts.* Katmandu, Nepal: South Asia Forum for Human Rights. 391pp.

A collection of articles by mainly Jumma and Bengali (from Bangladesh and West Bengal, India) authors covering all the relevant aspects of the CHT conflict, including the Indian policy regarding the CHT and the diaspora of the Jumma in N.E. India.

Chittagong Hill Tracts Commission (1991). *"Life is Not Ours": Land and Human Rights in the Chittagong Hill Tracts, Bangladesh.* Amsterdam/Copenhagen: Organising Committee CHT Campaign /International Work Group for Indigenous Affairs. 131pp.

Details and analysis of the findings of the investigation of the CHT Commission in the refugee camps in Tripura, India and the CHT in November/December/January 1990/91. The eight sections cover a wide array of topics/issues, including: key political and legal history, the militarization of the area, human rights violations, land issues, development projects, cultural and religious discrimination, and social problems. It concludes with a series of recommendations. (Downloadable from http://iwgia.org/sw29919. asp.)

Chittagong Hill Tracts Commission (1992, 1994, 1997, 2000). *"Life is Not Ours": Land and Human Rights in the Chittagong Hill Tracts, Bangladesh: Update 1, 2, 3, and 4.* Amsterdam/Copenhagen: Organising Committee CHT Campaign/International Work Group for Indigenous Affairs. Respectively 28, 41, 26, 101 pp.

Four updates of the original report of the CHT Commission on the various aspects of the CHT conflict. The first update (1992) covers the year after the government of Khaleda Zia came to power, the first elected government after fifteen years of military rule. The third update (1997) came out after Sheikh Hasina of the Awami League had won the national elections, while the last update (2000) covers three years after the signing of the Peace Accord. (All downloadable from http://iwgia.org/sw29919.asp.)

Guhathakurta, Meghna (undated). "Ethnic Conflict in a Post-Accord Situation: The Case of the Chittagong Hill Tracts, Bangladesh." http://www.uttorshuri.net/CHT.html. 14 pp.

A detailed account of the attack by the army and settlers on Jumma people in Mahalchari area, Khagrachari District in August 2003, and an analysis of the implications of the attack in view of the 1997 Peace Accord.

Guhathakurta, Meghna (2004). "Women Negotiating Change: The Structure and Transformation of Gendered Violence in Bangladesh." *Cultural Dynamics* 16 (2/3):193-211.

Guhathakurta explores the abduction by the army and disappearance of Kalpana Chakma, Organizing Secretary of the Hill

Women's Federation, in June 1996. In the analysis, issues of agency and resistance are addressed, as well as the means by which women negotiate and resist the subject position of "victim."

Hossain, Hamida, and Hossain, Sara. (2007). *Human Rights in Bangladesh 2006*. Dhaka: Ain o Shalish Kendra (ASK). 210 pp.
    Annual overview of violations of the various human rights perpetrated in Bangladesh. The book includes a chapter on the rights of Adibashis (as indigenous peoples in Bangladesh are called), with separate sections on indigenous peoples in the CHT and in the plains.

International Work Group for Indigenous Affairs (2008). *The Indigenous World 2008*. Copenhagen, Denmark: Author. 578 pp.
    Annual update (since 1997) on political developments and developments in human rights with regard to indigenous peoples worldwide. The Bangladesh section (pp. 342-350) deals both with the Chittagong Hill Tracts and indigenous peoples from the plains.

International Work Group for Indigenous Affairs (1986). *IWGIA Newsletter No. 46*. Copenhagen, Denmark, Author. 120 pp.
    This issue contains two articles on the CHT. The first article (pp. 1-8) is based on reports by the PCJSS that contain 278 cases of human rights violations involving murder, torture, rape, robbery, arson, abduction, forcible conversion and electoral fraud. The second article (pp. 9-13,) "Threats to Safety of Tribal Refugees in India as Government/JSS Negotiations Break Down," deals with instances of forced repatriation of thousands of Jumma refugees who fled to India after attacks on their villages by the army and settlers in 1984 and 1986. The *Newsletter* also contains an article on the threat of eviction of over one million indigenous people in India as a result of the, at that time still planned, construction of dams in the Narmada River (pp. 69-77).

Levene, Mark (1999). "The Chittagong Hill Tracts: A Case Study in the Political Economy of 'Creeping' Genocide." *Third World Quarterly*, 20 (2): 339-369.

Levene argues against terms such as ethnocide and cultural genocide as these suggest a distinct form of genocide and discourages comparison with others genocides. Noting the example of the genocide in the CHT, Levene argues that the (attempted) destruction of indigenous peoples is central to the pattern of contemporary genocide and by examining such specific examples, the general sources and processes of genocide can be more clearly delineated. The general efforts of the new nation-state of Bangladesh to overcome its structural weaknesses by attempting a consolidation and settlement of its resource rich frontier region and to integrate into the western-dominated international system closely mirrors other state-building, western-funded development agendas that have been confronted with communal resistance. Levene argues that it is in these efforts "to realize what is actually unrealizable" that the relationship between a flawed state power and genocide can be located.

Mey, Wolfgang (Ed.) (1984). *Genocide in the Chittagong Hill Tracts, Bangladesh. IWGIA Document 51.* Copenhagen, Denmark: IWGIA. 190 pp.

A collection of in-depth articles on the history of repression and resistance, tradition, land rights and resources in the CHT. It includes an account of exile by a Chakma and an interview with Upendra Lal Chakma, Member of Parliament for the CHT.

Mey, Wolfgang (Ed.) (1988). *Wir Wollen Nicht Euch—Wir Wollen Euer Land* (*We Do Not Want You, We Want Your Land*). Göttingen and Vienna: Gesellschaft für Bedrohte Völker. 136 pp.

This publication in German is a compilation of articles by mostly German authors and puts land as the central issue in the human rights violations. It is suggested that with nine percent of the total population of Bangladesh in control of 54 percent of all the land, the solution of the problem lies in radical land reform in Bangladesh.

Mohsin, Amena (1997). *The Politics of Nationalism: The Case of the Chittagong Hill Tracts, Bangladesh.* Dhaka: The University Press Limited. 253 pp.

Mohsin questions the efficacy of the organizing conceptions and institutions of the nation-state. These have become a tool of hegemony of the dominant forces and have alienated subordinate communities and thus given rise to sub-state nationalism. Political, economic and military policies have been adopted to consolidate the hegemony of the Bengalis and these have alienated the hill people. Mohsin argues that nationalism, used as a counter-hege-mony tool by the indigenous peoples in the CHT (who are not a homogenous community), will only reproduce hegemony and alienation. Mohsin posits that a recognition that nation refers to a cultural entity and state to a political entity would give space to a concept of a Bangladeshi (vs. Bengali) citizenship in which different ethnic groups retain their own identity. Lastly Mohsin lists the necessary measures at the constitutional and institutional levels that such a change would require.

Roy, Rajkumari Chandra (2000). *Land Rights of the Indigenous Peoples of the Chittagong Hill Tracts, Bangladesh. IWGIA Document 99.* Copenhagen: IWGIA
    Roy discusses how from colonial times onwards governments have infringed on the land rights of the Jumma peoples and how the latter have been struggling to regain control. Roy identifies and analyzes the major components of the land issue and provides recommendations for the short, medium and long term. Chapter 5 extensively documents the various international instruments that are available for indigenous peoples to assert their land rights, such as the Universal Declaration of Human Rights and ILO Conventions 107 and 169.

Schendel, Willem van (1992). "The Invention of the 'Jummas': State Formation and Ethnicity in Southeastern Bangladesh." *Modern Asian Studies*, 26(1): 95-128.
    By reconstructing ethnic persistence and innovation on the basis of historic documentation of the last 200 years, van Schendel seeks to explain why in recent years the new "Jumma" identity has been "invented" and found acceptance. Van Schendel concludes: "It was a bid for ethnic innovation, the creation of a new 'national'

collectivity, to cope with the political and economic consequences of loss of power, growing expendability to the state, and cultural marginalization."

Shelley, Mizanur Rahman (Ed.) (1992). *The Chittagong Hill Tracts of Bangladesh: The Untold Story.* Dhaka: Centre for Development Research, 200 pp.

This collection presents itself as an endeavor to provide "a correct and objective vision." However, it mainly represents government views and pictures government policies as a sincere commitment to a peaceful solution. The authors play down allegations of human rights violations as exaggerated and distorted, in particular the Logang massacre in April 1992. It seeks the root cause of the massacre in "a deliberate plan and provocative action by the Shanti Bahini." In reality, the army and settlers had killed at least 100 indigenous people after settlers alleged that the Shanti Bahini had killed a Bengali boy after he had tried to rape a Jumma girl.

Survival International (1984). *Genocide in Bangladesh: Survival International Annual Review No.43.* London: Author, pp. 7-28.

This *Review* contains three articles on Bangladesh. The first describes gross human rights violations in the CHT. The second article is on the southern Bandarban District and describes the process by which the government and military appropriated the indigenous peoples' land. The third article describes how the indigenous peoples in the north of Bangladesh have been systematically robbed of their land.

6

Genocide of Khoekhoe and San Peoples of Southern Africa

Robert K. Hitchcock and Wayne A. Babchuk

Introduction

In Southern Africa, like many other parts of the world including the Americas, Asia, Australia, New Zealand, and the Pacific, a
significant proportion of the genocides of indigenous peoples took
place during the course of colonial expansion (Gordon and Douglas, 2000; Gall, 2001; Hitchcock and Twedt, 2009). In 1652, when
Europeans established a full-time presence in Southern Africa,
there were some 300,000 San and 600,000 Khoekhoe in Southern
Africa. During the early phases of European colonization, tens of
thousands of Khoekhoe and San peoples[1] lost their lives as a result
of genocide, murder, physical mistreatment, and disease (Philip,
1828; Moodie, 1838, 1841; Theal, 1919; Elphick, 1977; Gordon,
1985, 1989, 2009; Gordon and Douglas, 2000; Skotnes, 1996a,
1996b; Morris, 1996; Gall, 2001; Brantlinger, 2003, pp. 68-93;
Crais and Scully, 2009). There were cases of "Bushman hunting"
in which commandos (mobile paramilitary units or posses) sought
to dispatch San and Khoekhoe in various parts of Southern Africa
(Wright, 1971; Marks, 1972; Penn, 1995, 2006).

Genocides also took place during wars between colonists and
Khoekhoe and San, one example being the "frontier war" of 1739

in which there were massacres of upwards of several hundred Khoekhoe and San (Penn, 2006, pp. 56-78). San were hunted down and killed in the Maluti-Drakensberg Mountains region of Lesotho and South Africa until what some people believed to be "the last Bushman" in the mountains was killed in 1873 (Stow, 1905; How, 1970; Wright, 1971). It is unlikely that this was the case, however, as there are people in the area today who claim to be San.

The conditions of South African indigenous peoples were so severe in the early part of the nineteenth century that the British Aborigines Protection Society drew attention to them, and concerns were also expressed by faith-based organizations such as the London Missionary Society (Philip, 1828; Brantlinger, 2003, pp. 68-93). The indigenous peoples of Southern Africa were characterized as being "on the road to extinction" and therefore, it was assumed, little could be done to prevent their "inevitable disappearance" (Brantlinger, 2003, pp. 3, 13, 42; 70-93).

The earliest genocide of the twentieth century took place in southwestern Africa, now Namibia. The targets were the Herero and the Nama and the perpetrators were members of the German military and German and other European settlers (Bridgman and Worley 2009; Schaller, this volume). Not long afterwards, between 1912 to 1915, another genocide was carried out in the same area that targeted San (Bushmen) peoples (Gordon, 2009). This latter genocide has largely been overlooked, in part because most of the victims were members of small-scale mobile groups in remote areas who depended primarily on hunting and gathering or on labor on small farms and who were considered by people of European descent to have relatively low status and few, if any, rights in Namibian society.

Allegations of genocide involving Khoekhoe and/or San peoples in contemporary times include ones involving San in Angola in the 1970s and 1980s and up through 2002 (Souindola, 1981; Robins, Brenziger, and Madzudzo, 2001; Pakleppa and Kwononoka, 2003; Akpan, Mberengwa, Hitchcock, and Koperski, 2004), Tyua San in western Zimbabwe in the early 1980s (Catholic Justice and Peace Commission of Zimbabwe and Legal Resources Foundation, 1997, 1999; Hitchcock, 1995; Hitchcock and Twedt, 2009), Khwe San in Namibia in 1999-2000 (National Society for Human Rights, 1996; Orth, 2003), and G/ui and G//ana San and Bakgalagadi of the Central Kalahari Game Reserve in Botswana in the 1990s and into the new millennium (Isaacson, 2004; Arce-Whyte, 2004; Saugestad, 2005).

In Botswana in 2002, after several hundred people were relocated involuntarily out of the Central Kalahari Game Reserve, the largest protected area in the country, representatives of non-government organizations and human rights groups accused the Botswana government of "ethnic cleansing," "slow genocide," "cultural genocide," and acts "tantamount to genocide" (see Isaacson, 2004; www.survival-international.org; www.iwant2gohome. com). Evelyne Arce-White, the executive director of International Funders for Indigenous Peoples, said, "There is a largely unpublicized genocide occurring in Botswana" (Arce-White, 2004, p. 1). Concerning the situation of the situation of the San in the Central Kalahari, Survival International, an indigenous peoples' human rights advocacy group, asserted that "They have experienced a genocide which has almost completely been ignored" website (www.survivalinternational.org, accessed on October 15, 2005). An op-ed writer, Mike Lavene, asked the question in a Botswana newspaper, "Can Botswana be Charged with Genocide?" (Lavene, 2002, p. 6).

Some local people also argued that what they saw as forced resettlement out of the Central Kalahari Game Reserve and denial of access to water by the government of Botswana was a deliberate policy aimed at inflicting harm and destroying them as people.

At one and the same time, there are others who questioned the sagacity of referring to what transpired as genocide. More specifically, two major groups in Botswana —both Ditshwanelo, the Botswana Center for Human Rights, and the Kuru Family of Organizations, the largest San non-government organization in Botswana – assert that to claim, that people in the Central Kalahari were killed deliberately because of who they were goes too far. Both of these organizations pointed out that using the term genocide to refer to a situation in which nobody was killed overstates the severity of what transpired in the Central Kalahari. Paul Kenyon (2005), a reporter for the British Broadcasting Corporation's program "Crossing Continents" also questioned whether what the San experienced was genocide. As one can readily see, the issue of genocide is clearly an important issue in contemporary debates in Southern Africa. The Botswana government categorically dismissed the allegations of genocide, forced removals, and ethnic cleansing on its website and in statements to the media (www.bot. gov/home.html).

It should be stressed that not all genocides of Khoekhoe and San were at the hands of Europeans. As will be shown below, there were also cases of massive human rights violations perpetrated against Khoekhoe and San by other African groups. There were also instances in which Khoekhoe and San engaged in genocide and massive human rights violations, as occurred, for example, in some of the resistance efforts of Khoekhoe and San in the seventeenth through nineteenth centuries in South Africa (Wright, 1971; Penn, 1995, 1996, 2001, 2006), and during military actions involving San in the South African Defense Force in Angola during the war in Angola in the latter part of the twentieth century. In other words, as Jones and Robins (2009) note, genocides and mass murder are not perpetrated exclusively by state actors but may also be perpetrated by subalterns or peoples — many of them minorities—who themselves have experienced oppression.

Khoesan Peoples in Southern Africa

Southern African populations are divided into a number of different named groups, including those designated as Khoesan (Khoisan) peoples (Schapera, 1930; Lee, 1976, 1979; Barnard 1992, 2007; Suzman 2001a). The San are variously known as Bushmen, or, in Botswana, as Basarwa (Mogwe, 1992; Saugestad, 2001; Cassidy, Good, Mazonde, and Rivers 2001; Hitchcock, Ikeya, Biesele, and Lee 2006; Thomas, 2006). The term Khoekhoe is sometimes used to refer to peoples who were referred to pejoratively in the past as Hottentots or, in some cases, as Nama (Elphick, 1977; Barnard, 1992; Penn, 2006, pp. 8-9). Khoekhoe traditionally were livestock-keepers and part-time foragers who occupied the coast and interior of southwestern and Southern

Africa at the time of European exploration and colonization (Elphick, 1977). The Aborigines Protection Committee formed by Lord Thomas Buxton in England in the 1830s was informed in 1837 that the "Hottentot" population in South Africa had been reduced from 200,000 (or more) to 32,000 (Brantlinger, 2003, p. 75). Today, Khoekhoe groups are found in Namibia, South Africa, and Botswana. Some of the Khoekhoe and San are involved in a pan-Khoekhoe social movement aimed at promoting their human rights (Bredekamp, 2001; Saugestad, 2001; Sylvain, 2002, 2005; Hitchcock, 2002).

There are several groups in Namibia that are considered by themselves and others to be indigenous to the country. These include not only the San, who are found in many parts of the country, especially in the central and northern areas and in urban settings such as Windhoek, but also the Himba, pastoralists who reside mainly in the Kunene region in the northwestern part of Namibia. Two other Namibian groups also consider themselves indigenous: the Nama, Khoe-speaking peoples who traditionally were small stock herders who live mainly in the central and southern parts of Namibia, and the Basters, a community of mainly Afrikaans-speaking people who reside in the south of the country. San are also found today in western Zambia, western Zimbabwe, and southern Angola (Suzman, 2001a; Akpan, Hitchcock, Mberengwa, and Koperski 2004). In South Africa today, there are some 7,500 San (Chennels and du Toit, 2004; Roger Chennels and Axel Thoma, personal communications, 2008) and there are at least 360,000 Khoekhoe.

At the time of colonization, Richard Lee (1976) estimated that there were some 300,000 San living in Southern Africa south of the Congo watershed (p. 12). There were also several hundred thousand Khoekhoe residing in what are now Botswana, Namibia, and South Africa (Boonzaier, Malherbe, Smith, and Berens, 1996; Henry Bredekamp, personal communication, 2001). Table 6.1 presents data on the numbers of San and Khoekhoe living today in Southern Africa. It can be seen that contemporary San live in six of the countries of Southern Africa, though in the past they were much more widespread. Khoekhoe today live in three countries,

Table 6.1
Numbers of San and Khoe in Southern Africa

Country	Population Size (July, 2008 estimate)	Size of Country (square kilometers)	Number of San and Khoe
Angola	12,531,357	1,246,700	3,500 San
Botswana	1,842,322	600,370 1,000 Khoekhoe	52,000 San,
Namibia	2,088,669	825,418	32,000 San, 36,000 Khoekhoe
South Africa	48,782,756	1,221,912	7,500 San, 360,000 Khoekhoe
Zambia	11,559,534	752,614	1,300 San
Zimbabwe	11,350,111	390,580	2,500 San
TOTALS	88,154,749 people in 6 countries	5,037,594 sq km	98,800 San, 396,000 Khoekhoe

Note: The numbers of Khoekhoe in South Africa include 300,000 Griqua who claim Khoekhoe identity

though, they, too, were likely to have been more widespread in the past. San and Khoekhoe are minorities in all of the states of Southern Africa.

There has been a long and complex history of mistreatment of Khoekhoe and San peoples. Indeed, friction between groups was a near-constant phenomenon on the frontiers of European settlement in Southern Africa, and periodically there were outbreaks of pitched battles and wars. Mistreatment of aboriginal groups was seen by the Select Aborigines Committee of the British Parliament in the 1830s "as a practice which pleads no claim to indulgence," one which "has been a burden on the [British] empire" (quoted by Brantlinger, 2003, p. 74).

Hunter-herder (forager-pastoralist) conflicts are by no means uncommon in Southern Africa, and this has been the case for hundreds of years. At issue is the degree to which these conflicts have been characterized by genocide and massive human rights violations, including rape and the removal of Khoekhoe and San children from their families. As livestock-owning colonists moved further north in South Africa in the eighteenth century, there were numerous conflicts, some of which led to retaliatory raids and the destruction of whole communities (Penn, 2006, pp. 24-55). It is important to note, as Penn (2006) does, that "It is no coincidence that the most intense fighting between the trekboers [colonists] and the Khoisan occurred during periods of transition from one resource area to another" (p. 19). As MacCrone (1937) pointed out, the commando system used against the Bushmen in South Africa reached a climax in "the elaborately organized campaign of 1774 in which the whole of the northern frontier from the Camdeboo to the Oliphants River was involved.... From this time on, the northern frontier remained in a state of chronic warfare and the Bushman became a sort of public enemy (No. 1) "to be shot at sight and out of existence" (p. 104). He went on to say, "The official policy itself had become one of 'extirpation of the said rapacious tribes" (MacCrone, 1937, p. 105). The Khoekhoe and San put up fierce resistance but eventually were overwhelmed by other groups (Marks, 1972; Elphick, 1977; Penn, 1995, 1996, 2001, 2006).

In 1869-1870, explorer and trader Edward Mohr said of the San in the area of what is now northeastern Botswana and western Zimbabwe, "The Bushmen are like hunted game in these districts" (Mohr, 1876, pp. 156-157). In 1874, explorer Frank Oates (1881) noted that "The Matabele were out on business of murdering a lot of poor Bushmen; the latter are constantly being killed, and their life is one long struggle for existence" (p. 122). Bryden (1893) said that the San in 1890 were "in a state of absolute slavery and of hopeless degradation" (p. 142). He went on to point out,

> Woe betide him if the hunting season has been bad, or if the wild Beasts have made havoc with flock and herd. He and his family must answer for it, in such a case, with heavy stripes, not seldom, indeed, a brutal death is the penalty. Even his children and women folk are not his own, but may be and are seized and carried away into domestic servitude or concubinage. (Bryden, 1893, p. 143)

Bryden (1893) argued that the San were on the decline as a result of extermination or forced migration. As he notes, "The tiny aboriginal Bushmen are now very scarce; they have been exterminated or driven by the ancient system of Boer commandos almost completely from the old colony, and although they here and there are still to be found along the Orange River or in the lower portions of the Kalahari, another hundred years will probably witness their final extinction" (Bryden, 1893, p. 246).

Some of the information on what happened to the Khoekhoe and San comes from letters from settlers and in reports of the local colonial administrative institutions (see, for example, the reports by Tagart, 1933; Joyce, 1938). As Penn (2006) puts it, "The almost total suppression of the Khoihoi voice within the legal discourse of the colony is itself indicative of their fate" (p. 4). Even the fine materials of the W. H. I. Bleek and Lucy Lloyd collections made among now-extinct /Xam San of South Africa in the 1870s contain relatively little information on the ways in which /Xam were affected by genocidal and other historical forces (see Bleek and Lloyd, 1911; Skotnes, 2008). One does see evidence, however, of violent deaths in the genealogies of some of the /Xam families (Penn, 2006, p. 5).

Some of the mistreatment is also recorded in fine historical treatments like that of Nigel Penn (2006) in his book *The Forgotten Frontier: Colonist and Khoisan on the Cape's Northern Frontier in the 18th Century*. There are records of human rights violations against San on the eastern Cape frontier (Marks, 1972) and in the eastern highlands regions of South Africa and Lesotho (Stow, 1905; How, 1970; Wright, 1971).

Archaeological and forensic human rights work has been carried out in places in Southern Africa where Khoekhoe and San were said to have been murdered. Such work has been done, for example, in the Tsholotsho and Bulalima-Mangwe Districts of Matabeleland Province in western Zimbabwe where several thousand people lost their lives during counter-insurgency operations by government forces between 1981 and 1987 (Catholic Peace and Justice Commission of Zimbabwe and Legal Resources Foundation, 1997, 1999). Mass graves were also discovered in Namibia that relate to the liberation struggle between 1965 and 1990. Other places where genocidal actions and massacres took place are found in various parts of Southern Africa (see table 6.2). There have yet to be any

Table 6.2

Places of Memory: Sites Where Genocidal Massacre Events Involving Indigenous Peoples Occurred in Southern Africa

Site and Country	Event(s) Commemorated or Consecrated	Reference(s)
Angola	Sites where San soldiers and non-combatants who disappeared were buried	Souindola (1981); Pakleppa and Kwononoka (2003);
Botswana	Places where massacres of San took place (e.g. on the Ramaquebana River)	Oates (1881); Hitchcock (1991, 1995); Botswana National Museum information
Lesotho	Sites where San were killed and buried, rock shelter sites, cemeteries	How (1970); Wright (1971); data from Lesotho Highlands Development Authority
Namibia	Sites where San were killed and buried, graves and cemeteries of Herero, Nama (1904-1907); mass graves from Namibian liberation struggle	National Society for Human Rights (1996); Gordon (2009); Gordon and Douglas (2000); Bridgman and Worley (2009); Legal Assistance Center information
South Africa	Sites where massacres of San and Khoekhoe took place and where trophy skulls are kept	Penn (1995, 1996, 2001, 2006); Morris (1996); Skotnes (1996a)
Swaziland	Sites where San were massacred	Information from Swaziland National Trust Commission
Zambia	Sites where Kxoe San were killed and buried	Robins, Madzudzo, and Brenziger (2001)
Zimbabwe, Tsholotsho District, Matabeleland Province	Burial sites of Ndebele and others killed during the 1982-87 attacks and executions by the Zimbabwe army (Fourth Brigade)	Catholic Justice and Peace Commission of Zimbabwe and Legal Resources Foundation (1997, 1999); Hitchcock and Twedt (2009)

charges brought against government officials in Southern Africa for genocide or war crimes at the International Criminal Court (ICC), although mentions were made of the human rights violations before the Truth and Reconciliation Commission in South Africa and in discussions in Zimbabwe and Namibia.

As Brantlinger (2003) notes, "Efforts were made by individuals such as John Philip to publish books (1828, Volume 1) that brought attention to the 'native tribes' with the purposes of obtaining for them the protection of the British Government" (p. 78). The British Colonial Office had appointed a commission of inquiry to look in to the "oppressed state" of the "natives" of South Africa which largely bore out Philip's claims (Brantlinger, 2003, p. 78). One of Philip's proposals was for more intervention on the part of the British government. As Philip (1828) put it, "The Hottentots, despairing of help from every other quarter, now look to the justice and humanity of England for deliverance" (p. 400, Volume 1). England, for its part, did outlaw slavery, and the British Parliament issued proclamations and reports on the situations facing indigenous peoples in various parts of the world, including Southern Africa. There were also players on the local scene who lobbied for fairer treatment of indigenous peoples.

Critical Challenges Facing the Field Today

Critical challenges facing the Khoekhoe and San today in Southern Africa include post-conflict reconstruction and transitional justice in Angola, the extremely difficult conditions in which Tyua San and their neighbors are living today in Zimbabwe, and the ways in which the Botswana government is dealing with the G/ui and G//ana San and Bakgalagadi who were removed from the Central Kalahari Game Reserve beginning in the 1990s up through 2002 (Saugestad, 2001, 2005; Good, 2009). During the Zimbabwean War of Independence (1965-1980), Tyua San and their neighbors along the border of Botswana and Zimbabwe were subjected to repeated military attacks by Rhodesian government forces. Many of the residents of the region were forcibly resettled into "protected villages" where they were not allowed to have weapons, carry out hunting activities, or even to protect their crops from marauding wildlife.

In the early 1980s, after Zimbabwe achieved its independence, tensions continued to be felt in Matabeleland, where one of the major groups of freedom fighters, the Zimbabwe African Peoples Liberation Army, the military wing of the Zimbabwe African Peoples Union (ZAPU), had its primary base of support. Some of the former guerrillas felt that they had not been treated appropriately by the new government under Robert Mugabe, and tensions erupted into conflict in late 1980 and early 1981. A number of former guerrillas returned to the bush and began what turned in to a low-level insurgency.

Beginning in 1981, and continuing into the mid-1980s, the new Zimbabwe government carried out counter-insurgency operations against what they termed "dissidents." These operations included military attacks on villagers, kidnappings of suspected terrorists, torture and murder of detainees, committing of a wide range of atrocities against the civilian population, and restriction of the movement of food into the area. Before it was over, as many as 3,000 people were killed, and some of their bodies dumped into old mines that dotted the area (Catholic Justice and Peace Commission and Legal Resources Foundation, 1997, 1999; Hitchcock and Twedt, 2009). By the late 1980s, the atmosphere had improved considerably and a peace accord was signed between the Ndebele and the government of Robert Mugabe. This situation lasted until 2000, when the Mugabe government again began pressuring the peoples of Matabeleland, including the Tyua, and there have been instances of murders and disappearances of Tyua as recently as mid-2009.

Real Probabilities of Success in the Field

On December 13, 2006, the Botswana High Court announced its decision on the long-running Central Kalahari legal case. The High Court judges, while divided on their opinions, ruled that the removals of people from the Central Kalahari were unlawful. A day after the High Court ruling was announced, the Attorney General of the Botswana government decreed that the government would not provide services, including water, to the people returning to the Central Kalahari.

In 2008-2009 there were incidents where San and Bakgalagadi entering the Central Kalahari Game Reserve were detained and allegedly abused for seeking to obtain water from sources inside of the reserve, including ones being used by mineral exploration companies. There were also cases where San and Bakgalagadi had their requests for land declined by district land authorities in Botswana, including certain settlements where people were resettled after having been removed from the reserve. In addition, there are reports from people in the settlements who were detained on suspicion of hunting illegally who maintain that they were arrested, jailed, and refused access to legal representation. In May, 2009, livestock belonging to San and Bakgalagadi that were found in the Central Kalahari Game Reserve were destroyed by the government, something that local people decried, saying that it was tantamount to depriving them of their livelihoods.

Conclusion

Khoekhoe and San see themselves as indigenous peoples, and as such they feel that they should have the same rights as other indigenous peoples around the world. The various governments of Southern Africa, however, take the position that all citizens of the state are indigenous. None of the Southern African states are signatories to the only international human rights instrument relating directly to indigenous peoples, Convention 169 of the International Labour Organization (ILO). They are, however, all signatories of the Declaration on the Rights of Indigenous Peoples, which was passed by the United Nations General Assembly on September 13, 2007. Khoekhoe and San argue that now the Southern African governments have committed themselves to the Declaration on the Rights of Indigenous Peoples, they should go about implementing the provisions of that declaration. They want fair treatment from the various judicial bodies of the countries in which they reside. They also feel that they are owed formal apologies from the governments of Southern Africa and the nation-states that supported South Africa and Rhodesia during the colonial and apartheid eras for the violations of their rights. They have also called for an end to impunity for individuals who harm indigenous peoples.

The indigenous peoples of Southern Africa and their supporters realize full well the need for greater attention to be paid to issues involving genocide and the deprivation of many of their basic human rights. They feel that they should be treated with respect, and that their rights to life, liberty, and dignity should be protected and promoted. The nation-states of Southern Africa, for their part, need to pay much greater attention to the needs, desires and rights of indigenous minorities and other peoples who are at risk in the region.

Acknowledgements

Information in this paper was compiled from a broad array of sources, including ones in national archives (e.g., those of Botswana, Namibia, and Zimbabwe), unpublished reports of non-government organizations and individuals, published sources, documents of human rights organizations, faith-based groups, and indigenous peoples' organizations, and interviews of government officials, civil society representatives, members of international organizations, and individuals in Botswana, Lesotho, Namibia, South Africa, Swaziland, Zambia, and Zimbabwe. We wish to thank all of the people and organizations who assisted us. We dedicate this paper to the indigenous peoples of Southern Africa who have sought to oppose genocide, oppression, and human rights abuses and to bring attention to social justice for all peoples.

Note

1. Southern African populations traditionally are divided into a number of different named groups, each with their own languages, cultures, histories, and identities. The San and the Khoekhoe are themselves broken down into a number of different named groups.

    Neither San nor Khoekhoe traditionally had overarching names for themselves as collective entities.

    The terms "San, "Bushmen," "Basarwa," and "Khwe" have all been used to refer to peoples of hunting and gathering origin in Southern Africa. The terms Khoekhoe, Khoekhoen, "Hottentots," and Nama have all been used to refer to those peoples who are of pastoralist (livestock herding) origin in Southern Africa. The two sets of groups are linked in that they both are yellow-skinned, small-in-stature, and speak languages containing click consonants. Together, they differ from the majority black African Negorid Bantu-speaking populations.

    The San, or Bushmen, are the best known and most numerous of the indigenous, hunting and gathering, peoples of Southern Africa. Recent human biological research suggests that they have biological links to other peoples who have hunting and gathering backgrounds in central Africa (the Pygmies or Batwa), and east Africa (the Hadza of Tanzania).

References

Akpan, Joseph; Mberengwa, Ignatius; Hitchcock, Robert K.; and Koperski, Thomas (2004). "Human Rights and Participation Among Southern African Indigenous Peoples," pp. 194-201. In Robert K. Hitchcock and Dinah Vinding (Eds.) *Indigenous Peoples' Rights in Southern Africa.* Copenhagen, Denmark: International Work Group for Indigenous Affairs.

Arce-White, Evelyne (2004). *Funding Indigenous Conservation: International Funders for Indigenous Peoples Strives to Protect Pristine Environments.* http:/www.internationalfunders.org/images2/conservation.pdf.

Barnard, Alan (1992) *Hunters and Herders of Southern Africa.* Cambridge: Cambridge University Press.

Bleek, W.H.I., and Lloyd, L. C. (1911). *Specimens of Bushman Folklore.* London: George Allen.

Boonzaier, Emile; Malherbe, Candy; Smith, Andy; and Berens, Penny (1996). *The Cape Herders: A History of the Khoikhoi of Southern Africa.* Cape Town and Johannesburg: David Philip, and Athens: Ohio University Press.

Brantlinger, Patrick (2003). *Dark Vanishings: Discourse on the Extinction of Primitive Races, 1800-1930.* Ithaca, NY: Cornell University Press.

Bredekamp, Henry C. Jatti (2001). "Khoisan Revivalism and the Indigenous Peoples Issue in Post-Apartheid South Africa," pp. 191-209. In Alan Barnard and Justin Kenrick, (Eds.) *Africa's Indigenous Peoples: "First Peoples" or Marginalized Minorities?* Edinburgh: Center of African Studies, University of Edinburgh.

Bridgman, Jon, and Worley, Leslie J. (2009). "Genocide of the Hereros," pp. 17-53. In Samuel Totten, and William S. Parsons (Eds.) *Century of Genocide: Critical Essays and Eyewitness Accounts*, third edition. New York: Routledge.

Bryden, H.A. (1893). *Gun and Camera in Southern Africa: A Year of Wanderings in Bechuanaland, the Kalahari Desert, and the Lake River Country, Ngamiland, with Notes on Colonization, Natives, Natural History, and Sport.* London: Edward Stanford.

Cassidy, Lin; Good, Ken; Mazonde, Isaac; and Rivers, Roberta (2001). *An Assessment of the Status of the San in Botswana.* Windhoek, Namibia: Legal Assistance Center.

Catholic Justice and Peace Commission of Zimbabwe and Legal Resources Foundation (1997). *Report on Massacres and Atrocities in Matebeleland, Zimbabwe, 1982-1987.* Harare, Zimbabwe: Author.

Catholic Commission for Justice and Peace in Zimbabwe and Legal Resources Foundation (1999). *Breaking the Silence, Building True Peace: A Report into the Disturbances in Matabeleland and the Midlands 1980-1988.* Harare, Zimbabwe: Author.

Chan, T.M. (2004). "The Richtersveld Challenge: South Africa Finally Adopts Aboriginal Title," pp. 114-133. In Robert K. Hitchcock and Diana Vinding (Eds.) *Indigenous Peoples Rights in Southern Africa.* Copenhagen: International Work Group for Indigenous Affairs.

Chennels, R., and du Toit, A. (2004). "The Rights of Indigenous Peoples in South Africa," pp. 98-113. In Robert K. Hitchcock and Diana Vinding (Eds.) *Indigenous Peoples Rights in Southern Africa.* Copenhagen: International Work Group for Indigenous Affairs.

Crais, Clifton, and Scully, Pamela (2009). *Sara Baartman and the Hottentot Venus: A Ghost Story and a Biography.* Princeton, NJ: Princeton University Press.

Dieckmann, Ute (2007). *Hai//om in the Etosha Region: A History of Colonial Settlement, Ethnicity, and Nature Conservation.* Basel: Basler Afrika Bibliographien.

Elphick, Richard (1977). *Kraal and Castle: Khoikhoi and the Founding of White South Africa*. New Haven, CT: Yale University Press.

Gall, Sandy (2001). *The Bushmen of Southern Africa: Slaughter of the Innocent*. London: Chatto and Windus.

Good, Kenneth (2009). *Diamonds, Dispossession and Democracy in Botswana*. Johannesburg: James Currey and Jacana Media.

Gordon, Robert J. (1985). "Conserving Bushmen to Extinction in Southern Africa: The Metaphysis of Bushman Hating and Empire Building," pp. 28-42. In Marcus Colchester (Ed*.) An End to Laughter? Tribal Peoples and Economic Development*. London: Survival International.

Gordon, Robert J. (1988). "The Rise of the Bushman Penis: Germans, Genitalia, and Genocide." *African Studies*, 57(1): 27-54.

Gordon, Robert J. (2009). "Hiding in Full View: The 'Forgotten' Bushman Genocides in Namibia." *Genocide Studies and Prevention*, 4(1):29-57.

Gordon, Robert J., and Douglas, Stuart Sholto (2000). *The Bushman Myth: The Making of a Namibian Underclass*, second edition. Boulder, CO: Westview Press.

Hays, Jennifer (2004). "Indigenous Rights in Education: The San of Southern Africa in Local and Global Contexts," pp. 228-248. In Robert K. Hitchcock and Diana Vinding (Eds.) *Indigenous Peoples Rights in Southern Africa*. Copenhagen: International Work Group for Indigenous Affair.

Hitchcock, Robert K. (1991). "Kuakaka: An Early Case of Ethnoarchaeology in the Northern Kalahari." *Botswana Notes and Records,* 23: 223-233.

Hitchcock, Robert K. (1995). "Centralization, Resource Depletion, and Coercive Conservation Among the Tyua of the Northeastern Kalahari." *Human Ecology* 23(2): 169-198.

Hitchcock, Robert K. (2002). 'We Are the First People': Land, Natural Resources, and Identity in the Central Kalahari, Botswana." *Journal of Southern African Studies*, 28(4):797-824.

Hitchcock, Robert K., and Twedt, Tara M. (2009). "Physical and Cultural Genocide of Indigenous Peoples," pp. 413-458. In Samuel Totten and William S. Parsons (Eds.) *Century of Genocide: Critical Essays and Eyewitness Accounts*. New York: Routledge.

Hitchcock, Robert K; Ikeya, Kazunobu; Biesele, Megan; and Lee, Richard B. (Eds.) (2006). *Updating the San: Image and Reality of an African People in the 21st Century*. *Senri Ethnological Studies* 70. Osaka, Japan: National Museum of Ethnology.

How, Marion Walsham (1970). *The Mountain Bushmen of Basutoland*. Pretoria: J. L. Van Schaik, Ltd.

Isaacson, Rupert (2002). *Last Exit from the Kalahari. The Slow Genocide of the Bushmen/San*. www.opendemocracy.net/content/articles/pdf/267.pdf.

Jones, Adam A., and Robins, Nicholas A. (2009). "Introduction: Subaltern Genocide in Theory and Practice," pp. 1-24. In Nicholas A. Robins and Adam Jones (Eds.) *Genocides by the Oppressed: Subaltern Genocide in Theory and Practice*. Bloomington and Indianapolis: Indiana University Press.

Joyce, J.W. (1938). *Report on the Masarwa in the Bamangwato Reserve, Bechuanaland Protectorate*. League of Nations Publications VI. B.: Slavery. Annex 6, pp. 57-76.

Kenyon, Paul (2005). "*Row Over Bushmen 'Genocide'."* BBC News, Crossing Continents Programs. London: BBC (11/06/2005).

Lavene, Mike (2002). "Can Botswana Be Charged with Genocide?" October. *Mmegi wa Dikang*, pp. 4-10.

Lee, Richard B. (1976). "Introduction," pp. 1-24. In Richard B. Lee and Irven DeVore (Eds.) *Kalahari Hunter-Gatherers: Studies of the !Kung San and their Neighbors*. Cambridge, MA: Harvard University Press.

Lee, Richard B. (1979). *The !Kung San: Men, Women, and Work in a Foraging Society.* Cambridge: Cambridge University Press.

LeRoux, Willemien, and White, Alison (2004). *Voices of the San: Living in Southern Africa Today.* Cape Town: Kwela Books.

London Missionary Society (1935). *The Masarwa (Bushmen): Report of An Inquiry by the South Africa District Committee of the London Missionary Society.* Alice, South Africa: Lovedale Press.

MacCrone, Ian Douglas (1937). *Race Attitudes in South Africa: Historical, Experimental, and Psychological Studies.* London: Oxford University Press.

Marks, Shula (1972). "Khoisan Resistance to the Dutch in the Seventeenth and Eighteenth Centuries." *Journal of African History,* 13(1): 55-80.

Marshall, John and Claire Ritchie (1984). *Where Are the Ju/Wasi of Nyae Nyae? Changes in a Bushman Society: 1958-1981.* Communications No. 9, Center for African Area Studies, University of Cape Town. Cape Town: University of Cape Town.

Mogwe, Alice (1992). *Who Was (T)here First? An Assessment of the Human Rights Situation of Basarwa in Selected Communities in the Gantsi District, Botswana.* Gaborone, Botswana: Botswana Christian Council.

Mohr, Edward (1876). *To the Victoria Falls of the Zambezi.* London: Sampson Low, Marston, Searle, and Rivington.

Moodie, Donald S. (1838). *The Record, or Series of Official Papers Relative to the Condition and Treatment of the Native Tribes of South Africa.* Photo Reprint. Cape Town: A.A. Balkema.

Moodie, Donald S. (1841). *The Evidence of the Motives and Objects of the Bushman Wars, 1769-77.* Cape Town: A.S. Robertson and London: J.M. Richardson.

Morris, Alan G. (1996). "Trophy Skulls, Museums, and the San," pp. 67-79. In Pippa Skotnes (Ed.) *Miscast: Negotiating the Presence of the Bushmen.* Cape Town: University of Cape Town Press.

National Society for Human Rights (1996). *The Rights of Indigenous Peoples: The Kxoe People of Namibia.* Windhoek, Namibia: National Society for Human Rights.

Oates, Frank (Ed.) (1881). *Matabele Land and the Victoria Falls: A Naturalist's Wanderings in the Interior of South Africa.* London: C. Kegan Paul and Company.

Orth, Ina (2003). "Identity as Dissociation: The Khwe's Struggle for Land in West Caprivi," pp. 121-159. In Thekla Hohmann (Ed.) *San and the State, Contesting Land, Development, Identity, and Representation.* Koln: Rudiger Koppe Verlag.

Pakleppa, Richard, and Kwononoka, Americo (2003). *Where the Last Are First: San Communities Fighting for Survival in Southern Angola. Report of a Needs Assessment of Angolan San Communities in Huila, Cunene, and Cuando Cubango Provinces from 17 June to 14 July 2003.* Windhoek, Namibia: Trocaire Angola, Working Group of Indigenous Minorities in Southern Africa (WIMSA), and OCADEC.

Penn, Nigel (1995). The Northern Cape Frontier Zone, 1700 – c. 1815. Ph.D. Dissertation, University of Cape Town, Rondebosch, Cape, South Africa.

Penn, Nigel. (1996). "Fated to Perish: The Destruction of the Cape San," pp. 81-91. In Pippa Skotnes (Ed.) *Miscast: Negotiating the Presence of the Bushmen.* Cape Town: University of Cape Town Press.

Penn, Nigel. (2001) "'Civilizing' the San: The First Mission to the Cape San, 1791 – 1806.* Working Paper No. 3. Basel: Basler Afrika Bibliographien.

Penn, Nigel (2006). *The Forgotten Frontier: Colonist and Khoisan on the Cape's Northern Frontier in the 18th Century.* Athens: Ohio University Press.

Philip, John (1828). *Researches in South Africa: Illustrating the Civil, Moral, and Religious Condition of the Native Tribes,* 2 volumes. New York: Negro Universities Press, 1969.

Robins, Steven; Madzudzo, Elias; and Brenzinger, Mathias (2001). *An Assessment of the Status of the San in South Africa, Angola, Zambia, and Zimbabwe.* Windhoek, Namibia: Legal Assistance Center.

Saugestad, Sidsel (2001). *The Inconvenient Indigenous: Remote Area Development in Botswana, Donor Assistance, and the First People of the Kalahari.* Uppsala, Sweden: Nordic African Institute.

Saugestad, Sidel (2005). "'Improving their Lives': State Policies and San Resistance in Botswana." *Before Farming,* 2005/4, 1-11.

Schapera, I. (1930). *The Khoisan Peoples of South Africa: Bushmen and Hottentots.* London: Routledge and Kegan Paul.

Skotnes, Pippa (1996a). "Introduction," pp. 15-23. In Pippa Skotnes (Ed.) *Miscast: Negotiating the Presence of the Bushmen.* Cape Town: University of Cape Town Press.

Skotnes, Pippa (Ed.) (1996b). *Miscast: Negotiating the Presence of the Bushmen.* Cape Town: University of Cape Town Press.

Skotnes, Pippa (2007). *Claim to the Country: The Archive of Wilhelm Bleek and Lucy Lloyd.* Johannesburg: Jacana Press.

Skotnes, Pippa (2008). *Unconquerable Spirit: George Stow's History Paintings of the San.* Athens: Ohio University Press, and Auckland Park: Jacana Media.

Smith, Andy; Malherbe, Candy; Guenther, Mat; and Berens, Penny (2000). *The Bushmen of Southern Africa: A Foraging Society in Transition.* Cape Town: David Philip, and Athens: Ohio University Press.

Souindola, Simao (1981). "Angola: Genocide of the Bosquimanos." *IWGIA Newsletter,* Volume 31-32, pp. 66-68.

Suzman, James (2001). *An Introduction to the Regional Assessment of the Status of the San in Southern Africa.* Windhoek, Namibia: Legal Assistance Center.

Suzman, James (2001b). *An Assessment of the Status of San in Namibia.* Windhoek, Namibia: Legal Assistance Center.

Sylvain, Renee (2002). "'Land, Water, and Truth'": San identity and Global Indigenism." *American Anthropologist* 104(4): 1074-1085.

Sylvain, Renee (2005). "Disorderly Development: Globalization and the Concept of 'Culture' in the Kalahari." *American Ethnologist* 32(3): 354-370.

Tagart, E.S.B. (1933). *Report on the Conditions Existing among Masarwa in the Bamangwato Reserve of the Bechuanaland Protectorate and Certain Other Matters Appertaining to the Natives Living Therein.* Pretoria, South Africa: Government Printer.

Theal, George McCall (1919). *Ethnography and Condition of South Africa before A.D. 1505.* Second Edition. Wynberg and Johannesburg: Juta and Company.

Thomas, Elizabeth Marshall (2006). *The Old Way: A Story of the First People.* New York: Farrar, Straus, Giroux.

Wright, John B. (1971). *Bushman Raiders of the Drakensberg, 1840-1870.* Pietermaritzburg, South Africa: University of Natal Press.

Annotated Bibliography

Barnard, Alan (1992). *Hunters and Herders of Southern Africa: A Comparative Ethnography of the Khoisan Peoples.* Cambridge: Cambridge University Press. 349 pp.

This book is a comprehensive anthropological assessment of the Khoekhoe and San peoples. It is a comparative and theoretical examination of subsistence, settlement patterns, kinship, social organization, politics, religion, language, and identity. Speaking of the Nama, the best-known of the Khoekhoe peoples, Barnard says that their quality of life "had deteriorated considerably as a result of warfare and subjugation under oppressive colonial rule." He goes on to say, "This oppression was to remain through a further sixty-seven years of South African control over Namibia" (p. 177). There was "extensive warfare" involving Khoekhoe peoples in Namibia in the latter part of the nineteenth century with the incursions of Bantu-speaking peoples, the Dutch, and the Germans, the ultimate result of which was "the almost total destruction of Nama tribal organization after the German colonization of South West Africa in the 1890s."

Barnard, Alan (2007). *Anthropology and the Bushman*. London: Berg. 179 pp.

This book addresses the interplay between the Bushmen (San) and the field of anthropology and the ways in which San have been represented over time. To some extent, it also addresses the social and political history of Southern Africa, a region in which San peoples have experienced killings, discrimination, commodification, impoverishment, takeovers of their land, accusations of thievery, and paternalistic treatment. He draws distinctions among Khoekhoe or "Hottentot" cattle and sheep herders, Khoekhoe-speaking San, and Non-Khoe-speaking San. Barnard notes that some San were "entirely peaceful" but some Khoekhoe and San were caught up in battles with Khoekhoe, San, Dutch, and Germans, and other African peoples in the seventeenth, eighteenth, and nineteenth centuries. Some San, he notes, were described by early observers such as John Barrow as having tense relations with other groups, in part because of cattle raiding, and were considered "brutal savages" as opposed to the twentieth-century viewpoint of San peoples as peace-loving and "harmless." There were, Barnard notes, violent confrontations and brutality that took place on the frontier of white settlement, and San were killed for sport, chased into mountainous areas, and enslaved. Some San responded to these events by retaliating, which resulted in a "negative, violent image" growing up around them which led to further mistreatment.

Catholic Commission for Justice and Peace in Zimbabwe and Legal Resources Foundation (1999). *Breaking the Silence, Building True Peace: A Report into the Disturbances in Matabeleland and the Midlands 1980-1988.* Harare, Zimbabwe: Catholic Commission for Justice and Peace in Zimbabwe and Legal Resources Foundation. 36 pp.

This report describes the ways that the Zimbabwe government dealt with the Ndebele, Tyua San, and other groups in Matabeleland and the Midlands areas after Zimbabwean independence in 1980. It documents the government's use of a special North Korea- trained military force, 5 Brigade, and other organizations such as the Police Support Unit and Youth Brigades which engaged in mass murders, individual killings, assassinations, rape, disappearances, and destruction of local people's villages and homes in the early to mid-1980s. The report is based on over 1,000 oral testimonies, archival research, interviews, and other sources of information compiled by the CCJPZ, the Legal Resources Foundation, lawyers, journalists, witnesses, faith-based groups and other civil society organizations. Some of the violence was directed toward what were termed "dissidents" by the Zimbabwe government and their supporters. In April 1983, the President of Zimbabwe said of those suspected of feeding dissidents, "We exterminate them." Thousands of civilians were terrorized in what the report described as "organized violence," with over 3,000 people killed and thousands more beaten, tortured, and denied medical treatment, food, or other humanitarian assistance. Bodies of victims were deposited in mass graves or left in the open. While one government-sponsored investigation of what transpired in Matabeleland and the Midlands took place in April, 1984, the report was not made public, and perpetrators of the violence were treated with impunity.

Dieckmann, Ute (2007). *Hai//om in the Etosha Region: A History of Colonial Settlement, Ethnicity, and Nature Conservation.* Basel: Basler Afrika Bibliographien. 398 pp.

A book that describes the experiences of the Hai//om San, the most populous of Namibian San peoples, and their interactions with other Namibian groups such as the Ovambo, Germans, South

Africans, the South West African administration, the Namibian state, and non-government organizations. In his introduction to Dieckmann's volume, Robert Gordon notes that "this book provides much evidence for genocide" (p. ix). The human rights violations that Dieckmann describes have been overlooked except for a few voices of protest. The book describes in detail how the Hai//om were dispossessed of their land, in some cases in the name of wildlife and nature conservation, with Etosha National Park, Namibia's largest protected area, as the centerpiece. Solutions to what were described as "the Bushman plague" by the Germans included resettlement, "education to work," forced labor, deportation, and the creation of a Bushman reserve (p. 79). Stock thefts and alleged attacks on migrant workers were used as justifications for reprisals against Hai//om and other San. Draconian measures were announced in 1911, leading to attacks on San communities, detentions, forcing of San adults into farm and mine labor, and removals of children from their families. The latter portion of the book deals with the ways in which Hai//om responded to the treatment that they received, including their participation in social movements aimed at promoting Hai//om rights in the 1990s and the early part of the new millennium.

Elphick, Richard (1977). *Kraal and Castle: Khoikhoi and the Founding of White South Africa.* New Haven, CT: Yale University Press. 266 pp.

This book describes in detail the early history of the Khoikhoi peoples of Southern Africa and their relations with other groups, including the San and the Dutch. It describes the range of variation in relationships that existed between Khoikhoi communities and others, ranging from cooperation to conflict and from reciprocal exchange and trade to negotiation and subjugation. Elphick provides useful insights into the causes of conflicts between the Khoikhoi and other groups, some of them ecological, some sociocultural, and some having to do with the ways in which the various groups viewed each other. The wars between the Khoikhoi and the Dutch are described, as are the factors involved in the evolution and decline of Khoikhoi societies in South Africa, including economic deprivation, disease, absorption into the colonial labor force, and cultural dissolution brought about by both internal and external forces.

Gordon, Robert J. (2009). "Hiding in Full View: The 'Forgotten' Bushman Genocides in Namibia." *Genocide Studies and Prevention*, 4(1): 29-57.

This article is one of the few that directly treats the issue of genocide of Bushman peoples, focusing on the period in Namibia between 1912 and 1915. This genocide, Gordon argues, has been largely overlooked by scholars and is not remembered by Namibian Bushmen themselves. Bushmen were shot on sight by German military personnel and settlers. They were deprived of their livelihoods, their mobility was restricted, and they were treated as vagrants if they could not demonstrate their means of support, all by government decrees, the most draconian of which were issued by the German government of South West Africa in August 1907. In part, because of attacks on farmers and labor migrants, Bushmen were hunted down by military patrols and police. The military sought and received dispensation to shoot Bushmen if they failed to stop on command, something that Gordon says was "a warrant for genocide." Policies pursued include what we now describe as ethnic cleansing; individuals were detained and hanged without trial; and entire Bushman communities were destroyed. Captured Bushmen were rounded up and turned over to the mines and farmers as laborers to ease a labor shortage. The article describes preconditions for genocidal violence, and it assesses academic, government, and media discussions of ways to deal with what became known as "the Bushman problem." It also considers the nature and range of variation in colonial genocides.

Gordon, Robert J., and Stuart Sholto Douglas (2000). *The Bushman Myth: The Making of a Namibian Underclass*, second edition. Boulder, CO: Westview Press. 342 pp.

This book provides detailed insights into the Bushman peoples of Namibia. It calls into question some of the representations of Bushman peoples, and it analyzes "the politics of labeling Bushmen." Noting that "the banality of evil and indeed of genocide is universal" (p. 10), Gordon says that he hopes that the material he documents will be used to develop a comparative study of genocide and the vulnerability of small-scale social formations. Gordon describes the treatment of Bushmen in Namibia in the early twentieth century by the colonial German government and settlers, a treatment which was in many ways genocidal. He goes on to discuss what he calls the "praetorianization" of the Bushmen in the latter part of the twentieth century in which Bushmen were incorporated into the military and how this process contributed to the decline in the well-being of Bushman communities in Namibia.

Marks, Shula (1972). "Khoisan Resistance to the Dutch in the Seventeenth and Eighteenth Centuries." *Journal of African History*, 13(1): 55-80.

This article addresses the ways in which Khoekhoe and San peoples responded to Dutch incursions into their lands. In doing so, Marks discusses the Khoisan peoples, noting that there is often a distinction between Khoikhoi ("Hottentot") herders and San hunter-gatherers. She points out that they are not discrete racial categories and notes the fluidity of their adaptations. She notes they "have all but disappeared from twentieth century South Africa, at least in their earlier guise" (p. 55), in part because some of them were assimilated into the larger society of South Africa and because of the conflicts that occurred with Khoikhoi and San peoples over land, livestock, labor, and trade.

Marshall Thomas, Elizabeth (2006) *The Old Way: A Story of the First People*. New York: Farrar, Straus, Giroux. 343 pp.

This beautifully written book is a wide-ranging discussion of the lifeways of the Ju/'hoansi San of the northern Kalahari Desert region of Namibia. Marshall Thomas describes a way of life that is rapidly disappearing. Part I of the book, which has eighteen chapters, describes key aspects of the traditional Ju/'hoan way life. In Part II, which has three chapters, Marshall Thomas documents the profound changes that have occurred among the Ju/'hoansi over the past fifty years. Beginning with an important turning point in the history of Nyae Nyae, the establishment in 1959 of the South West African government post at Tsumkwe, she traces events that are seemingly beyond Ju/'hoan control. She points out that sedentarization of the Ju/'hoansi was accompanied by widespread poverty, increased reliance on government rations and welfare, unemployment, disease, alcohol, unprecedented violence, and premature death. She concludes by saying that although the old way of life may be lost in terms of hunting and gathering as an effective adaptive strategy – the way of life that shaped homo sapiens—it remains strong in the way the Ju/'hoansi relate to one another, their mutual respect, decision-making by consensus, their ethos of sharing, generosity, cooperation, group living, and the collective resourcefulness to survive the challenges of their changing environment.

Mogwe, Alice (1992). *Who Was (T)here First? An Assessment of the Human Rights Situation of Basarwa in Selected Communities in the Gantsi District, Botswana*. Gaborone, Botswana: Botswana Christian Council. 51 pp.
     A report by the director of Ditshwanelo, the Botswana Center for Human Rights, on the human rights issues faced by the Nharo and other San of the Gantsi freehold farms and surrounding communal lands. She notes the ways in which the Botswana government deals with the Basarwa (the term for San in Botswana) which includes denying them indigenous identity and lack of recognition of land, resource and cultural rights, unequal treatment of Basarwa before the law, and failure to protect Basarwa from torture or inhuman or degrading punishment. It was this report that drew attention to the serious human rights situations faced by Basarwa in Botswana in the 1990s and which led to calls for change at the international level.

Moodie, Donald S. (1838). *The Record, or Series of Official Papers Relative to the Condition and Treatment of the Native Tribes of South Africa*. Photo Reprint. Cape Town: A.A. Balkema. 4 parts: 446 pp., 112 pp. 60 pp., and 27 pp.
     An important book by a colonial administrator that contains documents from the Dutch East Indian Company. The relations

particularly between the Khoikhoi and the Dutch are described in the papers, with some mentions of Bushmen (San). The book provides useful insights into the policies and practices of the Dutch East India Company and the settlers in what came to be South Africa.

National Society for Human Rights (1996). *The Rights of Indigenous Peoples: The Kxoe People of Namibia.* Windhoek, Namibia: National Society for Human Rights (NSHR). 30 pp.

This report provides an overview of the Kxoe (Khwe) of West Caprivi, Namibia with particular reference to the human rights challenges that they were facing in May-July 1996. The National Society for Human Rights (NSHR) argues that "The physical and cultural existence of virtually all Namibia's indigenous and tribal peoples could be described as very precarious, with some of them facing physical extinction." It goes on to say that San peoples are "the most endangered of all indigenous collectivities in the country" (p. 3). The survival of the Kxoe, who numbered between 4,000 and 6,000 in 1996, was "under a potential threat" as a separate social entity (p. 4). The NSHR points out that Kxoe were coping with discrimination, mistreatment, dispossession, inequitable social, political, economic, and legal policies, poor health conditions, and violations of their human rights, including the right to life.

Orpen, J.M. (1874). "Mythology of the Maluti Bushmen." *Cape Monthly Magazine* 9(49): 1-13.

A brief report on the rock art, mythology, and belief systems of San peoples in what is now Lesotho. The primary informant, a San named Qing, had "never seen a white man but in fighting" (p. 13).

Pakleppa, Richard and Americo Kwononoka (2001). *Where the Last Are First: San Communities Fighting for Survival in Southern Angola. Report of a Needs Assessment of Angolan San Communities in Huila, Cunene, and Cuando Cubango Provinces from 17 June to 14 July 2003.* Windhoek, Namibia: Trocaire Angola, Working Group of Indigenous Minorities in Southern Africa (WIMSA) and OCADEC. 91 pp.

A report on the contemporary situation of the 3,400 or so San of southern Angola based on a needs assessment carried out in 2003. The vast majority of Angolan San survive through a combination of working for Bantu-speaking groups, small-scale food production, foraging, and limited wage labor. As the authors note, "San communities throughout southern Angola experience social exclusion, discrimination, and economic exploitation." The authors go on to say that "Their human rights are routinely disrespected and violated." San live in "uneasy relationships of servitude and dependency with their Bantu neighbors." The report notes that during the several decade-long Angolan civil war, San peoples were excluded from receiving humanitarian aid; they lacked land and resource rights; and many San took refuge in other countries in an effort to avoid persecution.

Penn, Nigel (2006). *The Forgotten Frontier: Colonist and Khoisan on the Cape's Northern Frontier in the 18th Century*. Athens: Ohio University Press. 388 pp.

This book describes in detail the interactions and changes that occurred among Khoikhoi, San, and white colonists in the Cape region of South Africa in the 1700s. It evaluates the causes and consequences of the conflicts, collaboration, and competition among the Khoisan peoples of Southern Africa, white settlers and livestock producers, the Cape colonial administration, local military councils, and the Dutch East India Company. Penn assesses the various ways in which the Khoikhoi and San resisted what many of them saw as an onslaught. It also shows how the colonists treated Khoisan peoples along the northern Cape frontier, including engaging in warfare and sending out commandos, mobile paramilitary units aimed at recovering lost livestock, killing Khoikhoi and San, and capturing individuals who were incorporated into the colonial labor force. In the latter part of the book Penn also addresses what he calls "the civilizing of the San," efforts of humanitarians and missionaries to bring "civilization" to the Khoikhoi and San, a process that included encouraging them to settle down and engage in agriculture and commercial labor, pacification, and cultural modification.

Robbins, David (2006). *A San Journey: The Story of the !Xun and Khwe of Platfontein.* Kimberley: The Sol Plaatje Educational Trust. 45 pp.

   A report on the contemporary situations of San who were re-settled in South Africa in 1990 at the end of the war between the South West African government and the South African Defence Force against liberation forces in Namibia. The report describes briefly the history of the !Xun of Angola and Khwe of Namibia, with a discussion of the impacts of militarization and social change. As Robbins notes, the !Xun escaped into Namibia 1974 in order "to avoid being exterminated." Some !Xun and Khwe were re-cruited initially into the military as trackers and later as soldiers. At the end of the Namibian civil war, the San were given the op-tion of staying in Namibia or going to South Africa. Some 3,700 San opted to go to Schmidtsdrift, near Kimberley, South Africa, where they lived in tents for thirteen years before getting land of their own at Platfontein. Robbins points out that the impact of the move, "coming on the heels of centuries of gradual loss," were significant in terms of !Xun and Khwe cultural stability and well-being, and their situations in South Africa "changed rapidly, and generally for the worse" (p. 24).

Schapera, I. (1930). *The Khoisan Peoples of South Africa: Bushmen and Hottentots.* London: Routledge and Kegan Paul. 450 pp.

   This book describes what was known of the Khoikhoi and San peoples of Southern Africa up to the late 1920s, based on analyses of travelers' accounts, archival materials, ethnographies, and both official and unofficial reports. It addresses a wide range of issues, from social organization to subsistence and from politics to reli-gion. Schapera points out that the "Like the Bushmen, Hottentots must be regarded as a disappearing people" (p. 50), and he goes on to say that disease and war contributed to the decline in their numbers. He also says that "Their native culture, where it has not been completely displaced, has at least been considerably affected by the intrusion of European elements." His book is a classic account of the customs, traditions, practices, and belief systems of an important set of Southern African peoples.

Skotnes, Pippa (Ed.) (1996). *Miscast: Negotiating the Presence of the Bushmen*. Cape Town: University of Cape Town Press. 382 pp.

A well-illustrated and detailed book on the Bushmen of Southern Africa. In 30 chapters, this book portrays in word and image the varied situations of Bushmen peoples and the myriad and complex ways that they have been represented. In her introduction, Skotnes points out that in South Africa, "The destruction of people and the death of San culture and language was almost complete by 1910." She goes on to remark about the power relationships between Bushmen and other groups in Southern Africa, and says, "That these relationships resulted in the tragic loss of thousands of lives and communities in multiple language death and cultural genocide is evidenced by the images [shown in the book] of trophy heads, hangings, prison victims, and starvation" (p. 18). A number of other chapters in the book deal directly with issues surrounding genocide and ethnocide, notably those by Alan Morris, Nigel Penn, and Anthony Traill. Although the Bushmen were viewed, as George McCall Theal put it, as "fated to perish," this book is a testament to their resilience, adaptability, and vitality.

Stow, George W. (1905). *The Native Races of South Africa: A History of the Intrusion of the Hottentots and Bantu into the Hunting Grounds of the Bushmen, the Aborigines of the Country*. George McCall Theal (Ed.). London: Swan Sonnenschein. 618 pp.

This book is considered to be one of the first "ethnographies" of San peoples. Written by a geologist and trader, George William Stow, it documents in several chapters (pp. 1-231) and in twenty-two illustrations the lifeways and art of the Bushmen of Southern Africa. Part of the book is based on first-hand observations and interviews, but it is best-known for a second-hand account which states, "The last Bushman artist of the Malutis was shot in the Witteberg Native Reserve, where he had been on a marauding expedition, and had captured some horses.... Thus perished the last of the painter tribes of Bushmen!" (p. 230). Faced with competition with other groups, the Bushmen were "pursued and destroyed with a relentless and almost savage ferocity, clan after clan being annihilated; the men were shot down without mercy, and surviving women and children were dragged into a state worse than slavery" (p. 212). Thus, the Bushmen of South Africa and Lesotho were seen as "a disappearing people."

Tobias, P.V. (Ed.) (1978). *The Bushmen: San Hunters and Herders of Southern Africa.* Cape Town: Human and Rousseau. 206 pp.

This book provides a detailed overview of the San peoples of Southern Africa, taking into consideration their biology, prehistory, history, languages, material culture, religion, folklore, art, social organization, scientific and practical knowledge, and contemporary situations. Of the fourteen chapters in the book, two address in detail the ways in which San peoples were treated by other groups —one chapter is by Alex R. Willcox and the other is by M.D.W. Jeffreys. Willcox presents an outline of "what was virtually a war" between whites and Bushmen, which continued, "with increasing ferocity, for almost two centuries" (p. 78). The causes of the conflicts, according to Willcox and Jeffreys, were the "incompatibility of the means of livelihood," competition for resources, infringements on territory and hunting rights, and retaliation for attacks on livestock and people. The year 1715 was said to be a turning point, with the beginning of the commando system as a mobile mounted force with official state sanction to attack and kill Bushmen. In addition, Bushmen children were taken away from their parents and made "farm servants, a euphemism for slaves" (p. 79).

Wright, John B. (1971). *Bushman Raiders of the Drakensberg, 1840-1870: A Study of their Conflict with Stock-Keeping Peoples in Natal.* Pietermaritzburg, South Africa: University of Natal Press. 213 pp.

The author discusses the history of the Bushmen of the Drakensberg and Maluti Mountains and surrounding areas of southeastern

South Africa and Lesotho in the nineteenth century. Because of competition with other groups, Wright notes, eventually the Bushmen were driven to take one of three courses: to withdraw into areas not occupied by cattle-owners, to adapt to the new conditions being thrust upon them, or to fight to preserve their independent existence (pp. 4-5). It is argued that as the growing Bantu-speaking population began to strip the Bushmen of their means of survival, hostility between the two populations became more marked. Wright points out that it is difficult to determine the nature and extent of the hostility between the various groups because of the difficulty of interpreting the records left by European writers. In the 1820s, Bushmen were caught up in the fighting among different groups and many individuals were killed. As the numbers of whites expanded in the region, Bushmen who engaged in raiding and attacks on settlers and their "Hottentot" herders were retaliated against, and "the farmers and their retainers showed little mercy...shooting down men and women and carrying children off as servants" (p. 25). Wright notes that there was a correlation between years of drought in the interior and an intensification of raids along the northern frontier. It was not until 1862, however, that an inquiry was ordered by the government to investigate their fate, and the finding at the time was that the Bushmen had been dispossessed of their lands and resources, hundreds had been killed, and they had been "treated without mercy" (p. 31). The Bushmen were looked upon as pests, to be shot on sight "as if they were animals." Wright points out that treatment of the Bushmen varied both temporally and spatially, but because of the economic value of captives it never went as far as complete extermination.

7

The Ache of Paraguay and Other "Isolated" Latin American Indigenous Peoples: Genocide or Ethnocide?

Robert K. Hitchcock, Charles Flowerday, and Thomas E. Koperski

Introduction

Members of various indigenous groups, human rights organizations, observers, journalists, and researchers have asserted that some of the ways in which Latin American indigenous peoples have been dealt with over the past 500 years constitute genocide (De las Casas, 1992; Lewis, 1969, 1974, 1975; Dostal, 1972; Stannard, 1982; Montejo, 1987; Smith, 1987; Chalk and Johnassohn, 1990, pp. 173-180; Churchill, 1997; Maybury Lewis 1997, 2002; Robbins, 2005; Jones, 2006, pp. 70-72; Kiernan, 2007, pp. 72-100). This point was made by Miguel Chase-Sardi with reference to the Ache (Guayaki) of eastern Paraguay at the Symposium on Inter-Ethnic Conflict in South America held in Barbados from January 25 to January 30, 1971.

Mark Munzel (1973, 1974), a German anthropologist who worked in eastern Paraguay in 1971-1972, published two reports on what he described as the genocide of Ache peoples. In his reports he described what the Ache experienced: massacres; individual murders by settlers and government forces; "manhunts" (Munzel,

1985) and forced slavery. Ache children were also taken away from their families. In general, the Ache experienced massive human rights violations and were treated inhumanely by settlers and by the Paraguayan government.

The Ache suffered not only collective mass killing but also other kinds of threats that Fein (2007) describes as "life integrity rights" (pp. 2, 5-8). As Ward Churchill (1999), noted, "Approximately 85 per cent of Paraguay's remaining native population, mostly Aches, were quite literally butchered with machetes during the 1960s and 1970s to make way for the progress embodied in timbering, ranching, and large-scale agriculture" (p. 434). By the time that the book *Genocide in Paraguay* (Arens, 1976) was published, the Ache had become a *cause célèbre*, an example of an indigenous people who were documented as being exposed to massive human rights violations that fit the United Nations definition of genocide (United Nations, 1948).

The Ache case is important because it is one of the few in which efforts were made to bring charges against government officials for genocide and human rights violations against an indigenous people at the international level (Arens, 1976a, b, 1978; Inter-American Commission on Human Rights, 1978, 1987, 2001; Parellada and de Ancantara, 2008). It is also important because of the attention it brought to the plight of indigenous peoples in the Gran Chaco and in Latin America more broadly (Brysk, 2000, pp. 68-69, 110; Parellada, 2007). As a result of the treatment to which they were subjected, the Ache and other indigenous groups, along with human rights organizations and support groups and journalists, applied unceasing pressure on the Stroessner government, ultimately contributing to its demise (Horst, 2003).

It is possible to distinguish specific types of genocide involving indigenous populations. The first type, which can be termed *socioeconomic genocide*, comes about the context of colonization or exploitation of resources in areas occupied by indigenous groups. The perpetrators of socioeconomic genocide range from government organizations established ostensibly to assist indigenous peoples to settlers who receive subsidies from the state and from large landowners to peasant farmers. Another type of genocide where indigenous peoples are victims is *retributive genocide*, in which actions are taken against collectivities that are perceived as threats or as representing opposition to state ideology and interests. This kind of genocide occurs in contexts in which there is civil conflict, or there are challenges to the legitimacy and authority of a dominant class or group. Indigenous peoples in a number of Latin American countries have been the victims of retributive genocide in the twentieth and twenty-first centuries. A list of cases of genocides and genocidal massacres of Latin American indigenous peoples is provided in Table 7.1. Data on these and other cases have been provided by governments and non-government organizations, opposition groups, anthropologists, and indigenous people themselves. This information has sometimes resulted in further investigations into the treatment of indigenous peoples. The problem, however, is that the findings of these investigations have not always led to improvements in the situations facing indigenous populations. In some cases, the follow-ups to the reports have had the effect of tempering government treatment of indigenous groups and the groups that support them.

In the not too distant past, a significant proportion of the genocides of indigenous peoples occurred during the course of colonial expansion. In Brazil, Davis (1977, p. 5) estimated that more than 80 Indian tribes that came in contact with the national society between 1900 and 1957 were destroyed, and the indigenous population dropped from approximately a million to less than 200,000. Indigenous peoples in the Brazilian Amazon continue to be exposed to genocidal actions, as can be seen, for example, in the case of what came to be known as the Hashimu massacre of Yanomami Indians in northern Brazil in 1993 (Survival International, 1988a; Chagnon, 1993; Albert, 1994; Sponsel, 1997). Latin American indigenous groups have also died out as a result of overwork, hunger, disease, and stress (Hurtado et al., 2005; Survival International, 2007).

Isolated indigenous peoples – those who live in out-of-the way places in Latin America—are some of the most vulnerable groups in the world today (Castillo, 2004; Paralleda, 2007). As Beatriz Huertas Castillo (2004) points out, over the past century isolated

Table 7.1
Genocides and Human Rights Violations of Indigenous
Populations in Latin America

Population	Country	Year(s)
Ache	Paraguay	1965-79
Akuntsu	Brazil	2007-2008
Arara	Brazil	1992
Araucanian	Argentina	1870s
Arhuaco (Ika)	Colombia	2003-2004, 2008
Arsario	Colombia	2004
Ashaninka	Peru	1986
Awa	Brazil	2008
Cuiva	Colombia	1967-71
Kogi	Colombia	2004
Huaorani	Ecuador	1960s, 1986-92
Maya	Guatemala	1964-1996 (1981-84)
Makuxi	Brazil	2008
Miskito	Nicaragua	1981-1986
Nambiquara	Brazil	1986-87
Nunak	Colombia	1991
Paez	Colombia	1991
Pai Tavytere	Paraguay	1990-91
Pilaga	Argentina	1947
Pewenche	Chile	1996
Rama	Nicaragua	1981-1986
Tagaeris	Ecuador	2000
Ticuna	Brazil	1988
Ulwa	Nicaragua	1981-1986
Yanomami	Brazil	1988-89, 1993

Note: Data obtained from the International Work Group for Indigenous Affairs (www.iwgia.org), Survival International (www.survival-international.org), Cultural Survival (www.cs.org), Amnesty International (www.amnesty.org), Human Rights Watch (www.hrw.org), Minority Rights Group International (www.minorityrights.org), Antislavery International (www.antislavery.org), and the annual United States Country Reports on Human Rights.

indigenous peoples of the Peruvian Amazon experienced overt and purposeful violence aimed at destroying them In response, isolated indigenous peoples sometimes had to abandon their traditional areas and move to new places. They also responded by organizing themselves and attempting to get recognition at the local, regional, national, and international levels. In some cases, they used the media to good effect, appealing to the international community to put pressure on the government to treat them more humanely.

In Latin America, some of the genocides of indigenous peoples occurred in the context of armed conflicts in which either the government forces or the opposition groups or both targeted local people. A classic example is the treatment of Quiche Maya in Guatemala by the government and paramilitary forces especially in the 1980s (see Jones, 2006, p. 77; Totten, this volume). Isolated indigenous peoples generally have been subjected to genocidal massacres and human rights violations in the context of the expansion of the state, some of which has been military in nature but which has also been done as a means of pacifying remote areas in order to enhance development initiatives.

The Ache Case in Paraguay

The Ache (Guayaki) of eastern Paraguay in some ways represent a classic example of an isolated Latin American indigenous people. In the 1960s, a sizeable percentage of the Ache consisted of small groups of nomadic hunter-gatherers who moved from place to place in remote areas of eastern Paraguay (Clastres, 1972, 1998; Melia et al., 1973; Hill and Hurtado, 1989, 1995). The Ache resided in and moved over tracts of dry tropical forest in areas that they recognized as their own and to which they had customary rights. Interactions with other groups varied, with some Ache groups preferring to avoid contact and others engaging in exchange of goods and, in some cases, farm labor.

In the mid-1960s, the Ache territory in eastern Paraguay was opened up through the construction of a new road. The Ache in the area, who numbered some 600-700 people at the time, faced encroachment from the outside from the state and from European settler groups. After contact occurred, some of the Ache ended up on reservations, while others migrated into towns or lived in the compounds of ranchers, settlers or missionaries. The Paraguayan military established an Ache reservation where people were confined, allegedly by force (Arens, 1976; Lewis, 1976). Allegedly, food and medicines were deliberately withheld from the Ache residents of the reservation.

In 1974, the Ache case was brought before the Inter-American Commission on Human Rights. The IACHR requested information on the situation from the Paraguayan government, which did not reply. On March 8, 1974, U.S. Senator James Abourezk of South Dakota denounced, on the floor of the United States Senate, what he described as genocidal activities in Paraguay. In August 1974, a representative of Anti-Slavery International (AAI) addressed the UN Sub-Commission on Prevention of Discrimination demanding a United Nations investigation of the charges made against Paraguay while, as he put it, the "Indians could still be saved."

In 1974, the International League for the Rights of Man submitted a statement to the Secretary-General of the United Nations calling for the Stroessner government in Paraguay to be charged with genocide, slavery and torture. The Director of the Paraguay Indian Affairs Department was cited as being one of those involved in the exploitation of young Ache women as slaves (Arens, 1976, pp. 12).

The Catholic Church took a strong stance on Paraguayan indigenous peoples' rights, partially in response to the information on the treatment of the Ache. The government of Paraguay rejected the charges of genocide outright Chase-Sardi (1972) asserted that in a number of articles published in the local Paraguayan press. Luis Albospino tried to alert the Paraguayan public to what was going on, to little avail (p. 195).

The Inter-American Commission on Human Rights (IACHR) of the Organization of American States (OAS) also considered the Ache case (see Inter-American Commission on Human Rights, 1978, 1987, 2001). Other organizations that looked into the Ache case included the Anti-Slavery Society (now Anti-Slavery International, AAI), the U.S. Catholic Conference, the Conference of Catholic Bishops, the National Council of Churches, the Anti-

Defamation League, the International Association of Democratic Lawyers, and the United Nations Sub-Commission on Prevention of Discrimination and Protection of Minorities (Arens, 1976; Inter-American Commission on Human Rights, 2001; Parellada and Beldi de Alcantara, 2008). Virtually all of the organizations working on the Ache case claimed either that genocide had occurred or that massive human rights violations had been perpetrated against them, including killings, disappearances, children being taken forcibly from their families, purposeful prevention of access to food and medicines which were necessary to maintain decent standards of health and nutrition.

The Debate over Genocide and Ethnocide

Anthropologists and faith-based groups weighed into the discussions about what had transpired among the Ache, including those working with or for some of the indigenous peoples' human rights organizations: the International Work Group for Indigenous Affairs, founded in 1968, Survival International, founded in 1969, and Cultural Survival, founded in 1972 (Melia et al., 1973; Smith, Smith, and Melia, 1978; Hill and Hurtado, 1995; Horst, 2000, 2003, 2007). A bitter debate arose over the ways in which members of indigenous peoples' advocacy groups portrayed the treatment of the Ache in the early 1990s (see Survival International, 1993). Some of Survival International's arguments stemmed from disagreements with an initial draft of a report on the Indian peoples of Paraguay by Maybury-Lewis and Howe (1980). This report covered both the plight and the prospects of Paraguayan indigenous peoples, and it addressed issues ranging from purposeful killings of Indians to the withholding of medical care. Maybury Lewis and Howe (1980) argued that "the Indians of the Paraguayan Chaco have undergone a tremendous and largely negative transformation since the turn of the century" (p. 25). They went on to say that only a few of Paraguay's indigenous peoples were still hunter-gatherers, and that they were eking out a marginal existence on the fringes of the economy and society of the Chaco.

When Maybury Lewis and Howe's (1980) report questioning whether genocide had occurred in the case of the Ache was published, Survival International wrote to Cultural Survival expressing their concern. Meetings took place between representatives of the two organizations; these addressed a number of issues, including the nature of the reporting, with Cultural Survival maintaining that their report was "academic" as opposed to the more "journalistic" reports produced by Survival International and the International Work Group for Indigenous Affairs (Survival International, 1993). Another issue of concern revolved around what was meant by the term "genocide," which implies, according to the United Nations Convention on the Prevention and Punishment of the Crime of Genocide, the issue of "intent." A third concern that was raised in the discussions related to the nature of the evidence, including the degree to which first person testimony was utilized, when and how it was obtained, and who was responsible for the interviews and information (Survival International, 1993).

As noted above, much of the debate about whether or not the Ache were subjected to genocidal treatment relates to the issue of government intent. As David Maybury-Lewis and James Howe (1980) put it in their report, "The charge that the Paraguayan government has had an official policy of genocide against the Indians seems to us unlikely as well as unproven" (p. 40). The defence on the part of the Paraguayan government under Alfredo Stroessner was that the government never had a systematic policy to exterminate the Ache or other Indian groups; instead, the government argued, the approach to dealing with Indians was one of attempting to help them. The establishment of settlements was seen as one way of providing assistance to Indian peoples, though many Indians would disagree with that position, given the conditions under which they lived in those settlements. The U.S. media in particular was criticized for failing to pay greater attention to the "tragedy of the Ache" (Arens, 1976, pp. 5-6). The Ache, it was argued by those who believed that genocide was being perpetrated, had to cope with a two-pronged policy, one of physical extermination on the one hand and enslavement and forced enculturation (ethnocide) on the other.

Debate continues about the Ache case, with some analysts suggesting, based on interviews and detailed field and archival work, that the original reports by Mark Munzel were overstated or, even worse, outright lies (see, for example, Horst, 2000, p. 7). Anthropologists Kim Hill and Magdalena Hurtado (1995), for example, who worked intensively with the Ache for a number of years, questioned the application of the term genocide to the Ache case on the basis of their field data on Ache demography (pp. 168-169). They pointed out that the most common cause of death was one where a person was killed by another Ache individual. This was as true in pre-contact warfare, they asserted, as it was post-contact. The colonists, they noted, did not want to exterminate the Ache but rather preferred to take their land and use the Ache as laborers on that land.

According to Hill and Hurtado (1995), one of the reasons that people opted to go to the reservations was to avoid warfare and conflict. Their data suggest that the Ache population was not in danger of extinction but rather that their population was growing rapidly at the time of the alleged genocide. Hill and Hurtado (1995) also questioned the accuracy of Munzel's figures on deaths and captures of children, saying that Munzel's number was almost twice the size of the entire Northern Ache population in 1968 (p. 169). Hill and Hurtado also maintain that the Ache were persuaded, as opposed to being coerced, into settling down in reservations and villages.

In 1989, a military coup ended the thirty-five-year-long dictatorship of Alfredo Stroessner, and this led to the possibility of obtaining additional information on the Ache case. A number of different groups and organizations have worked with the Ache since that time, including conservation organizations such as the Nature Conservancy and the Moises Bertoni Foundation of Paraguay, which helped to gain enhanced protected status over the Mbaracayu, a forest area in eastern Paraguay that had been in the hands of the International Finance Corporation (IFC) since 1979.

In spite of the publicity, the documentation, the requests for investigations and the various hearings that were held, no sanctions were imposed on the Paraguayan government by the United Nations, the Inter-American Commission on Human Rights or by the United States, at that time Paraguay's major financial donor. The Paraguayan minister of defense, General Marcial Samaneigo, in the 1970s, attempted to browbeat representatives from religious organizations, government institutions and non-government organizations into making a public statement that the accusations by Mark Munzel had been false. He was unsuccessful in this effort.

Today, the Ache number approximately 1,600 people (Parellada and Ancantara, 2008). The percentage of Ache compared to the population of Paraguay as a whole is extremely small. In July, 2008, Paraguay had a population of 6,831,306 in a country 406,750 sq km in size. In 2008, there were at least eight villages and reservations where Ache resided, some of them state-sponsored and others associated with faith-based institutions. These villages included Alta Parana, Caaguau, Chopapou, Cerro Moroti, Puerto Barre and Tupa Rendu. Ache residing in these areas had a mixed subsistence system and they engaged, in some cases, in wage labour. Some Ache children attended school. A fairly sizable number of Aches also attended church.

There are numerous issues facing the contemporary Ache. In a report published in 2006 by Anti-Slavery International (Kaye, 2006), it was noted that some 8,000 indigenous peoples in the Chaco region were involved in forced labour on the estates of well-to-do farmers. The reason for this situation, it was argued, was due to a combination of few employment opportunities, low rates of literacy among indigenous peoples (less than 50 percent), the desire for cheap labour on the part of farmers, and overt racism. Low wages were paid to workers, who also had to pay high prices to local store owners for goods. Because the indigenous peoples lacked transport, they could not go to places where goods were cheaper. Consequently, members of indigenous communities took out loans which they were unable to pay back. The owners of the estates pressed the people who had debts into service as what, in essence, were bonded labourers. As Kaye (2006) notes, debt bondage is one of the principal means of coercion used around the world to control migrant workers.

Critical Challenges Facing the Field Today

There continue to be cases where individual Ache and members of other isolated indigenous peoples are killed, tortured, captured and pressed into service, essentially as slaves, and where children are taken away from their families. Some Ache continue to assert that they are being subjected to human rights violations both by the government of Paraguay and organizations working in Ache areas. They also believe that what transpired in the past was tantamount to genocide, and that the actions to which they were subjected are in line with the definition found in the UNCG. They also claim that they have been subjected to policies of assimilation that are aimed at depriving them of their culture. When asked if they faced genocide or ethnocide, some Ache, though not all, answer that they faced both, purposeful destruction of them as people, and purposeful destruction of their culture.

The Ache, like other Latin American indigenous peoples, state that protection from perpetrators of human rights violations is imperative, and that they wish to see the perpetrators punished. If this is to happen, then substantial efforts will need to be made in order to gain detailed knowledge of the situation on the ground before such interventions are attempted.

Some positive impacts of the publicity surrounding the treatment of Ache include pressures being brought to bear on the government for greater indigenous peoples' rights. Also non-government organizations have increased their efforts to work with Ache and other Paraguayan Indian communities. At the same time, the international recognition of the plight of the Ache led to other organizations working on behalf of Ache and other groups in the Gran Chaco, a process that has had some positive impacts in terms of enhancing access to development and to greater recognition of their rights at the national level in Paraguay.

Some anthropologists, genocide scholars, educators, native leaders and members of religious organizations continue to feel that the treatment of the Ache was ethnocide, if not genocide. They also believe that the debate over the Ache case has been positive in terms of bringing greater pressure to bear on the Paraguayan government and groups operating in Paraguay to change their policies.

Real Probabilities of Success in the Field

If contemporary Latin American isolated indigenous peoples are going to be able to cope with the challenges facing them in terms of genocide and massive human rights violations, they will have to be in positions where they and their advocates can influence government and international policies regarding indigenous peoples. One way to do this is to work with the existing international indigenous rights institutions, such as the United Nations Permanent Forum on Indigenous Issues (UNPFII), the UN Special rapporteur on the human rights and fundamental freedoms of indigenous peoples, and the UN Expert Mechanism on the Rights of Indigenous Peoples. They will also have to have cases that they bring before regional organizations such as the Inter-American Commission on Human Rights taken seriously.

Latin American isolated indigenous peoples will also have to be given the opportunity to remain isolated if they so choose. One way that some Latin American countries have attempted to assist isolated indigenous peoples is to set aside large areas – the equivalent of cultural parks for isolated indigenous peoples – which are off-limits to outsiders (Castillo, 2004; Parellada, 2007; Parellada and de Ancantara, 2008). The key issue here is for governments to ensure that the rules about non-entry are enforced

Another way that success can be achieved is for the international community to do a better job of monitoring cases of suspected genocides and ethnocides of isolated Latin American indigenous peoples. As noted previously, it is exceptionally difficult to obtain reliable and detailed information on genocides of indigenous peoples. This is particularly true when it comes to locating first-person accounts of genocides involving such groups (Totten, 1991; Totten, Parsons, and Hitchcock, 2002). One reason for this situation is that many contemporary indigenous groups who have been subjected to genocidal treatment tend to live in out-of-the-way places that are often inaccessible for environmental (i.e., remote locations, lack of roads), social, or political reasons. Documentation of genocidal events against indigenous communities is also rare since those groups residing in remote locations tend not to write very much about their experiences, focusing instead on oral documentation.

Gathering data on genocides of indigenous peoples is also difficult because in many cases the gross violations of human rights are ongoing. Because of the conditions, it is rare for outside observers to be in places where massive human rights violations are occurring. At the same time, individuals in these contexts are often reluctant to talk for fear of reprisals.

One of the difficulties faced by anthropologists and others investigating genocidal acts is that most of the existing accounts are not from indigenous groups but rather come from the government, the military, or other agencies who have come in contact with these groups. Fortunately, indigenous peoples themselves are recording their experiences and telling their stories more often now than was the case in the past.

A crucial type of information on genocides and ethnocides of indigenous people consists of oral testimony obtained from indigenous peoples made to researchers or investigators, some of whom may be anthropologists, as was the case with Mark Munzel, Miguel Chase Sardi, David Maybury Lewis, or Kim Hill. An advantage of these oral histories and ethnographic accounts is that they sometimes are obtained during or not long after the incidents to which people are referring occurred, thus ensuring that the effects of gradual memory loss are minimized. Collecting of oral testimony also reduces the chances that subsequent reports and media coverage will influence individual perceptions.

Another critical type of information on indigenous peoples is detailed demographic data which can be obtained through careful interviews, genealogical documentation, and life history studies of individuals, as was collected by Kim Hill and Magdalena Hurtado in their work among the Ache. It is also useful for researchers and development workers to go back in to areas where genocides and ethnocides were reported to have taken place and to obtain new information from witnesses and others, as was done by Alejandro Parellada and his colleagues in eastern Paraguay (Parellada and de Alcantara, 2008).

Clearly, there is a tremendous need to obtain additional accounts of cases of genocides of indigenous peoples, including first-person accounts and detailed scientific assessment. Having more detailed and nuanced information on genocides and human rights violations will facilitate the process whereby early warning systems can be developed. Analysis of case materials such as those on the Ache and other isolated Latin American populations can help in the determination of the accuracy and reliability of the information collected and can lead to a better understanding of the conditions under which the rights of indigenous peoples are violated and facilitate the development of strategies to alleviate them.

References

Albert, Bruce (1994). "Gold Miners and Yanomami Indians in the Brazilian Amazon: The Hashimu Massacre" pp. 47-55. In Barbara Rose Johnson (Ed.) *Who Pays the Price? The Sociocultural Context of Environmental Crisis*, Washington DC and Covelo, California: Island Press.

Arens, Richard (1978). *The Forest Indians in Stroessner's Paraguay: Survival or Extinction?* Survival International Document Series, No. 4. London: Survival International.

Arens, Richard (Ed.) (1976). *Genocide in Paraguay*. Philadelphia, PA: Temple University Press.

Brysk, Alison (2000). *From Tribal Village to Global Village: Indian Rights and International Relations in Latin America*. Stanford, CA: Stanford University Press.

Castillo, Beatriz Huertas (2004). *Indigenous Peoples in Isolation in the Peruvian Amazon: Their Struggle for Survival and Freedom*. Copenhagen: International Work Group for Indigenous Affairs.

Chagnon, Napoleon A. (1993). Anti-Science and Native Rights: Genocide of the Yanomami. *Human Behavior and Evolution Society Newsletter* 2(3):1-4.

Chase-Sardi, Miguel (1972). "The Present Situation of the Indians in Paraguay," pp. 173-217. In Walter Dostal (Ed.) *The Situation of the Indian in South America*. Geneva: World Council of Churches.

Churchill, Ward (1997). *A Little Matter of Genocide: Holocaust and Denial in the Americas, 1492 to the Present*. San Francisco, CA: City Lights Books.

Churchill, Ward (1999). "Genocide of Native Populations in South America," pp. 433-434. In Israel W. Charny. (Ed.) *Encyclopedia of Genocide, Volume II*. Santa Barbara, CA and London: ABC-Clio.

Clastres, Pierre (1972). "The Guayaki," pp. 138-174. In Bicchieri, M.G. (Ed.) *Hunters and Gatherers Today*. New York: Holt, Rinehart, and Winston.

Clastres, Pierre (1998). *Chronicle of the Guayaki Indians*. Paul Auster, translator. New York: Zone Books.

Dostal, Walter (Ed.) 1972. *The Situation of the Indian in South America*. Geneva: World Council of Churches.

Fein, Helen (2007). *Human Rights and Wrongs: Slavery, Terror, Genocide*. Boulder, CO and London: Paradigm Publishers.

Hill, Kim, and Hurtado, Ana Magdalena (1989). "Hunter-Gatherers of the New World." *American Scientist* 77(5): 436-443.

Hill, Kim, and Hurtado, Ana Magdalena (1995). *Ache Life History: Ecology and Demography of a Foraging People*. Chicago, IL: Aldine de Gruyter.

Hitchcock, Robert K.; Koperski, Thomas E.; and Flowerday, Charles (2008). "Genocidio Y Etonocidio de Pueblos Indigenas: El Caso de Los Ache del Paraguay," pp. 43-54. In Alejandro Parellada and Maria de Lourdes Beldi de Alcantara, (Eds.) *Los Ache del Paraguay: Discusion de un Genocido*. Copenhague: Grupo International de Trabajo Sobre Asuntos Indigenas (IWGIA).

Horst, Rene Harder (2000). "Political Advocacy and Religious Allegiance: Catholic Missions and Indigenous Resistance in Paraguay, 1982-1992." Paper presented at the 2000 annual meetings of the Latin American Studies Association, Miami, Florida.

Horst, Rene Harder (2002). "The Catholic Church, Human Rights Advocacy, and Indigenous Resistance in Paraguay, 1969-1989." *Catholic Historical Review* 88(4):723-744.

Horst, Rene Harder (2003). "Consciousness and Contradiction: Indigenous Peoples and Paraguay's Transition to Democracy," pp. 103-132. In Erick D. Lange with Elna Munoz (Eds.) *Contemporary Indigenous Movements in Latin America*. Wilmington, DE: Scholarly Resources.

Hurtado, A. Magdalena; Lambourne, Carol A.; James, Paul; Hill, Kim; Cheman, Karen; and Baca, Keely (2005). "Human Rights, Biomedical Science, and Infections Diseases among South American Indigenous Groups." *Annual Review of Anthropology* 34:639-677.

Jackson, Jean E., and Warren, Kay B. (2005). "Indigenous Movements in Latin America, 1992-2004: Controversies, Ironies, and Directions." *Annual Review of Anthropology* 34, 549-573.

Kaye, Mike (2006). *Contemporary Forms of Slavery in Paraguay*. London: Anti-Slavery International.

Jones, Adam (2006). *Genocide: A Comprehensive Introduction*. New York and London: Routledge.

Kiernan, Ben (2007). *Blood and Soil: A World History of Genocide and Extermination from Sparta to Darfur*. New Haven, CT: Yale University Press.

Lewis, Norman (1969). "Genocide-From Fire and Sword to Arsenic and Bullet, Civilization Has Sent Six Million Indians to Extinction." *Sunday Times Magazine* [London], February 23, 1969.

Lewis, Norman (1974). *Genocide: A Documentary Report on the Conditions of Indian Peoples*. Berkeley, CA: Indigena and the American Friends of Brazil.

Lewis, Norman (1975). "Shock Report." *The Sunday Times of London*, January 26, 1975.

Lewis, Norman (1976). "The Camp at Cecilio Baez," pp. 58-68. In Arens, Richard (Ed.) *Genocide in Paraguay*. Philadelphia, PA: Temple University Press, pp. 58-68.

Maybury-Lewis, David (1997). *Indigenous Peoples, Ethnic Groups, and the State*. Boston, MA: Allyn and Bacon.

Maybury-Lewis, David (2002). "Genocide against Indigenous Peoples," pp. 43-53. In Alexander Laban Hinton (Ed.) *Annihilating Difference: The Anthropology of Genocide*. Berkeley, CA and Los Angeles: University of California Press

Maybury-Lewis, David, and James Howe (1980). *The Indian Peoples of Paraguay: Their Plight and Their Prospects*. Cambridge, MA: Cultural Survival Inc.

Melia, B.; L. Miraglia; M. Munzel; and C. Munzel (1973). *La Agonia de los Ache-Guayaki: Historia y Cantos*. Asunción: Centre de Estudios Antropológicos, Universidad Católica.

Montejo, Victor (1987). *Testimony: Death of a Guatemalan Village*. Willamantic, Connecticut: Curbstone Press.

Munzel, Mark, (1973). *The Ache Indians: Genocide in Paraguay*. IWGIA Document No. 11. Copenhagen, Denmark: International Work Group for Indigenous Affairs.

Munzel, Mark (1974). *The Ache: Genocide Continues in Paraguay*. Copenhagen, Denmark: International Work Group for Indigenous Affairs.

Munzel, Mark (1985). "The Manhunts: Ache Indians in Paraguay," pp. 351-403. In Willem A. Veenhoven (Eds.) *Case Studies on Human Rights and Fundamental Freedoms: A World Survey, Volume 4*. The Hague: Nijhoff.

Parellada, Alejandro (Ed.) (2007). *Pueblos Indigenous en Aislamiento Voluntario y Contacto Inicial en la Amazona y el Gran Chaco*. Copenhagen: Grupo International de Trabajo Sobre Asuntos Indigenas (IWGIA).

Parellada, Alejandro and Maria de Lourdes Beldi de Alcantara (Eds.) (2008) *Los Ache del Paraguay: Discusion de un Genocido*. Copenhagen: Grupo International de Trabajo Sobre Asuntos Indigenas (IWGIA).

Robbins, Nicholas (2005). *Native Insurgencies and the Genocidal Impulse in the Americas*. Bloomington and Indianapolis: Indiana University Press.

Smith, Roger W. (1987). "Human Destructiveness and Politics: The Twentieth Century as an Age of Genocide," pp. 21-38. In Isidor Wallimann and Michael Dobkowski, (Eds.) *Genocide and the Modern Age: Etiology and Case Studies of Mass Death*. Westport, CT: Greenwood Press.

Smith, R.; J. Smith; and B. Melia (1978). *Genocide of the Ache-Guayaki?* London: Survival International.

Stannard, David E. (1992). *American Holocaust: Columbus and the Conquest of the New World*. New York and Oxford: Oxford University Press.

Survival International (1988a). *Brazil: Ticuna Massacre*. Urgent Action Bulletin, UAB/BRZ/11, April, 1988. London: Survival International.

Survival International (1993). *The Denial of Genocide*. London: Survival International.

Survival International (2000). *The Awa. Brazil: Uncontacted Indians Face Extinction*. Urgent Action Bulletin, July, 2000. London: Survival International.

Survival International (2001). *Ayoreo: Paraguay: Uncontacted Indians in Danger*. Urgent Action Bulletin, September, 2001. London: Survival International.

Survival International (2007). *Progress Can Kill: How Imposed Development Destroys the Health of Indigenous Peoples*. London: Survival International.

Totten, Samuel (Compiler/Editor) (1991). *First Person Accounts of Genocidal Acts Committed in the Twentieth Century*. Westport, CT: Greenwood Press.

Totten, Samuel; Parsons, William S.; and Hitchcock, Robert K. (2002). "Confronting Genocide and Ethnocide of Indigenous Peoples: An Interdisciplinary Approach to Definition, Intervention, Prevention, and Adequacy," pp. 54-91. In Alexander Labhan Hinton (Ed.) *Annihilating Difference: The Anthropology of Genocide*. Berkeley and Los Angeles: University of California Press.

United Nations (1948). *United Nations Convention on the Prevention and Punishment of the Crime of Genocide*. General Assembly Resolution 260A (iii) of December 9, 1948, entered into force on January 12, 1951. New York: United Nations.

Varese, Stefano (2006). *Witness to Sovereignty: Essays on the Indian Movement in Latin America*. Copenhagen: International Work Group for Indigenous Affairs.

Annotated Bibliography

Arens, Richard (Ed.) (1976). *Genocide in Paraguay*. Philadelphia, PA: Temple University Press. 171 pp.

This book, which contains ten chapters, describes the ways in which the Ache Indians were dealt with by the Paraguayan government, settlers, and non-government organizations. The editor and some of the authors argue that the Ache were physically exterminated in acts that amounted to genocide; they were subjected to the deliberate creation of conditions under which they suffered starvation and psychological stress and where Ache culture was "deliberately and demeaningly extinguished" (p. 10); and Ache children were taken away from their families by force and sold as slaves. Aimed at raising awareness of what was occurring in Paraguay in the 1970s, the book criticizes not only Paraguay but also the American media, the U.S. government for its support of the Stroessner regime, and the international community for failing to take action against Paraguay.

Hill, Kim, and Hurtado, Ana Magdalena (1995). *Ache Life History: Ecology and Demography of a Foraging People.* Chicago, IL: Aldine de Gruyter. 561 pp.

This book is a detailed ethnographic and behavioral ecological study of the Ache of eastern Paraguay by two anthropologists. The authors examine Ache population dynamics, subsistence practices, and farming, among other issues. In 1978 Hill had the opportunity "to observe firsthand the disastrous effects of first contact" (p. 55). Subsequently, Hill, Hurtado, and their colleagues undertook careful social and ecological studies of forest-living and reservation Ache, living and travelling with them, participating in their daily lives, and observing them closely. They note that mission evangelical activities resulted in permanent changes in Ache behavioral patterns, including ones "biased toward serving male interests" (p. 76). Based in part on their demographic data (e.g. causes of death), Hill and Hurtado call into question the conclusion that the Ache experienced genocide, saying, "The data do not suggest that the Ache population was ever in danger of extinction from external warfare before 1970 (in fact that population was growing rapidly during the time they were allegedly being exterminated), nor is there evidence any group of people (government, corporation, military, etc.) ever intended to exterminate the Ache" (p. 168). They admit that the Ache contact situation resulted in extremely high mortality, but conclude that "This was due to carelessness and incompetence rather than intention" (p. 168).

Horst, Rene Harder (2000). Political Advocacy and Religious Allegiance: Catholic Missions and Indigenous Resistance in Paraguay,

1982-1992. Paper presented at the 2000 annual meetings of the Latin American Studies Association, Miami, Florida.

This paper considers the ways in which the Catholic Church used human rights advocacy to increase its influence among indigenous peoples in Paraguay. Indigenous peoples, for their part, took advantage of this support in their struggles against the policies of the Stroessner regime. Horst notes that after the Stroessner government was denounced by German anthropologist Mark Munzel in 1971 for attempted genocide against the Ache, Catholic activists used the Ache situation as a way the criticize state integration policies and treatment of indigenous groups. In May 1974, the Conference of Catholic Bishops called for an exhaustive inquiry of the Ache case, "whose survival is seriously imperiled" (p. 6). Paraguayan government security forces cracked down on Catholic activists and indigenous leaders, but ultimately their collaboration helped bring an end to the Stroessner regime in 1989.

Munzel, Mark (1973). *The Ache Indians: Genocide in Paraguay.* IWGIA Document No. 11. Copenhagen, Denmark: International Work Group for Indigenous Affairs. 80 pp.

This report, by German anthropologist Mark Munzel, was one of the first widely disseminated discussions of the treatment of Ache Indians by the Paraguayan state and other groups. He argued that the Ache were being exterminated intentionally and that they had to cope with what he called "manhunts" which saw members of Ache groups taken away and forced into slavery. These manhunts, he suggested, "have increased in volume and in violence during recent years" (p. 13). He said that in the early 1970s there were raids on Ache camps by people who were "specialists in killing Ache" (p. 16), and he discussed ways in which Ache men, women, and children were dealt with, from rape to torture and from starvation to forced labour. Munzel noted that the people in charge of the reserves on which Ache were placed were directly responsible for the violation of Ache rights and that the Native Affairs Department of the Paraguayan government was aware and tolerant of the situation. He also said that the Ministry of Defense had been made aware of massacres of Ache but they had done nothing to stop them. In his report, Munzel cited first-hand and eyewitness accounts of cases where armed raiding parties had hunted down and killed Aches. He concluded by saying that "only international protest" might make the Paraguayan government change its policies (p. 63).

Munzel, Mark (1974). *The Ache: Genocide Continues in Paraguay.* Copenhagen, Denmark: International Work Group for Indigenous Affairs. 32 pp.

This report summarized some of the findings of Munzel's earlier work, which he described as a "specific case of genocide" (p. 3), and outlined what had happened in Paraguay from 1972 on. He discussed the public outcry that had ensued about the Indian situation in Paraguay, and he noted the fact that academics, church officials, journalists, and others had published articles and letters about what was happening to the Ache and other Indians. As Munzel put it, "The reason for these protests is the fear that this genocide may continue" (p. 6). He noted that the Ache reservation had been taken over by the New Tribes Mission, something that led to a rise in material standards but also to cultural changes among reservation residents. He pointed out that the new managers of the reserve were engaged in manhunts aimed at bringing additional Ache to the reserve. Munzel concluded that the international attention paid to "the genocide of the Ache" led to improvements in the situations of the Ache but that there was still much left to do (pp. 19-20).

Parellada, Alejandro (Ed.) (2007). *Pueblos Indigenous en Aislamiento Voluntario y Contacto Inicial en la Amazona y el Gran Chaco.* Copenhagen: Grupo International de Trabajo Sobre Asuntos Indigenas (IWGIA). 386 pp.

This book, which is entitled, "Voluntarily Isolated Indigenous Peoples and Initial Contact in Amazonia and in the Gran Chaco," contains a series of papers presented at the Regional Seminar held at Santa Cruz of the Sierra (Bolivia) from November 20-22, 2006. There were participants at the meeting from the seven countries with isolated peoples and those that have been initially contacted:

Bolivia, Brazil, Colombia, Ecuador, Paraguay, Peru and Venezuela. As noted in the introduction, one result of this seminar, besides the dialogues and interactions that took place among the participants, who included representatives of indigenous groups and organizations, government administrators, non-government organization members, and experts, was the formulation of an "Appeal of Santa Cruz of the Sierra." It is hoped that the appeal and the book publication will contribute to greater recognition and enhanced protection of the rights of these diverse Amazonian and Gran Chaco peoples. These groups, variously described as "isolated," "in a situation of isolation," "voluntarily isolated," "wild people," "un-contacted peoples," "hidden," or "free" (people), are the most vulnerable of all indigenous peoples.

In spite of the human rights campaigns conducted by civil society groups and advances in the international recognition of the fundamental rights of indigenous peoples, members of indigenous organizations say that killings and mistreatment of isolated indigenous peoples persist, processes which have contributed to pressures to form an International Alliance for the Protection of Isolated Indigenous Peoples. The UN Permanent Forum on Indigenous issues urged governments, the United Nations system, civil society, and indigenous organizations to work toward an immediate ban of acts of aggression and genocide and called for new kinds of development strategies and programs aimed at the protection of the rights of isolated peoples and their territories.

The book contains thirty-one chapters, twenty-four of which deal with the diverse experiences of the seven countries that contain isolated and recently contacted indigenous peoples. National policies on isolated peoples are examined, and recommendations are made for ways to deal with these vulnerable groups, including the passage of laws aimed specifically at protecting the rights and physical and cultural integrity of isolated peoples, the establishment of "no-go" zones, capacity-building of indigenous organizations, and the use of surveillance systems.

Parellada, Alejandro y Maria de Lourdes Beldi de Alcantara (Eds.) (2008) *Los Ache del Paraguay: Discusion de un Genocido.* Copenhague: Grupo International de Trabajo Sobre Asuntos Indigenas (IWGIA). 286 pp.

This book, which contains eight chapters, addresses both past and contemporary issues faced by the Ache Indians of eastern Paraguay. It reproduces some of the classic papers on Ache genocide and ethnocide, two written by German anthropologist Mark Munzel which were published originally in English by the International Work Group for Indigenous Affairs in 1973 and 1974, and one by Bartomeu Melia, the director of Catholic Missions in Paraguay who in 1969 had conducted doctoral fieldwork among the Mbya and Ava Guarani. It was Melia who said in the early 1970s that "The Ache reservation is an Ache graveyard" and who, along with other Catholic human rights activists, said that the Ache experienced both physical and cultural genocide.

It is noted in the book that in 1968, the Ache's territory was made accessible by a new road. The possibility of exploiting forestry resources and the expansion of agricultural activities, combined with government policies toward indigenes peoples, resulted in raids, murders, kidnappings, and enslavement. Survivors of the "manhunts' were concentrated at the Guayaki National Reserve and many children, largely girls, were sold, some of them for sexual purposes. It was these and related events that led to the charges of genocide by Munzel, Melia, and others.

On the occasion of IWGIA's fortieth anniversary, IWGIA decided to review what had happened to the Ache. In mid-April, 2008, Alejandro Parellada was able to make a brief visit to Paraguay to meet with Paraguayan anthropologist Jorge Servín, visit an Ache community, and speak to an Ache woman, Margarita Mbywangi who as a child had been sold. Mbywangi later studied to be a nurse and in 2006 was a candidate for the Paraguayan Senate, losing by only a few votes. Based in part on this work, combined with perspectives of researchers, activists, and development workers, this book assesses what happened to the Ache since the 1960s and 1970s, outlines the various development initiatives in which they have taken part, and describes their efforts to promote Ache rights.

Sponsel, Leslie E. (1994) "The Yanomami Holocaust Continues," pp. 37-55. In Barbara Rose Johnston (Ed.) *Who Pays the Price? The Sociocultural Context of Environmental Crisis.* Covelo, CA: Island Press.

This article deals with the problems faced by the Yanomami, one of the largest and best-known of Latin America's indigenous peoples. Numbering some 20,000, the Yanomami reside in a mountainous and lowland tropical forest watershed area on the Brazil-Venezuela border. Sponsel argues that the Yanomami have had to cope with the "shock and stress of Western contact" which has resulted in their becoming "increasingly an endangered people." He says that "The federal and provincial governments of Brazil have been intentionally and systematically violating the human rights of the Yanomami to the extent of committing ecocide, ethnocide, and genocide" (p. 38). He describes the spread of disease, the negative effects of infrastructure and development projects, and the invasions of tens of thousands of gold miners whose activities have resulted in deforestation, game depletion, biodiversity reduction, displacement, soil erosion, river siltation, and pollution, especially from mercury. He says that genocide of the Yanomami is both direct (in terms of lethal violence) and indirect (though the introduction of disease). He goes on to point out that "Ethnocide involves all levels and aspects of the society and culture of the Yanomami" who, he argues, have been left "disoriented, demoralized, decultured, and dehumanized" (p. 39). Sponsel concludes his paper with a set of recommendations on strategies to ensure the protection of Yanomami human rights.

8

Genocide of the Nuba

Samuel Totten

Introduction

The Nuba people are "black" and "African," and indigenous to the Nuba Mountains in Sudan where they continue to reside. While different groups speak different dialects, the lingua franca of the Nuba is Arabic.[1] Some Nuba are Muslim, some are Christian. Many mix elements of their traditional religious beliefs with their "newly acquired" Muslim and Christians beliefs and rituals. Rahhal (2001) has observed that ""[b]efore the war came to the mountains, Islam, Christianity and local beliefs were practiced side by side without prejudice or pressure, creating a remarkable religious tolerance among the Nuba. It was common to find more than one religion in a single family"[2] (p. 40).

The Nuba live in central Sudan in the Kordofan Province, home of some eighty-plus hill communities in the Nuba Mountains. The expanse of area, which constitutes the richest agricultural land in Sudan, covers some 30,000 square miles.

It is thought that the Nuba may "represent the remnants of indigenous populations that once lived far more widely across Sudan" (African Rights, 1995, p. 15). To the Nuba people themselves, the term "Nuba" refers "to the myriad cultures and traditions of the more than fifty different tribal groups in the Nuba Mountains"

(African Rights, 1995, p. 5). On the other hand, "for the dominant class in Sudan, and in particular the ruling National Islamic Front [NIF], 'Nuba' refers to second class citizens—'primitive' black people, servants and labourers" (African Rights, 1995, p. 5).[3]

The Nuba, along with many other groups who live in the so-called "peripheries" of Sudan (that is, outside of the riverine valley where the "elites" reside and govern), are disenfranchised in just about every way imaginable. Just like other indigenous peoples, "the Nuba were not incorporated into Sudan's mainstream political culture" (Salih, 2999, p. 37). Furthermore, those in power perceive the Nuba as inferior beings (the same as they do the black Africans of Darfur), be it culturally, educationally, religiously, et al. African Rights, a London-based human rights group, asserts that "The central theme of Nuba history is the tension between political incorporation into the state of Sudan and maintenance of local identity" (quoted in Winter, 2000, n.p.). The Nuba's main desire is self-determination.

Like any case of genocide, the genocide of the Nuba is complicated. Among some of the many factors at work in this case are: systemic racism; the government's Islamic extremist agenda; the struggle over land; and ongoing discrimination against the Nuba in the realms of the economy, education, health, and political representation.

Systemic Racism

The racist policies of the current government of Sudan (GoS) are nothing new to the Nuba. Ironically, in an attempt to protect the culture and identity of the Nuba (and those residing in Southern Sudan), the British, in the 1920s, established the so-called "Closed District policy" that virtually segregated Arabs from the Nuba. While this policy accomplished its goal, it also precluded the Nuba from gaining a sound education, taking part in the administration of the country, and benefiting from development projects. "This policy opened up gaps between the people of the north and the people of the peripheries, which eventually contributed to the civil conflict which has torn apart the Sudan for most of the [past] 45 years" (Rahhal, 2001, p. 43).

More often than not the Nuba are perceived as so-called "abids" (a highly derogatory meaning "slaves") by those residing in the peripheries. It is used to draw a distinction between those who are Arab and non-Arab, and is a way to make non-Arabs feel diminished as human beings.

Moreover, a key tactic of the GoS and its militia was the rape of the Nuba females. The mass rape, which constituted a policy of rape, "served as a measure intended both to destroy the fabric of the targeted communities and to create a new generation with 'Arab' paternity" (de Waal, 2006, p. 1). Further, as de Waal (1995) noted:

> [as] Khalid el Husseini explained: "the reason for the men and women being distributed in different camps is to prevent them marrying, the reason being that if the men and women are together and get married and have children, that itself is contrary to government policy....The members of the Arab tribes are allowed to marry them in order to eliminate the Nuba identity." The phrase "allowed to marry" amounts to "encouraged to rape" in the context of the absolute power held by the camp officials and guards over the females in their charge. (222)

The Government's Islamic Extremist Agenda

Muslims and Christians, alike, reside in the Nuba Mountains. Tellingly, both groups were targets of ongoing GoS' attacks. Even before the war in the Nuba Mountains began, Christians were attacked by GoS security forces, largely as a result of "a polarized political context, with Islamic extremism in the ascendant" (African Rights, 1995, p. 281). Churches were desecrated and/or destroyed (many were burned to the ground), and Christians were harassed, vilified, beaten, tortured, and even killed by GoS troops and their proxies. Muslims in the area were informed that the Christians were godless and out to destroy Sudan.

When Muslims in the Nuba Mountains did not support the government's actions against the Christians and refused to take part in the desecration and destruction of the churches they were then targeted and their places of worship, mosques, were attacked. Additionally, those Muslims who did not adhere to the more extremist versions of Islam were targeted as infidels. Furthermore, "...despite the fact that the SPLA [Sudan People's Liberation Army] forces in the Nuba Mountains have been very largely led by Moslems, successive governments have portrayed the guerillas as fighting against Islam. In order to do so they have withdrawn the legitimacy of Islam in the SPLA held areas, in effect declaring all Moslems who are not with them to be infidels, and thus the legitimate target for a *Jihad*" (African Rights, 1995, p. 288).

Significantly, the GoS's push for Arabization and Islamization across Sudan also threatened the survival of the traditional Nuba religion, *Kujurism*. Should there be any question as to the seriousness of such, Saeed (2001) notes that should the religious beliefs of Kujurism be undermined or torn asunder, "the whole social structure [of the Nuba] will collapse" (p. 13).

At one and the same time, Arabs have received preferential treatment by the GoS, often to the detriment to the Nuba. A classic example is that while nomads, under laws established by Anglo-Egyptian condominium, were prohibited from using the Nuba's agricultural land for grazing their herds prior to harvest, the laws began to be ignored by both the nomads and the GoS. This resulted in serious conflicts between the Nuba and Arab nomads, and as time went on the conflicts increased in number and intensity.[4]

On a different but related note, the ever-increasing number of weapons that flowed into the area and into the hands of the Murahaliin (GoS-supported Arab militia) in the late 1970s contributed to the violence perpetrated against the Nuba.

Addressing the ultimate goals of the GoS, Rahhal (2001) asserts that "The regime is intolerant of any culture or beliefs other than its own variant of Islamic and Arabic culture. The NIF government seeks to Islamize all Sudanese in order to form the first Islamic state south of the Sahara as a springboard for spreading Islam to the rest of the continent. The Nuba's strong separate identity is a major obstacle to this project" (p. 48).

Marginalization and Disenfranchisement of the Nuba

As previously alluded to, just like the other areas constituting the peripheries in Sudan, the Nuba Mountains suffered years of severe marginalization and disenfranchisement. This was true in a wide variety of areas, including but not limited to education, health and social service, communication, roads and other types of infrastructure, economic development, and political representation.

As far back as 1964, Nuba intellectuals formed the General Union of the Nuba (GUN) in order to discuss their grievances (Mekki, 2001, p. 30). In an attempt to make its needs known, GUN put up candidates for the 1965 parliamentary elections. The Nuba won eight seats in Parliament; and as a result, there was great hope that the GoS would begin to better meet the needs of the Nuba. That, however, was not to be and the peripheries, including the Nuba Mountains and Darfur, continued to suffer marginalization.

Shortly after Jafaar al-Nimeiri came to power as a result of a coup d'état in 1969, his government applied pressure on the Nuba to abandon their traditions. For example, extreme pressure was applied to force them to begin wearing clothes. Regulations were established that required clothing and sellers were forced to refuse the sale of any goods to those not wearing clothing. Then, in 1983, Nimeri imposed strict Islamic law (*Shari'a*) throughout the country, and in doing so the government continued to apply pressure on the Nuba to give up other traditional practices.

Rahhal (2001) reports that "During the spells of democratic government, the people of the Nuba Mountains, the Beja Hills and Darfur were politically undermined and marginalized by the two main parties despite the strong showing of regional parties in the 1965 elections....[The regions were neglected while an accelerated rate of development in northern Sudan led to greater exploitation of young Nuba migrants who had no recourse against racial discrimination" (p. 38).

Marginalization, discrimination, disenfranchisement, and exploitation, then, were the roots causes of Nuba disenchantment with the GoS, and, at one and the same time, the reason behind their openness to the goals of the SPLA.

Forced Removal from Their Ancestral Land

Land, too, has been at the center of the conflict between the Nuba and the powers that be in Sudan. In this regard, Salih (1999) asserts that

[e]ven though the present crisis in the Nuba Mountains is politically-driven, the real factors underlying the conflict have originated in land. From their earlier period of settlement in the Nuba Mountains, the Jellaba took [an] interest in agriculture and

became cotton growers, first by borrowing Nuba land and later by purchasing the most fertile lands.... The Nuba were infuriated and began to show signs of revolt during the mid-1960s when the Jellaba took control over larges portions of their cultivable lands. Jellaba appropriation of Nuba cultivable land continued well into 1968 when the Mechanized Farming Corporation (MFC) began to implement large-scale mechanized schemes privately owned by wealthy Jellaba and a few Baggara oxservicemen and civil servants. (p. 37)

Then, in the early 1970s, believing that Sudan could serve as the "bread-basket of the Arab world" (Rahhal, 2001), the Government of Sudan chose to "expand mechanized farming from the irrigated lands along the Nile westwards into the fertile rain-fed pastures of South Kordofan" (Rahhal, 2001). This effort was underwritten, in part, by the World Bank. The impact on the Nuba and other peoples was nothing short of devastating:

The [GoS] introduction of MFC [Mechanized Farming Corporation] projects had a disastrous effect on the Nuba. Their land was seized, and they were evicted and driven from their ancestral land without compensation.... Most of the fertile land in the eastern part of the Nuba Mountains has been allocated to commercial farmers, including PDF leaders. Many Nuba have become impoverished wage laborers on the farms of absentee landlords and the sustainable agriculture of the Nuba has been replaced by over-intensive farming of thin soil. (Rahhal, 2001, p. 47)

All of this would have been bad enough, but there is another factor that makes it even more devastating: part and parcel of Kujurisim, the traditional religion of the Nuba, is "the veneration of Ancestral Spirits, a veneration that comes close to worship, [which] forms the basis of Nuba religion of those still living. [It is believed that after the death of their loved ones, not only do ancestral spirits continue to reside on the land but that they directly impact the lives of those still living, including all benefits they accrue and all the disasters they suffer.] This also explains the Nuba's exceptional tribal patriotism, [and] *their reluctance to leave their ancestors' home...*" (Saeed, 2001, p. 11, emphasis added).

Furthermore, after being forced off their land, the Nuba, jobless, were, as noted above, forced into taking on menial and poor paying tasks that those in power and in favor did not want to do. As a result, in addition to suffering ongoing marginalization and disenfranchisement, the Nuba increasingly suffered exploitation.

Over the years, "Nuba resistance to the state's appropriation of their land to mainly Jellaba and Baggara has increased, especially since they discovered that they are losing land at an accelerated rate" (Salih, 1999, p. 37).

Outbreak of War

The war that would tear asunder the lives of the Nuba people erupted in 1985. Reportedly, up "until that point, South Kordofan was a peaceful and tranquil area. Relations between the Nuba and the Arabs of South Kordofan were generally good despite minor clashes over cattle grazing and water holes that were usually settled peacefully" (Rahhal, 2001, p. 36). Ultimately, in 1985, "latent conflicts exploded into violence" (Rahhal, 2001, p. 36).

It was in 1985 that the southern-based rebel Sudan People's Liberation Army made their way into the Nuba Mountains. According to Human Rights Watch (1999), early on, the SPLA carried out a raid on a cattle camp of Baggara Arab nomads, which was located near the north-south "internal boundary." In response, the Sudanese government hired the Baggara as a militia to help fight the SPLA and to punish any civilians who were believed to be "sympathetic" to the SPLA. African Rights (1995) reports that

[w]hile the SPLA was not present *in force* [in the Nuba Mountains] until 1989, militia attacks became routine and an army crackdown became intense.... The first stage of the war was marked by militia raids, to loot cattle, kill and occasionally to burn villages. In areas where SPLA units penetrated, the army also undertook mass reprisals, always targeted at villages and civilians.... The war intensified with the arrival of the SPLA...in 1989. It quickly over-ran large areas of the Nuba Mountains and unleashed a ferocious response from the militia and army. Between 1989 and 1991 scores of villages were burned and thousands of villagers killed in joint army and militia assaults. (7, italics added)

Due to ongoing discrimination, marginalization, and ostracism at the hands of the GoS (largely, a "process of assimilation [that became too violent, too racist and too exploitative" [De Waal, 2001, p. 4]), many Nuba joined the ranks of the rebels. As Rahhal (2001) notes, "The resentment and frustration caused among the people of the marginalized regions convinced many that armed struggle was the only way to end northern domination and achieve their political objectives" (p. 43).

Instead of merely attacking the rebel groups, including the Nuba fighters, the GoS carried out a scorched earth attack against all Nuba (just as the GoS would do beginning in 2003 against all black Africans in Darfur). In addition to attacking and destroying Nuba villages, killing Nuba of all ages, and raping the females, the GoS also banned humanitarian aid, with the aim of starving to death those Nuba who sought sanctuary up in the Nuba Mountains. Ultimately, tens of thousands of Nuba perished.

Early on (1986-1989), those suspected of supporting the SPLA were often arrested, tortured, mutilated and killed by security forces. Furthermore, "the Arab-militias, and after 1987, increasingly the regular army as well, were unleashed on defenseless Nuba villages" (Rahhal, 2001, p. 47).

An early focus of the attacks was the systematic effort to wipe out both the educated and the leaders of the Nuba. Reportedly, "…hundreds of chiefs, teachers merchants, civil servants, priests, lawyers, health workers – in fact anyone with an education who might be a spokesman for the people – have been killed" (African Rights, 1995, p. 2).

Following the 1989 coup d'état that placed Omar al Bashir in power as president of Sudan, the Nuba people asked the GoS to help protect them from the Arabs militias; but, instead of providing the requested assistance, the GoS not only gave the militias its imprimatur to do as they wished but purportedly provided them with more weapons "to drive the Nuba from their land" (Rahhal, 2001, p. 47). In fact, "to the dismay of the Nuba, one of the first actions of the new government was to pass the Popular Defense Act, which formally recognized the militias as part of the Popular Defense Forces" (Rahhal, 2001, p. 47). Ultimately, "the systematic nature of the violations under the NIF regime against the Nuba reached an unprecedented scale" (Rahhal, 2001, p. 47).

Following the aforementioned coup d'état in 1989, the GoS established a "cordon sanitaire," virtually cutting the Nuba Mountains off from the rest of the world. As Winter (1999) notes, "Few outsiders were able to visit, and no one could do so freely. NGO personnel and others such as those of the UN's Operation Lifeline Sudan (OLS) were authorized at times to conduct relief operations to fulfill government policy objectives (e.g., to assist "peace camps" in government-controlled areas); [but] they have never been authorized to observe the conflict or assist civilians in SPLA-controlled sectors as is grudgingly allowed in parts of the South" (n.p.).

As for the attacks on the Nuba villages, once the government troops and militias looted and destroyed them, the perpetrators abducted hundreds of thousands of people and forced them into so-called "peace camps." In this way, the government depopulated the rural areas, controlled the actions and movement of civilians, deprived the SPLA of potential assistance, and undertook an effort to alter the Nuba's way of life in fundamental ways. The "peace camps" ended up being places of great abuse, including beatings, rapes, and the deprival of food. Describing the so-called "peace camps," African Rights (1995) reported that

> [t]he innocuously named "peace camps" are concentration camps in the true sense of the word. They are where the rural population is forcibly concentrated so they can be controlled and *their political and cultural identity can be changed.*
>
> Peace camps are the location of mass and systematic rape of women. They are where children are separated from their parents and "educated" to become extremist Moslems in the mold of the ruling Nationalist Islamic Front, *in a process of forced acculturation.* (African Rights, 1995, p. 3, emphasis added).

Genocide of the Nuba

Perhaps the most telling indication that the GoS intended to commit genocide in the Nuba Mountains is this statement by Khalid Abdel Karim Saleh, former head of security in the Office of the Governor of Kordofan: "The ongoing order given to the troops is to kill anything that is alive, that is to say to kill anybody, to destroy the area, to implement a scorched earth policy, to destroy everything, to burn the area, so that nothing can exist there" (African Rights, 1995, quoted on page 137).

In October of 1990, the GoS virtually closed off access to the South Kordofan area, which essentially cut the Nuba Mountains "off from the rest of the world" (Rahhal, 2001, p. 47). At one and the same time, the government attacks against the Nuba continued unabated.

Then, in January 1992, Abdel Krim al-Husseini, the governor of Kordofan, "declared a Jihad in the Nuba Mountains" (Rahhal, 2001, p. 48). More specifically, a large number of armed forces including Mujahadiin and Arab militias were sent to the Nuba Mountains. Backed by indiscriminate aerial bombing and shelling, the army destroyed villages, looted, abducted women and children, killed tens of thousands of men and women and displaced hundreds of thousands of Nuba – forcing more than a hundred thousand into camps on the outskirts of Kadugli, Dilling and Lagowa as a prelude to resettlement in so-called "peace camps" in North Kordofan. Many died in these camps from hunger, disease and exposure. (Rahhal, 2001, p. 48)

Lieutenant Khalid Abdel Karim Salih, the brother of the governor of Kordofan and a former security office in South Kordofan, estimated that between 60 and 70,000 Nuba were killed as a result of the attacks and indiscriminate shelling.

Speaking of this jihad, Sudan expert Alex de Waal (2007) reported that

In 1992, the Sudan Government launched what was almost certainly the most ambitious campaign of forced social change in modern Sudanese history. It was proclaimed a *jihad*. The scale of the military assault on the Nuba was larger than anything seen before or subsequently in the Sudanese wars. The battle of Tullishi was fought around the clock for almost four months. The ambition of entirely emptying the Nuba Mountains of the Nuba people, and forcibly relocating them to "peace camps" away from their homelands, had no parallel. The aim was nothing less than the complete relocation of the Nuba and the eradication of their traditional identities. The policy of separating men from women and preventing the Nuba reproducing by "marrying" the women to Arab men was also something unique. Of all the cases in which activists have debated whether to use the word "genocide" in Sudan, the Nuba case is the most compelling instance. (1)

The policy of allowing Arab men to "marry" the Nuba women in effect legitimized the rape of the latter. This policy "served as a measure intended both to destroy the fabric of the targeted communities and to create a new generation with 'Arab' paternity" (de Waal, 2006, p. 1). Speaking of the latter, African Rights (1995) argues that rape "[broke] the fundamental bond of the family, the relationship between husband and wife, and [broke] down the trust, confidence and sense of identity not just of the woman who ha[d] been raped, but the family and community. When women bear children as a result of rape, they do not have a known, legitimate patrilineage – and so they lack an acceptable social identity" (African Rights, 1995, p. 222).

The children of many Nuba were taken from their parents and educated, in a process of forced acculturation, to become Muslim extremists. If carried out with the intent to destroy in whole or in part an [in this case] ethnic or religious group, as such, this constitutes genocide under the UNCG.

Clear evidence that the government was largely successful in its mission is not only the large number of villages its men and hired hands utterly destroyed, but the famine they created as a result of destroying the crops and stealing and burning the foodstuff stored by the people for the year to come. As Rahhal (2001) commented: "The prevention of food relief [became] one of the government's main weapons for depopulating the mountains. It [was] more effective than bullets, with the starving Nuba forced to choose between death from hunger or life in one of the peace camps" (p. 52).

By September 1992, "the peak of the genocidal onslaught was over. What followed was a slower, but systematic war aimed at grinding down Nuba resistance" (Rahhal, 2001, p. 49).

By 1995, "the campaign of 1992 had failed and was replaced by a thoroughly nasty, if lower-level counter-insurgency" (de Waal, 2008, p. 2). To describe the subsequent situation, de Waal used the term "genocide by attrition." He notes that he used that term "not because the government still harboured genocidal intent, but because the outcome of the war, continued indefinitely into the future, would have been the elimination of Nuba identity" (de Waal, 2008, p. 2).

de Waal (2008) argues that the jihad failed for three key reasons: (1) the armed resistance of the Nuba; (2) the split within the GoS: "the militant *jihad*ists who wanted a campaign of ethnic cleansing could not prevail over those who wanted to defeat the rebellion and leave it at that. Most army officers, for example, supported the war but not the forced displacement to peace camps" (p. 2); and (3) horror, disgust and outrage among the Sudanese citizenry, "especially the residents of towns in Kordofan who had Nuba people literally dumped on their doorstep" (p. 2).

Still, the GoS continued its siege of the Nuba, and in doing so continued to cause immense hardship and suffering:

The government of Sudan has never permitted access by the U.N. or any relief agency to the SPLA areas of the Nuba Mountains. While even preventing ordinary traders from doing civilian business with these rebel areas, the government has facilitated

U.N. assistance to garrison towns, particularly to the "peace camps" where captured Nubas from rebel areas are interned and are subjected to abuse. The government's strategy is to starve the estimated 400,000 civilians in SPLA areas, presumed to be the SPLA "support base," out of their traditional lands and into these "peace camps." (Human Rights Watch, 1999, p. 1)

Even that, though, was not the full extent of the GoS's efforts. In fact, the GoS's attacks continued unabated throughout the 1990s and into the 2000s. In addition to aerial bombardments, the GoS strategically planted anti-personnel mines along well-traveled paths, in those areas where people fetched water, and near military garrisons. The area continues to be strewn with these horrific instruments of war and constitute an ongoing and deadly menace to the Nuba.[5]

Tellingly, when called upon to cease and desist, the GoS acted much the same way it has the past six years in Darfur—made repeated promises only to break them time and again. For example, in 1999 Human Rights Watch reported that "Sudan's Foreign Minister promised U.N. Secretary General Kofi Annan on May 20, 1998, that the U.N. could conduct an assessment mission in the rebel areas of the Nuba Mountains. That promise has never been kept. The governments' continued refusal of all access mocks the U.N" (p. 1).

As late as 2001, de Waal asserted that "[t]here was and still exists a programme bent on the eradication and crushing of the Nuba identity, in the name of the 'civilization project' of the Sudan government" (pp. 3-4).

On November 14, 2001, the U.N. World Food Program began its first major relief operation in decades in the Nuba Mountains. At that time, the WFP (2001) reported that

[t]he Nuba population has been severely hurt by drought conditions in the country, and a combination of drought and insecurity has reduced food production by almost 60 percent, pushing as many as 93,000 into extreme poverty. A recent escalation of hostilities between the government and rebels also left 65,000 people completely devastated, losing their homes, food stocks, tools, seeds and fertile land. There is also widespread malnutrition reported among the Nuba population, and since May, Nuba civil authorities have reported 450 hunger-related deaths, 271 of which were children. (p. 1)

The Efforts of NGOs to Assist the Nuba

While the United Nations did little to nothing to actually help the Nuba, the London-based human rights group Africa Rights played an instrumental part in both reaching out to the Nuba as well as bringing their plight to the attention of the international community. Up until the varied efforts of African Rights, most, including other human rights groups, knew little, if anything, about the plight of the Nuba. Roger Winter (1999), a canny and well-informed human rights expert based in the U.S. and the former executive director of the U.S. Committee on Refugees, reported that he knew nothing about the Nuba, and that for the most part their plight was "invisible" to the rest of the world.

In regard to African Rights remarkable efforts to help the Nuba, Winter (1999) commented as follows: "An unusually creative and energetic human rights organization, in coordination with Nuba outside of the Sudan, undertook in 1994 to breach the secrecy blanket that blocked the war against the Nuba from international view. African Rights spearheaded an effort to establish a human rights monitoring project covering the seven districts in the region, using trained Nuba as monitors with radio capacity to communicate events to outside constituencies such as human rights groups, NGOs [nongovernmental organizations], and Nuba organizations such as the Nuba Relief, Rehabilitation and Development Society, based in Nairobi, and the Nuba Mountains Solidarity Abroad in Britain" (n.p.).

Significantly, African Rights also helped journalists, scholars, and NGOs gain access to the Nuba Mountains, which, in turn, helped to spread the word about the plight of the Nuba.

Such efforts by African Rights also provided human rights activists and others with "the first real chance to see genocide at work in the area" (Winter, 1999, n.p.). Be that as it may, "the response of the international community [was] effectively nonexistent, but it [was] not for lack of information" (Winter, 1999, n.p.).

Julie Flint, a British freelance journalist, entered the war ravaged Nuba Mountains in the early 1990s and in 1995 produced the first major documentary about the oppression and atrocities to which the Nuba had been, and were being, subjected. The film drew a great deal of attention to the Nuba's plight. Of Flint's efforts, Winter (1999) observed, with admiration: "Julie Flint…visually blew the lid off the *cordon sanitaire*. The documentary film, 'The

Nuba: Sudan's Secret War,' was broadcast on the BBC in July. The Sudanese Government had repeatedly asserted there was no war in the Nuba Mountains and that African Rights made up its reporting from whole cloth, never having been on-site. Flint's video demonstrates the Government's unabashed use of the big lie" (n.p.).

In 1995, Alex de Waal, an Oxford-educated social anthropologist and an expert on the Sudan who was working with Africa Rights, wrote a major report for Africa Rights entitled *Facing Genocide: The Nuba and Sudan*. That work drew additional attention to the plight of the Nuba, but did not, for some reason (possibly the on-going focus on the 1994 Rwandan genocide and the crisis in the former Yugoslavia), draw activists to the cause.

Subsequently, African Rights, with de Waal and others, "started a low-profile humanitarian air bridge in support of the Nuba Relief, Rehabilitation and Development Organization, with a handful of NGOs that were ready to operate in a discreet way, foregoing publicity in order to promote Nuba ownership of their programs. A year or so later some high-profile religious NGOs began operating in the Nuba Mountains, and several years later the UN and USAID provided assistance" (p.2). Ultimately, in 2002, a ceasefire was agreed to by the various actors.

Writing in 1999, Winter commented on the dearth of attention and assistance focused on the plight of the Nuba:

> The normal human rights and humanitarian mechanisms the world uses to target and respond to such tragedies have failed the Nuba. Operation Lifeline Sudan has been irrelevant; the UN Department of Humanitarian Affairs and International Committee of the Red Cross absent; the NGO community ignorant; the UN Security Council silent; interventions like that of Jimmy Carter's "cease fire" in Sudan neglectful. That some Nuba survive free is entirely due to their own efforts....[I]n the end, despite the fact that ample data and very credible analysis are now available, the Nuba are still waiting for the world community to respond to their plight. Relief is not the major issue, though medical and development assistance are needed. What is needed is an expression of outrage by the international community that genocide is in fact occurring in the Nuba Mountains, complemented by an effort to take the pressure off the Nuba people. (n.p.)

In June 1999, following the ten-year blockade of the Nuba Mountains, the United Nations Development Programme (UNDP) finally gained access in order to carry out a Humanitarian Needs

Assessment. Subsequently, the UNDP, along with various NGOs, began working on obtaining full and unhindered access in the Nuba Mountains. Various joint UN/INGO missions were carried out in both GoS and SPLM areas of the Nuba Mountains to conduct technical assessments, carry out polio vaccination efforts, and to provide emergency supplies. Those efforts, however, were soon stymied due to ongoing fighting.

Bombings of the Nuba people continued well into 2000. One of the most brutal was the GoS attack, on February 8, 2000, on the Holy Cross School in Kauda in the Nuba Mountains. Describing the carnage of the NIF aerial attack, Eric Reeves (2005), a U.S. scholar, wrote the following:

> ...crashing into the midst of these students were high-explosive bombs, wrapped in shrapnel, which would wreak immediate and horrific carnage. Thirteen children and a teacher were torn apart and killed on the spot; others would die subsequently from the wounds they sustained. And many more children would be severely and permanently maimed, losing hands and arms or enduring severe burns. All the dead children were under seventeen years of age.
>   An Antonov "bomber" of the National Islamic Front regime in Khartoum had deliberately targeted Holy Cross School as part of its ongoing assault on the people of the Nuba, dropping on this occasion four bombs in the area of the school. (p. 2)[6]

In 2001, the Nuba Survival Foundation reported that "The recent offensive has intensified with dire consequences for the civilian population and for the food situation in the Nuba Mountains. There are signs of impeding famine already in the areas; the price of livestock is falling as people sell their assets to buy food. In addition, the price of food is rising astronomically and surplus food is being consumed. Tens of thousands of displaced people in Nagurban County are already living on wild fruits" (Nuba Survival, 2001, p. 2).

Attempts at Peace

As far back as 1993 attempts were made to establish a peace in the Nuba Mountains, but most did not prove fruitful. Finally, as previously noted, a ceasefire agreement was put into effect in 2002. Be that as it may, the Nuba peoples' desires and rights were largely sidelined as the GoS and the leaders of Southern Sudan wrangled over major and minor issues as they worked to pound out the 2005 Comprehensive Peace Agreement (CPA). Unlike the people of Southern Sudan, the Nuba did not gain the right to self-determination. That was, and is, a devastating blow to the Nuba. As Minorities at Risk (2005) put it, "The Nuba occupy a precarious position as a buffer zone [a "transitional" area in the language of the CPA] between North and South Sudan. While politically aligned with Southern Sudan, they are geographically located in an area considered part of Northern Sudan [and thus under the thumb of the GoS]. [As a result,] the agreement with the South has considerably weakened the position of the Nuba" (p. 1).

In January 2005, the Nuba Survival Foundation issued a press release that summed up the frustration of the Nuba Peoples vis-à-vis the so-called peace agreements:

> Having carefully examined all the Peace Agreements signed in Navaisha so far, including the Agreement signed last week on 31 December 2004 by the Parties, we have come to conclusion that all these agreements have failed to address the fundamental rights of the people of the Nuba Mountains. The people of the Nuba Mountains have been consistently demanding the right of self-determination and self-rule during and after the interim period, which will give them the right to maintain, control and govern their ancestral land. The two negotiating Parties [the GoS and the leadership from Southern Sudan] instead of recognizing and accepting the basic rights for the people of Nuba Mountains, including the right of self-determination similar to that given to the people of Southern Sudan and Abyei, they agreed upon, denied these very same rights. They came up with what is called "Popular Consultations" for the people of the Nuba Mountains, which is an ambiguous clause and does not lead to anything except denying the people of the Nuba Mountains the right to determine their own future like others in Sudan. (p. 1)

The GoS and the leadership in Southern Sudan can, if they wish, overlook the frustration and sense of injustice felt by the Nuba, but most assuredly the Nuba cannot, and most likely will not, let the issue of self-determination fade away. This is particularly true as they continue to be buffeted by the winds of change in Sudan and the oppressiveness of being under the thumb of the riverine elites.

As for the so-called "peace" that was manufactured at the expense of the Nuba's freedom and self-determination, it has already begun to crack and splinter. Tellingly, as recently as July 28, 2008, a Nuba SPLA colonel, Haza Jemri, uttered the following words to a reporter visiting the Nuba Mountains: "Go tell the world that the so called peace only exists on paper" (Emase, 2008, p. 2).

In August 2008, the Switzerland-based Small Arms Survey research group issued a report noting that both northern and southern forces in Sudan were contravening the 2005 Comprehensive Peace Agreement by recruiting new troops in the Nuba Mountains region. Strife has emerged as each side has accused the other of ignoring and/or breaking various aspects of the peace agreement. Fighting has already broken out and resulted in major battles. Under the CPA, the southern army was supposed to redeploy out of the Nuba Mountains area and northern forces were supposed to reduce their numbers to pre-war levels.

The report concludes with these ominous words:

> It is clear that security is the biggest immediate challenge in the Nuba Mountains. A combination of weak political will, an international community distracted by Darfur, and UNMIS's underperformance, has led to the failure of CPA implementation in South Kordofan. Ethnic tensions are mounting in the region, and recovery and development plans are overshadowed by the danger of a return to open conflict. Discontent over the CPA's failure to deliver economic development is turning to anger, and many now view war in the Nuba Mountains as inevitable. An emerging local narrative sees parallels with the events that led to the Darfur conflict. (Small Arms Survey, 2008, pp. 9-10)

On January 14, 2009, armed irregular forces (reportedly from different clans within the Arabic-speaking Hawazma tribe who were heavily armed) carried out attacks on Nuba villages and SPLA military camps in Southern Kordofan. According to reports some nineteen people were killed. "Other reports suggest that some 400 police and members of the Popular Defense Forces—the type of militias once mobilized for the war in South Sudan and now in Darfur—attacked the Joint Integrated Unit in Khor El Delib" (Sudan Tribune, 2009, p. 1).

The Critical Challenges and Issues Facing the Nuba Today

Certainly the most critical issue facing the Nuba today is the danger posed by the most recent attacks and battles in the area. The international community must bring this situation under control and do its utmost to get both sides to honor each and every aspect of the CPA.

While the issue of security is predominant, there are numerous other challenges and issues that need to be addressed and solved.

In the "Open Letter to General Lazarus Sambeyweo from Nuba Civil Society Organizations, Regarding the Machakos Protocol," dated August 14, 2002, the authors urged those engaged in the ongoing negotiations being brokered by IGAD to take into mind the aspirations of the Nuba people. Among the many critical issues that they asserted had to be addressed were as follows:

[A] significant proportion of the Nuba people would not be satisfied with a peace settlement at any price. It is assumed therefore that any successful negotiated settlement will have to include genuine and satisfactory improvements in terms of political representation, sustained and equitable access to resources, and legal guarantees that Nuba societies will have the freedom to express their identity on their own terms.

The key point now is that there is no longer any illusion that such satisfactory improvements could realistically be achieved if the Nuba Mountains Region or Southern Blue Nile, were to come under the jurisdiction of the current Government of Sudan.

The reasons for our lack of trust in the Northern elite's governments, especially the present regime, in Khartoum are well known and many. To highlight but a few of these policies: the overt fundamentalist nature of the NIF; the imposition of Islamic *Sharia* law and a fundamentalist type of Islam; its lack of any genuine democratization, linked to its clear Arabist, self-serving policies that expressly deny the right of self-expression or self identification; domination and control of national wealth and economic exploitation of the people they have impoverished, in addition to a catalogue of well documented human rights abuses against the Nuba including ethnic and cultural cleansing, genocide and massive dislocation of Nuba people from their motherland. The appalling conditions in which the vast majority of Nuba people currently trying to survive in the north (whether in the camps of Kordofan or the shanty towns of Khartoum) are further testimony to reality of the unacceptable tendencies of the northern regime. (p. 1)

The Nuba have made it very clear that they wish to be considered part of the south versus part of the north in Sudan. Not only do they mistrust the leaders of the north and believe they would continue to suffer marginalization, disenfranchisement and exploitation at the hands of the riverine peoples and the leaders of Sudan, but they feel closer to those in the south (particularly since they fought with the south against the north). In this regard, the authors of Open Letter noted above assert the following:

Ethnically, culturally and socially the Nuba are much closer to the black African people of Southern Sudan and Southern Blue Nile than to the Northern Arabs who have marginalized the Nuba and other Africans for so long....

The Nuba people cannot live in harmony and coexist peacefully with the peoples of the North. Our strong adherence to religious tolerance, our strong African cultural identity and traditions, and our keen interest in freedom of belief are in direct contrast and conflict with the intolerant, dominating, and exclusive culture of the Arabs in the North (p. 1).

Ultimately, then, the challenges faced by the Nuba are as follows:

- The Nuba's right to self-determination must be recognized and acted upon;
- The return of the Nuba's land to their rightful owners;
- The end to the disenfranchisement and marginalization of the Nuba;
- The end to religious persecution;
- The end to racial discrimination and social segregation;
- The end to all human rights violations by the GoS;
- The clearing of land mines from the Nuba Mountains area;

What are the Real Probabilities of Progress Facing the Nuba

As far as making solid progress versus that which is more cosmetic and/or politically expedient, the situation seems, at best, tentative. This is true for at least six basic reasons: (1) The GoS is intent on having its way—meaning that it wants to establish a stronghold all across Sudan and impose Arabization and Islamization on the various peoples and cultures; (2) The CPA is not holding up the way many had hoped, and violent conflicts are now on the rise. Until this situation is brought under control, both the Southern and Northern governments are placing the Nuba in a very precarious position; (3) As long as the peace agreement between the GoS and South Sudan is shaky, it is highly unlikely that any other peace agreements will be solidified; (4) As long as the crisis in Darfur continues, it is unlikely that the GoS is going to willingly cede power, self-determination or honor basic human rights to other groups such as the Nuba; (5) As long as land and other resources in the Nuba Mountains continue to be coveted by the riverine elite and the GoS it is highly unlikely that the GoS and its followers will leave the Nuba people in peace; and (6) The peace agreements signed thus far between the GoS and the Nuba peoples have not withstood the test of time, and nothing suggests that the immediate future is likely to be all that different.

The simple but profound fact is that the Nuba people are extremely nervous about the prospect of coming under the direct rule of the people of "the north" (that is, the riverine elite) (Taylor, 2008, p. 1). Indeed, they want no part of that.

Conclusion

It seems as if there are some significant messages for genocide scholars and anti-genocide activists inherent in the case of the Nuba. First, once a regime has a taste of genocide and gets away with it, there is a fairly good chance it will be prepared to carry it out again if and when it perceives "the need" to do so. In other words, impunity for major human rights violations (be they crimes against humanity or genocide) is something that must not continue unabated. Second, when a nation closes off an area (the way the Khmer Rouge did between 1975 and 1979 as it carried out its genocide against its own people, the way the GoS did when it carried out its genocide by attrition against the Nuba, and the way, to a certain and significant extent, the GoS has operated during its genocidal attacks on the black Africans of Darfur between 2003 and 2005 and beyond), there cannot be a much clearer early warning signal that something grossly wrong is taking place within the area. Third, there is a need for some sort of international convention and law dealing with regimes that seal off parts of its country. Granted, this is much easier said than done since it impinges directly on state sovereignty, but it also brings to the fore the concept of the responsibility to protect—and what it means in reality—for the people on the ground who are destined to be victimized by such a situation.

Notes

1.   Salih (1999) notes that "Although the Nuba have marked linguistic and cultural differences among themselves, they use their collective name, 'Nuba,' to distinguish themselves from the Baggara and Jellaba. The Baggara and Jellaba are Arabic-speaking Muslims who migrated to the Nuba Mountains, in several waves since the turn of the 17th century, for slave raiding and trade" (p 37).
2.   Continuing, Rahhal (2001) remarks that "this religious freedom ended with the coming to power of the National Islamic Front (NIF), which is attempting to Islamize the whole of Sudan through repression and coercion while harboring ambitions of spreading its Islamic revolution to neighboring countries as well" (p. 40).
3.   As Salih (1999) comments, "the Nuba, as a group, do not accept Islam as their religious ideology or 'Arabism' as their racial ideology. These two notions of exclusion are often used by the state to justify the oppression and appropriation of Nuba land and natural resources" (p. 37).
4.   Rahhal (2001) notes that "Following the overthrow of Field-Marshal Gaffar Nimeiri in April 1985, the Nuba-conflict intensified and entered a new phase of hatred and hostility. The transitional government of Sowar al-Dahab began arming the Arab

militias, ostensibly to protect their interests in the area against the SPLA, which had made its first incursion into the mountains at al-Gardoud in 1985" (p. 41). The nomads, though, often made use of their newly acquired weapons to harass, threaten and maim Nuba during the aforementioned conflicts over land usage. Continuing, Rahhal (2001) reports that "This event [the incursion of the SPLA] *lit* the spark of war in the Nuba Mountains" (emphasis added) (p. 41).

5.   In an article entitled "The Landmine Situation in the Nuba Mountains," Peter Moszynski (2001) wrote as follows: "Outside the scrutiny of the international community Sudan government forces appear to feel free to treat the Nuba Mountains as a 'free fire zone' conducting military operations regardless of the cost to civilians. The government's forced villagization policy attempts to depopulate the land and keep the people in "peace villages" both through blockade and scorched earth tactics, of which the continuing use of banned anti-personnel mines form an integral part.

"Mines are used both to prevent SPLA attacks on government garrisons and to keep the local population incarcerated in their protected villages. They are also used to prevent people from returning to their own villages to salvage their property after raids out of the garrison towns....

"Soldiers of the 5th Division regularly use AP mines to prevent pursuit following raids, but also use them for ambushes along purely civilian routes such as paths to water holes, markets and orchards. Despite Khartoum being a signatory to the Ottawa Convention banning the use of anti-personnel mines, captured government military engineers responsible for recent mine laying apparently had no awareness of their prohibition" (p. 1).

More recently, according to the UN Office for the Coordination of Humanitarian Affairs, a South African based de-mining company, MECHAM, has joined with a Sudanese-created NGO, Operation Save Innocent Lives (OSIL), to demine the Nuba Mountain area. From April 2003 to March 2004, for example, OSIL claimed that "an area of 10,478,437 square km had been cleared in both the Nuba Mountains and in southern Sudan. More than 1,500 miles of roads have been cleared as well. However, a field co-ordinator for Humanitarian Mine Action [an OSIL department], Akech Athieu, told IRIN that it is difficult to determine the scope of the problem in terms of numbers of mines since there is no legitimate record of where or how mines were used" (UN Office for the Coordination of Humanitarian Affairs, 2004, p. 1).

6.   In an article about the bombing of the school, "Slaughter of the Innocents," published on April 18 2000, journalist Nat Hentoff wrote the following:

Roman Catholic Bishop Macram Max Gassis is all too well acquainted with the slavery, starvation, and murder of his people in central and southern Sudan—caused by the National Islamic Front government in the north. The killing fields that fall within his jurisdiction include the Nuba Mountains. He is in exile, although he slips back from time to time to report on the atrocities inflicted on black Christians, animists, and Muslims. These horrors are largely ignored by the world, including the president of the United States [George W. Bush]...

Because of the civil war in Sudan between the government and the resistant forces in the south, the children of the Nuba Mountains have been without schools for a generation. And so the bishop established the Holy Cross School in Kauda. This is from a report I received from the bishop on February 19:

"On Tuesday, February 8, forces loyal to the Khartoum regime [the government of Sudan] launched an air attack on [the Holy Cross School], part of the Roman Catholic diocese of El Obeid."

A Russian-built Antonov bomber targeted the heavily populated area around Kauda, including the school with its 339 students.

His report continues: "The Antonov aircraft dropped four shrapnel-laden bombs that landed near the school while outdoor lessons were going on, killing 15 children and wounding 17, some critically. A 22-year-old teacher was also killed. Most of the victims were first-grade students who were in the middle of an English lesson when the attack occurred. [Subsequently five more students died of their wounds.] Nuba eyewitnesses also reported that eight bombs fell on nearby villages during the attack.

"According to a February 11 Reuters report, Sudanese government officials defended the attack, saying that schools are a legitimate target in the country's long-running civil war.

"'The bombs landed where they were supposed to land,' Dirdiery Ahmed, an official in the Sudanese embassy in Nairobi, told Reuters" (pp. 1-2).

References

African Rights (1995). *Facing Genocide: The Nuba of Sudan*. London: Author.
de Waal (2006). "Averting Genocide in the Nuba Mountains, Sudan," pp. 1-6. Brooklyn, NY: Social Science Research Council.
de Waal, Alex (2008). "Kordofan, Making Sense of Darfur (Not Forgetting the Nuba War)." August 9. Accessed at: http://www.ssrc.org/blogs/darfur/2008/08/09/truth-telling-nuba/ -
de Waal, Alex (2001). "The Right to be Nuba," pp. 1-5. In Suleiman Musa Rahhal (Ed.) *The Right to Be Nuba: The Story of a Sudanese People's Struggle for Survival*. Lawrenceville, NJ: The Red Sea Press.
Emase, Phillip (2008). "Education Provides Hope for Sudan's Neglected Nuba." *News from Africa*. July 28. Accessed at: http://www.newsfromafrica.org/newsfromafrica/articles/art_11243.html
Hentoff, Nat (2005). "Slaughter of the Innocents: The World is Strangely Silent." *The Village Voice News*, April 18. Accessed at: http://www.villagevoice.com/issues/0016/hentoff.shtml
Human Rights Watch (1999). *Famine in Sudan, 1998: The Human Rights Causes*. New York: Author.
Minorities at Risk (2005). "Risk Assessment: Sudan (Nuba)." Accessed at: http://pards.org/2005/Sudan(Nuba)AtRisk.doc
Moszynski, Peter (2001). "The Landmine Situation in the Nuba Mountains." *The Nuba Vision*, June, 1(1):1-2. Accessed at: http://www.nubasurvival.com/Nuba%2520Vision/Vol%25201%2520Issue%25201/4.%2520landmines.htm
Nuba Survival Foundation (2005). "Naivasha Accord Fails to Address Nuba Grievances." January 4. *Sudan Tribune*. Accessed at: http://www.sudantribune.com/spip.php%3Farticle7354
Nuba Survival Foundation (2001). "United Nations Activities in the Nuba Mountains." *The Nuba Vision*, June, 1(1):1-2. Accessed at: http://www.nubasurvival.com/Nuba%2520Vision/Vol%25201%2520Issue%25201/6.%2520UN%2520activies.htm

"Open letter to General Lazarus Sambeyweo from Nuba Civil Society Organizations, regarding the Machakos Protocol." Accessed at: http://home.planet.nl/~ende0098/Articles/20020814a

Rahhal, Suleiman Musa (2001). "Focus on Crisis in the Nuba Mountains" pp. 36-55. In Suleiman Musa Rahhal (Ed.) *The Right to Be Nuba: The Story of a Sudanese People's Struggle for Survival*. Lawrenceville, NJ: The Red Sea Press.

Rahhal, Suleiman Musa (Ed.) (2001). *The Right to Be Nuba: The Story of a Sudanese People's Struggle for Survival*. Lawrenceville, NJ: The Red Sea Press.

Reeves, Eric (2005). "Children within Darfur's Holocaust." December 23. Accessed at http://www.genocidewatch.org/SudanChildrenWithinDarfurDec05.htm

Saeed, Ahmed Abdel Rahman (2001). "The Nuba," pp. 6-20. In Suleiman Musa Rahhal (Ed.) *The Right to Be Nuba: The Story of a Sudanese People's Struggle for Survival*. Lawrenceville, NJ: The Red Sea Press.

Salih, M. A. R. M. (1999). "Land Alienation and Genocide in the Nuba Mountains, Sudan." *Cultural Survival*, 22(4):36-38.

Small Arms Survey (2008). *"The Drift Back to War: Insecurity and Militarization in the Nuba Mountains." Sudan Issue Brief*. No. 12, August. Geneva: Author. August. Accessed at: http://www.smallarmssurvey.org/files/portal/spotlight/sudan/Sudan_pdf/SIB-12-drift-back-to-war.pdf -

Sudan Tribune (2009). "Fighting Erupts in Nuba Mountains, 19 Killed." January 14. *Sudan Tribune*. Accessed at: http://sudantribune.com/spip.php%3Farticle29874

Taylor, Darren (2008). "Anxiety and Tension Builds in Nuba Mountains of Sudan." Voice of America. September 2. Accessed at: http://www.sudan.net/news/posted/16242

UN Office for the Coordination of Humanitarian Affairs (2004). "Laying Landmines to Rest? Humanitarian Mine Action." *IRIN*. November. Accessed at: http://www.irinnews.org/InDepthMain.aspx%3FInDepthId%3D19%26ReportId%3D62841%26Country%3DYes

U.N. World Food Program (2001). "WFP Launches First Major Nuba Mountains Relief Operation in Years." Thursday, November 15. Accessed at http://www.unwire.org/unwire/20011115/21743_story.asp

Winter, Roger (1999). "The Nuba People: Confronting Cultural Liquidation," n.p. In Jay Spaulding and Stephanie Beswick (Eds.) *White Nile Black Blood: War, Leadership, and Ethnicity from Khartoum to Kampala*. Lawrenceville, NJ: The Red Sea Press.

Annotated Bibliography

Articles, Books, Reports

African Rights (1997). *A Desolate Peace: Human Rights in the Nuba Mountains*. Sudan. London: Author. 27 pp.

A discussion of the horrific situation the Nuba continued to face at the hands of the GoS.

African Rights (1995). *Facing Genocide: The Nuba of Sudan*. London: Author. 344 pp.

This highly informative book constitutes the first major and detailed report on the plight and fate of the Nuba. It provides an overview of the history of the conflict, an in-depth commentary on the actors involved, the atrocities perpetrated, the actions and reactions of the victims, and how and why the Sudanese Government's actions constitute "genocide by attrition." One of the co-authors of the report/book is Alex de Waal, a noted specialist on Sudan.

African Rights (1997). *Justice in the Nuba Mountains of Sudan: Challenges and Prospects*. London: Author. 43 pp.

Subtitled "A Report on African Rights' Involvement with Access to Justice in the Nuba Mountains, 1995-1997," this is an examination of the difficulties that were continuing to plague the Nuba as well as the challenges and potential for gaining some sort of justice for the Nuba in the region.

African Rights (1995). *Sudan's Invisible Citizens: The Policy of Abuse Against Displaced People in the North*. London: African Rights. 60 pp.

This report is comprised of the following chapters: "Internal Migration in Sudan"; "Forced Acculturation and the Moslem Brother's Project for Transforming Sudan"; "Demolition, Forced Removal and Removal and Population Transfer"; "Discrimination and Abuse: The Daily Struggles of the Displaced"; and "Response and Resistance."

African Rights and Justice Africa (2001). "Voices from the Nuba Mountains," pp. 59-84. In Suleiman Rahhal (Ed.) (2001). *The Right to Be Nuba: The Story of a Sudanese People's Struggle for Survival*. Trenton, NJ: Red Sea Press.

This chapter contains four first-person testimonies, each of which addresses a different issue faced by the Nuba people: abduction and rape, the beginning of the war in the Nuba Mountains, extrajudicial executions, and the burning of a mosque. It also contains a section entitled "stories from an offensive" ("softening up," full-scale assault, scorched earth policies and actions, shelling, land mines, abduction to garrisons and peace camps, killings, hunger and displacement) in which different individuals relate their personal experiences.

African Watch (1991). *The Secret War Against the Nuba.* New York: Author, n.p.
An early report that addresses the unremitting attacks by the Sudanese Government against the Nuba people, their culture, and way of life.

Africa Watch (1992). "Sudan: Eradicating the Nuba: Africa Watch Calls for the United Nations to Investigate Killings, Destruction of Villages and Forced Removals." *News from Africa Watch* September 9. 4(10).
A clarion call for action.

Africa Watch (1991). "Sudan: Destroying Ethnic Identity: The Secret War against the Nuba." *News from Africa Watch*, December 10, 3(15):9.
A short piece that provides insight into the GoS' attempted destruction of the ethnic identity of the Nuba.

Amnesty International (1993). *Sudan: The Ravages of War: Political Killings and Humanitarian Disaster.* London: Author. 29 pp.
In part, this report presents information on major human rights violations (including "ethnic cleansing") perpetrated by Government of Sudan troops and their militia cohorts against the Nuba people.

Amnesty International (1995). *Sudan: "The Tears of Orphans." No Future Without Human Rights.* London: Author. 132 pp.
This report includes information about the Government of Sudan's "ethnic cleansing" in the Nuba Mountains. Additionally, it includes key information about major human rights violations in Sudan, including disappearances, killings, and torture, and the abduction of children.

Bradbury, Mark (1998). "Sudan: International Responses to War in the Nuba Mountains." *Review of African Political Economy*, September, 25(77):463-474.

Bradbury examines the effectiveness of the international response to the Government of Sudan's war against the Nuba, and finds that that it was minimal at best.

Burr, Millard (1993). *A Working Document: Quantifying Genocide in Southern Sudan and the Nuba Mountains, 1983-1993*. Washington, DC: American Council for Nationalities Service. 66 pp.

In this report, the author estimates, based on his experience as director of logistics operations for the U.S. Agency for International Development (USAID) in Sudan, that 1.3 million people had died in southern Sudan due to war and war-related causes. That death total was nearly twice as large as earlier estimates. The conclusions of the study were generally accepted and used by policymakers, international media, humanitarian and human rights workers, and many Sudanese themselves.

Burr, Millard (1998). *Working Document II: Quantifying Genocide in Southern Sudan and the Nuba Mountains, 1983-1998*. Washington, DC: U.S. Committee for Refugees. 84 pp.

This report updates and expands on the first study (see above) by Burr. Burr suggests that approximately 600,000 additional people perished in southern and central Sudan since 1993, raising the toll to 1.9 million deaths. This updated report expands the scope of research to include the Nuba Mountains area of central Sudan.

Burr states that this report was "based on a review of thousands of articles and studies. Rather than simply quantifying incidents both by province and by year, three new elements were added to the study. The first dealt with the purposeful government aerial bombardment of civilian populations. The second new element, a chapter titled 'The Nuba Genocide,' describes the degradation and massacre of Nuba Mountains tribes by Government forces....The third new element in the updated study was a section titled 'Genocide in Bahr al-Ghazal.' It discusses the activity of Government forces and the Government's Arab militia (Murahihleen) to depopulate the Kiir River region of northern Bahr al-Ghazal."

de Waal, Alex (2006). "Averting Genocide in the Nuba Mountains, Sudan." 12 pp. Accessed at: ttp://howgenocidesend.ssrc.org/de_Waal2/
An update of *Facing Genocide: The Nuba of Sudan*, the latter of which de Waal wrote for African Rights. De Waal describes the events in the Nuba Mountains and discusses the status of the Nuba in the ten years after he wrote the initial report.

Human Rights Watch (1999). *Famine in Sudan, 1998: The Human Rights Causes*. New York: Author. n.p.
One section of this report is entitled "Nuba Mountains: Under Siege by the Government." In part, it discusses the GoS's strategy to starve the Nuba people into submission.

Human Rights Watch (1994). *Sudan: "In the Name of God" – Repression Continues in Northern Sudan. Human Rights Watch Report*, November, 6(9). Accessed at: http://www.hrw.org/reports/1994/sudan
The authors state that "This report highlights excerpts from the diary kept by a resident of Kordofan from late 1992 to April 1993 that describes the large-scale displacement of Nubans, their forcible relocation under intolerable conditions, the abduction of children, the forced recruitment of boys as young as thirteen into military service, the destruction of churches, the abuse of women in displaced persons' camps, and the manipulation of relief for Islamic proselytization purposes, among other abuses. This diary reinforces the findings on the situation in the Nuba Mountains presented in the February 1994 report of the U.N. Special Rapporteur on Human Rights in Sudan.

"This report also covers the plight of displaced persons and squatters in urban areas of northern Sudan, including Nubans and southerners displaced by the war. In 1992 hundreds of thousands of the displaced and urban squatters were summarily evicted from their homes in urban areas. Their property was destroyed under a purported urban renewal campaign which targeted the large non-Arab and non-Muslim population of the capital. This campaign continued in 1993, and in 1994 an estimated 160,000 more people were similarly displaced from Khartoum and moved to unprepared sites far from water, work, or education" (n.p.).

International Women's Committee in Support of Nuba Women and Children (1997). "Nuba Mountains Letter." *Africa Policy E-Journal*. October. Accessed at: http://www.africaaction.org/docs97/sud9710.nub.htm
    A letter of protest regarding the ongoing onslaught against the Nuba people. It includes information from various sources vis-à-vis the "genocidal human rights abuses" by the Government of Sudan in the Nuba Mountains region.

Jok, Madut, Jok (2001). *War and Slavery in Sudan.* Philadelphia: University of Pennsylvania Press. 211 pp.
    This study of war and slavery in Sudan examines the contemporary practice of slavery in Sudan through the lens of the long history of the conflicts between those residing in the north (Arabs with power) with those in the south, "the black African peoples" (many of whom are disenfranchised and comprised of both Christians and Muslims). It addresses, in part, the issue of slavery in the Nuba mountains, and, more specifically, how the Nuba people have been historically viewed as slaves.
    The book is comprised of the following parts and chapters: "Introduction: Slavery in Sudan: Definitions and Outlines"; Part I: The New Slavery (1. "The Revival of Slavery During the Civil War: Facts and Testimonies"; 2. "Slavery in the Shadow of the Civil War: Problems in the Study of Sudanese Slavery"; 3. "The Suffering of the South in the North-South Conflict"); and Part II: Underlying Causes of the Revival of Slavery in Sudan (4. "The Legacy of Race"; 5. "The South-North Population Displacement"; 6. "The Political-Economic Conflict"; and "Conclusion: Has No One Heard Us Call for Help? Sudanese Slavery and International Opinion."

Manger, Lief (1993). *From the Mountains to the Plains: The Integration of the Lafofa Nuba into the Sudanese Society*. Uppsala: Nordiska Afrikainstituet. 173 pp.

In this study of the Lafofa Nuba, Manger examines the interaction between Nuba and Arab groups, illuminating the impact of Arabization and Islamization.

Mohamed, Mona A., and Fisher, Margaret (2002). "The Nuba of Sudan," pp. 115-128. In Robert K. Hitchcock and Alan J. Osborn (Eds.) *Endangered Peoples of Africa and the Middle East: Struggles to Survive and Thrive*. Westport, CT: Greenwood Press.

In addition to providing a "cultural overview" of the Nuba (The People, The Setting, Traditional Subsistence Strategies, Social and Political Organization, Religion and Worldview), this chapter also discusses "the threats to survival" faced by the Nuba (including the attacks carried out against them by the Government of Sudan). In a subsection entitled "Response: Struggles to Survive Culturally," the authors assert that "From the Perspective of the Nuba, the most pressing issues they are facing are survival, resistance to genocidal policies, sovereignty, the right to make their own political decisions, and the right to practice their own cultural traditions and speak their own languages" (p. 123).

Nazer, Mende, and Lewis, Damien (2003). *Slave: My True Story*. New York: Public Affairs. 350 pp.

This book presents the story of Mende Nazer, a young Nuba woman, who was kidnapped in 1993 by Arab raiders and sold into slavery. It relates her years as a "black slave," as she was called by her wealthy Arab owners, and relates the physical, sexual and mental abuse to which she was subjected up until she regained her freedom.

Rahhal, Suleiman (2001). "Focus on Crisis in the Nuba Mountains," pp. 36-55. In Suleiman Rahhal (Ed.) (2001). *The Right to Be Nuba: The Story of a Sudanese People's Struggle for Survival*. Trenton, NJ: Red Sea Press.

This chapter is a must read for those who wish to begin to understand the origins and evolution of the crisis facing the Nuba people.

Among the issues covered herein are: a succinct overview of events leading up to the conflict; the roots of the conflict (the religious factor, the racial factor, issues over power-sharing, the lack of economic development, land sequestration, human rights violations); that which ignited the conflict; the jihad against the Nuba; extrajudicial killings; food as a weapon of war; and the international response.

Rahhal, Suleiman (Ed.) (2001). *The Right to Be Nuba: The Story of a Sudanese People's Struggle for Survival.* Trenton, NJ: Red Sea Press. 136 pp.

This highly informative book delineates the plight faced by the Nuba people and their struggle for survival as the Sudanese government continued to perpetrate major human rights abuses against them. It is comprised of pieces by prominent Nuba scholars, Nuba activists, and Nuba leaders, as well as others.

The book is comprised of the following chapters: 1. "The Right to Be Nuba" by Alex de Waal; "The Nuba" by Ahmed Rahman Saeed; "The Nuba of South Kordofan" by George Rodger; 4. "Things Were No Longer the Same" by Yousif Kuwa Mekki; 5. "Focus on Crisis in the Nuba Mountains" by Suleiman Musa Rahhal; 6. "The State of Sudan Today" by Peter Woodward; 7. "Voices from the Nuba Mountains" 8. "The Survival of the Nuba" by David Stewart-Smith; "The Nuba Relief, Rehabilitation and Development Organization" by Neroun Phillip Kuku; 12. "Nuba Agriculture: Poverty or Plenty?" by Ian Mackie; 11. "Democracy under Fire in the Nuba Mountains" by Julie Flint; 12. "Unity in Diversity: Is it Possible in Sudan" by Abmed Ibrahim Diraige; and 12. "What Peace for the Nuba?" by Suleiman Musa Rahhal. Note: Select chapters are annotated separately in this annotated bibliography:

Saeed, Ahmed Abdel Rahman (2001). "The Nuba," pp. 6-20. In Rahaal Suleiman (Ed.) *The Right to Be Nuba: The Story of a Sudanese People's Struggle for Survival.* Trenton, NJ: Red Sea Press.

This chapter provides a succinct but informative overview of who the Nuba are, early Nuba history, Nuba customs and traditions, the traditional religion of the Nuba, status of women in the Nuba community, and the impact of Islam in the Nuba Mountains.

Salih, M. A. R. M. (1999). "Land Alienation and Genocide in the Nuba Mountains, Sudan." *Cultural Survival*, 22(4)4: 36-38.
The author argues that "the current situation of indigenous peoples in the Sudan is the result of the independent state's adoption of land and other policies identical to those introduced by colonialists more than a century ago. The Sudanese state has unwittingly maintained some colonial coercive institutions and brutally deployed them against its indigenous peoples."

Salih, Mohamed. A. M. (1995) "Resistance and Response: Ethnocide and Genocide in the Nuba Mountains, Sudan." *GeoJournal*, 36(1):71-78.
This paper delineates the origins of Sudan's abuse and oppression against the Nuba and spells out how the government's policies and actions constitute both ethnocide and genocide.

Small Arms Survey (2008). "Insecurity and Militarization in the Nuba Mountains." *Sudan Issue Brief*. No. 12, August. Geneva: Author. August. 22 pp.
A highly informative report on an outbreak of fighting between GoS troops and the Sudan People's Liberation Army of the South.

Special Rapporteur of the Commission Human Rights (1993). *Interim Report on the Situation of Human Rights in the Sudan.* A/RES/48/147. 85th Plenary Meeting. December 20.
This UN report decries the grave human rights abuses by the Government of Sudan against its people residing in various parts of Sudan. It includes a line that reads: "…it is essential to put an end to the serious deterioration of the human rights situation in the Sudan, including that in the Nuba Mountains."

Suliman, Mohamed (1997). "Ethnicity from Perception to Cause of Violent Conflicts: The Case of the Fur and Nuba Conflicts in Western Sudan." Talk at the CONTICI International Workshop. Bern, Switzerland, July 8-11. Accessed at: http://www.ifaanet.org/ifaapr/ethnicity_inversion.htm

In speaking of the Government of Sudan's attacks against the Fur and Nuba in Western Sudan, the author argues that" "Most violent conflicts are over material resources, whether these resources are actual or perceived. With the passage of time, however, ethnic, cultural and religious affiliations seem to undergo transformation from abstract ideological categories into concrete social forces. In a wider sense, they themselves become contestable material social resources and hence possible objects of group strife and violent conflict." The section on the Nuba ("The Armed Conflict in the Nuba Mountains") is comprised of the following sections: The People, The History of the Nuba People, The Baggara Enter the Mountains, The Post-Independence Period, The Conflict, The Response of the Jellaba Government, the Causes, Resource Depletion, Against Mechanized Farming in the Nuba Mountains, Climate Variations, and Conflict Resolution.

Suliman, Mohamed (1999). "The Nuba Mountains of Sudan: Resource Access, Violent Conflict, and Identity," n.p. In Daniel Buckles (Ed.) *Cultivating Peace: Conflict and Collaboration in Natural Resource Management*. Washington, DC: ICRC/World Bank, n.p. Accessed at: http://www.idrc.ca/en/ev-27982-201-1-DO_TOPIC.htm

This chapter "attempts to explain the complex web of cooperation and conflict that binds the Nuba and the Baggara [the (Arab group used by government as militia to fight the Nuba]. It also documents three peace agreements reached between the two warring groups."

Winter, Roger (1999). "The Nuba People: Confronting Cultural Liquidation," n.p. In Jay Spaulding and Stephanie Beswick (Eds.) *White Nile Black Blood: War, Leadership, and Ethnicity from Khartoum to Kampala*. Lawrenceville, NJ: The Red Sea Press.

Winter, the former director of U.S. Committee for Refugees and a former administrator at USAID, provides a highly readable and engaging overview of the plight of the Nuba people as it stood in the late 1990s. In doing so, he provides key facts, addresses major issues, and interweaves the latter with personal stories and observations based on his visits to Sudan and the Nuba Mountains.

Films

Nuba: Pure People (Distribution: Bela Film, Beljaska 32, 1000 Ljubljana, Fax: (00 386 1) 515 00 25, E-mail: ida.belafilm@siol. net or Nuba Survival; PO Box 486 Hayes; Middlesex, UB3 3WZ; United Kingdom;e-mail: nubasurvival@googlemail.com).

"Award-winning documentary about the illegal journey of the Slovene writer Tomo Kriznar to the Nuba Mountains in Sudan [in order to capture] the story of the unknown genocide perpetrated for fifteen years against the Nuba people."

Nuba Conversations (52 minutes; produced in 2001; Nuba Survival; PO Box 486 Hayes; Middlesex, UB3 3WZ; United Kingdom;e-mail: nubasurvival@googlemail.com).

Described by the New York *Village Voice* as "A film that works both as searing journalism and a passionate first-person account of the unaccountable, a document of what has to many Western eyes remained an invisible cataclysm."

The Right to Be Nuba (35 minutes, videocassette; VHS; produced in 1993; Distributed by Filmmakers Library).

The struggles of the Nuba people are presented herein as they are caught in the middle of a civil war between Government of Sudan and the Sudan People's Liberation Army.

9

The Darfur Genocide

Samuel Totten

Introduction

The genocide of the black Africans of Darfur, Sudan, by the government of Sudan (GoS) troops and *Janjaweed*[1] (Arab militia) began in early 2003. Although the process of killing (bombings from airplanes, automatic weapons fire, the torching of villages and their inhabitants), the poisoning of wells, and forcing the victim population from their villages and homes has remained constant over the years, the rate and extent of the killing ebbed and flowed greatly as the GoS engaged in brinkmanship with the international community. The height of the killing took place between early 2003 and early 2005. Additional deaths resulted from "genocide by attrition." To date, it is estimated that over 250,000 people have been killed and/or perished as a result starvation, dehydration, and unattended injuries.[2]

Darfur, a region in west Sudan, is comprised of three states (Northern Darfur, Western Darfur, and Southern Darfur). The three-state region is approximately the size of France (or, put another way, Texas), and shares borders with the Central African Republic, Chad, and Libya. The vast majority of the people of Darfur, both the so-called "black Africans" and the Arabs, are Muslim.

Darfur is one of the most under-developed and isolated regions of Sudan, the latter of which constitutes one of the twenty-five poorest countries in the world. Over 90 percent of Sudan's citizens live below the poverty line, barely eking out an existence.

Until quite recently, the most productive land in Darfur was largely occupied by sedentary farmers and cattle owners who tended to be non-Arabs. At certain times of the year, though, the pasture land was used, as a result of mutual agreement between the sedentary black Africans and Arab semi-nomadic and nomadic peoples, by nomadic groups and their stock. This resulted in a symbiotic relationship of sorts; while the Arabs' animals were allowed to feed and be watered, the herds fertilized the ground owned by the black Africans, thus renewing the soil for subsequent growing seasons.

In the not too distant past, when conflicts erupted in Darfur the disagreements were generally resolved by the intervention and mediation of local leaders (*umdas* and *sheiks*). While neither conflict nor violence were uncommon, it rarely resulted in wholesale violence that went on for months, let alone years. If called for, "blood money" was paid to the victim, be it for family members who were killed, animals killed or stolen, or for some other transgression.

Notably, there was a certain amount of intermarriage amongst and between the various peoples of Darfur, including non-Arabs and Arabs. As a result, different groups of people cohabited as neighbors, friends and even relatives—and not as sworn enemies due to ethnic, racial, or any other type of classification/category.

Background to the Genocide

Among the issues and events that coalesced in Darfur and resulted in genocide are as follows: extreme drought; increased desertification; Arab supremacism; authoritarianism; extreme nationalism; an ever-increasing bellicosity in the region (within Sudan, Darfur and beyond its borders); and the disenfranchisement of black Africans at the hands of the Sudanese government.

Extreme Drought and Desertification

Since the early 1970s, numerous droughts (including the "great drought" of 1984-1985), resulted in ever-increasing desertification across Darfur. The desertification of the land in Darfur, accompanied by fierce sand storms, resulted in a dramatic decline in the yield of produce, loss of pastureland, and a loss of livestock. Increasingly, this resulted in conflict over land usage and access to water between the nomadic/semi-nomadic Arab groups and the sedentary/farming groups of non-Arabs. The drought affected other countries in the region as well, and nomads from Chad and Libya migrated to Darfur in large numbers in search of grazing land, which put further pressure on the scant resources available.

Not only did the drought and famine result in nomadic groups sweeping further south to locate sustenance for their herds, but it resulted in their remaining in such areas for longer periods of time. Concomitantly, farmers became increasingly protective of their land, resulting in even more hard feelings and conflict.

Arab Supremacism

Arab supremacism is an ideology that promotes and adheres to the notion that Arab beliefs and lifestyle are superior to all others. Essentially, and, ultimately, it calls for Arab dominance in all aspects of life—culturally, politically, economically, judicially, and socially. In Sudan, this has led to both the demonization and disenfranchisement of certain groups.

The origins of Arab supremacism "lay in the Libya of Colonel Gaddafi in the 1970s" and "the politics of the Sahara" (Flint and De Waal, 2005, p. 50). Gaddafi, in fact, fantasized about establishing an "Arab belt" across Africa. To accomplish this goal, he created, with his oil riches, various mechanisms, including "the *Faliq al Islamiyya* (Islamic Legion), which recruited Bedouins from Mauritania to Sudan; the *Munazamat Da'awa al Islamiyya* (Organization of the Islamic Call), which fostered Islamic philanthropy and evangelization; and sponsorship of the Sudanese opposition National Front, including the Muslim Brothers (or Muslim Brotherhood) and the *Ansar* (the *umma's* military wing). The Muslim Brotherhood's primary goal in Sudan was to "institutionalize Islamic law" (Mertz, 1991, n.p.). In 1964, it established its first political party.

Over time, the Brotherhood established a close relationship with young Darfurians, convincing the latter that the Brotherhood's push for the establishment of Islamic law was positive and that, as an organization, it was largely void of the prejudice and discrimination practiced by the Sudanese government when it came to ethnic and tribal differences. Ultimately, these same young people came to trust and support the secretary general of the Brotherhood, Hassan al Turabi.

Beginning as a peaceful civilian movement, the Brotherhood gradually morphed into a powerful and radical rebel group. Following a coup d'état in 1969, in which Colonel Jaafar Nimeri became prime minister of Sudan, Turabi's Islamist Party was dissolved. Immediately, though, the Islamists began planning its own rebellion. The attempted rebellion, however, was quashed by the Sudanese military in March 1970. The combined effort of the Sudanese air force and ground troops resulted in the deaths of hundreds of Islamists fighters. Many survivors sought exile in Libya, where they established military-type camps in preparation for a later attempt to dislodge the Nimeri government. As Flint and De Waal (2005) note, "Their [the Islamists'] plan [while undergoing training] was an armed invasion of Sudan from bases in Libya, crossing Darfur and Kordofan to storm the capital. [I]n July 1976, the Ansar-Islamist alliance very nearly succeeded ... but the army counterattacked and the rebels were defeated" (pp. 22-23).

Turabi, an astute political operative, disassociated himself from the failed invasion and ingratiated himself with Nimeiri—eventually serving as his attorney general in 1977. Furthermore, in his quest to establish an Islamic state, "[Turabi] infiltrated Islamist cadres into the armed forces, including elite units such as the air force" (Flint and De Waal, 2005, p. 23).

In 1983, intent on imposing his Islamist vision on Sudan, Turabi headed an effort to implement *shari'a* (Islamic law) in Sudan. In 1985, due to a combination of distrust, anger and fear at the brutality meted out by the government as a result of its *shari'a*-induced legislation and actions, Nimeiri was overthrown and parliamentary rule was subsequently reinstated. Subsequently, Turabi helped to establish the National Islamic Front (NIF), a political party that was controlled by the Muslim Brotherhood.

But then, in 1989, with Turabi in the shadows but playing an integral role as a power broker, the military overthrew the elected government, and Omar al Bashir was installed as president of Sudan. As Sudan entered a period of increased turbulence, Turabi is said to have been the real power behind the scenes.

In the early 1990s, the Sudanese Islamists began a full-frontal effort to Islamicize Sudan. At the forefront of the effort were Turabi and Ali Osman Mohamed Taha, an ardent Islamist and an on again-and-off again government figure. In 1990, as part of this effort, Turabi established the Popular Arab Islamic Conference (PAIC), which was basically a regional organization for political Islamist militants. In his position as secretary general of PAIC, Turabi prodded the Sudanese government to create "an open door policy for Arabs, including Turabi's Islamist associate Osama bin Laden, who made his base in Sudan in 1990-1996" (Human Rights Watch, 2002, p. 1). Ultimately, though, Turabi concluded that if he was to succeed in gaining power through the elective process, he needed to part ways with the Brotherhood. He came to such a conclusion due to the fact that the Brotherhood perceived Islamism and Arabism as one and the same, and many of those residing in Darfur were not Arab; and since Turabi believed he needed the votes of those in the West who were not Arab, he, calculatingly, severed his ties with the Brotherhood.

By the early 1990s, traditional dispute resolution approaches were proving to be inadequate. Arab nomadic attacks against black Africans were becoming more brazen, more frequent, more vicious, and more costly in terms of lives lost and villages, farm land, and orchards destroyed. In August 1995, for example, Arab raiders attacked and burned the non-Arab village of Mejmeri in West Darfur, stealing 40,000 cattle and massacring twenty-three civilians. By late 1998, more than 100,000 non-Arab Massalit had fled to Chad to escape the violent attacks (Flint and De Waal, 2005, p. 69).

In 1999, Turabi set out to become the major power in Sudan. But, once again, his grand plans came to naught. Not only did Ali Osman Taha break with Turabi as a result of looking askance at Turabi's ploys, schemes, and intrigues, but al Bashir announced a state of emergency and removed Turabi from office (thus, destroying Turabi's powerbase within the government). Ultimately, "the Bashir-Turabi split lost Darfur for the government, but made it possible to make peace in the South" (Flint and de Waal, 2005, p. 41).

Authoritarianism

From 1989 to the present, Sudan has been under the authoritarian rule of Omar al Bashir. When Turabi was a power behind the scenes, it meant that the Islamists were, like puppeteers, largely directing all aspects of Sudanese life. Those living in what is commonly referred to as the "peripheries" in Sudan (that is, those areas outside of Khartoum or the "center" which is the powerbase in Sudan), were (and are) perceived and treated as second class citizens. Everything, from behavior to dress and from speech to assembly with others, was dictated by the government. Those who did not comply or broke one of the seemingly innumerable rules were arrested (if not "disappeared") and/or tortured.

Disenfranchisement

Significantly, Darfur is not only one of the poorest regions in Sudan but one of the poorest regions in all of Africa. A single section of Sudan, the North (where Khartoum, the capital, is located), which comprises just over five percent of the population of the country, virtually controls all of Sudan. Almost all of those who hold major posts within the country have come from the North, including all of the presidents and prime ministers.

For years on end, the black Africans of Darfur requested the building of more schools, medical facilities, and roads—all of which are either minimal in number and sorely under-funded, or, as is true in the case of roads, largely nonexistent. The vast majority of the black Africans' requests for assistance fell on deaf ears in Khartoum.

For numerous years as well, the black Africans of Darfur also decried the hegemony of the North, as well as the fact that they (those residing in western Sudan) suffered prejudice, discrimination and disenfranchisement at the hands of those at the center. Another major problem is the fact that "water development is currently reserved for the ever-expanding capital Khartoum. The rest of the country is left out, dying of thirst as well as diseases like malaria, kalazar, bilharsiasis, and other water-borne diseases" (Justice and Equality Movement, 2000, p. 41).

In May 2000, *The Black Book: Imbalance of Power and Wealth in Sudan* mysteriously appeared in Khartoum. As photocopies of the book were "spontaneously" produced, the *Black Book* began to appear throughout the country and abroad. The *Black Book,* which was the work of the Islamicists in the country, was dedicated, in part, to "... the Sudanese people who have endured oppression, injustice and tyranny" (n.p.). de Waal (2004b) argues that *The Black Book* essentially "condemned the Islamist promise to Darfur as a sham. The *Black Book* was a key step in the polarization of the country along politically constructed 'racial' rather than religious lines, and it laid the basis for a coalition between Darfur's radicals, who formed the SLA, and its Islamists, who formed the other rebel organization, the Justice and Equality Movement" (p. 8). *The Black Book* may have constituted a key step in the polarization of country along politically constructed "racial" lines, but it was hardly the first or *the* major step. In light of the ongoing attacks since the early 1990s by various Arab groups (nomads, semi-nomads and then, collaboratively, by Arab herders and GoS troops) against black African villages, it seems obvious that the "racial divide" was certainly evident, and being acted up, many years prior to the appearance of *The Black Book.* In that regard, it seems that *The Black Book* was more the messenger versus the instigator of the polarization along "racial lines."

Ongoing and Increasing Insecurity and Bellicosity in the Darfur Region

Beginning in the early 1990s, Arab herders began carrying out attacks against entire villages of sedentary black African farmers. Over time, such attacks involved both GoS troops and the

Arab herders working in tandem. Such attacks were vicious and destructive, but not as systematic as the scorched earth attacks that became increasingly common in 2003 and beyond. As mentioned earlier, the latter attacks have ebbed and flowed over the years, up through today (early 2010).

The initial increase in violent conflict within the region was due to a host of issues. For example, in the 1980s, the GoS, under President Nimeri, abruptly replaced the tribal councils, the traditional bodies that helped mediate conflicts, with government oversight of the region. The GoS, however, failed to provide adequate resources to the regional government offices, and thus the offices and expected services largely became hollow shells. Exacerbating matters was the fact that riverine Arabs held the vast majority of government posts (including those as police and court officials in Darfur), further alienating the black Africans of Darfur.

As groups of Arab nomads bought into the beliefs of Arab Supremacism, they began to act as if they were superior to the black Africans. (Arab nomadic groups were and are not, of course, of a single mind and thus should not be construed as a monolithic group or movement.) Along with the huge influx of weapons into Darfur (resulting, in large part, due to the various wars in the region, including the Libya/Chad conflict, the prolonged war in southern Sudan, and a war in Eritrea), more and more herders began carrying weapons. Ultimately, the GoS also provided such groups with weapons with the expectation that the Arab herders would, in various cases, serve as their proxies in dealing with the black Africans. As the Arab herders increasingly engaged in conflicts with the black Africans over land and water usage, they (the Arabs) made it clear that they were ready and willing to use their weapons. Thus, with the difficulties presented by the droughts and desertification of pasture land, the influence of Arab Supremacism, and the Arab herders' experiences as mercenaries, it is not surprising that many of the Arab nomadic groups became increasingly cavalier and aggressive in their use of the sedentary people's lands in the early- to mid-1990s.

Not only did the Arab nomads increasingly and purposely neglect to seek permission to use the land, but they frequently refused to apologize for trespassing when confronted by the black African farmers. And when confronted by the farmers, it was not uncommon for the nomads to threaten the lives of the farmers—and, in many cases, they carried out their threats.

Due to increasing fear and anger over the repeated attacks on their villages, along with the gradual realization that the Arab marauders had tacit approval from the local government officials to do as they wished, the black Africans began to form self-defense groups.

Overview of the Genocide

Government of Sudan troops and the *Janjaweed* are the actors who carried out the actual killing, mass and gang rape, and the wholesale destruction of black African villages. In most cases, the attacks involved bombings by GoS aircraft, followed by a ground attack involving hundreds of *Janjaweed* on camels and horses and four-wheel vehicles (some mounted with machine guns) carrying both GoS troops and *Janjaweed*.

The *Janjaweed* comprise semi-nomadic and nomadic Arab herders. Many had fought in one or more of the wars in the region. Increasingly, many Arab herders have been forced—upon the threat of death to themselves and harm to their families—to join in the attacks against the black Africans. It is also significant to note, and recognize, that many Arab herders are not involved in the attacks, are not members of the *Janjaweed*, and do not necessarily support—and may, in fact, look askance at—the actions of the GoS and *Janjaweed*.

The main victim groups among the black Africans are the Fur, Massaleit, and Zaghawa. Like most of the issues surrounding the Darfur crisis, the composition of the population of Darfur is a complex one. Indeed, although "African" and "Arab" are common terms used in describing and, at least in part, explaining the conflict, neither term does justice to the diversity of ethnic groups that make up Darfur nor to "the nuanced relationships among ethnic groups" (Human Rights Watch, 2004, p. 1 of "The Background").

There are many, in fact, who claim that there is virtually no difference between the so-called black Africans of Darfur and the

Arab population (Mamdani quoted in Sengupta, 2004, p. 1; De Waal 2004a; de Waal, 2004c). Mamdani (2004), for example, asserts that "…all parties involved in the Darfur conflict—whether they are referred to as 'Arab' or as 'African'—are equally indigenous and equally black" (p. 2) He has also argued that "from the cultural point of view, one can be both African and Arab" (Mamdani, 2004, p. 2). Mamdani and de Waal, among others, argue that since all live in Africa they are all African. In this regard, de Waal (2004a) has asserted that "characterizing the Darfur war as 'Arabs' versus 'Africans' obscures the reality. Darfur's Arabs are black, indigenous, African Muslims—just like Darfur's non Arabs, who hail from the Fur, Masalit, Zaghawa and a dozen smaller tribes" (p. 1).

Some also argue that since there has been a great deal of intermarriage among the groups it is almost impossible to definitively state whether a person is from one ethnic group or another. Likewise, some assert that "where the vast majority of people [in Darfur] are Muslim and Arabic-speaking, the distinction between 'Arab' and 'African' is more cultural than racial" (UN Office for the Coordination of Humanitarian Affairs, 2003, n.p.; IRIN, 2007, p. 2). Mamdani, for one, argues that "the real roots of combat are not racial or ethnic but political and economic" (quoted in Hill, 2006). It is also not uncommon for individuals, who have, over time, attained a certain amount of wealth, to actually "choose" to become "Arab."

Be that as it may, both the perpetrators and the victims, themselves, *do make a distinction between* those who are purportedly "Arab" and those who are purportedly "black African." Numerous studies/reports (Human Rights Watch, 2004; Physicians for Human Rights, 2005; U.S. State Department, 2004) comprised of first-person testimony by internally placed persons (IDPs) and refugees from Darfur contain statement after statement about the "ethnic"/"racial" distinctions made by the very people involved in the crisis. For example, in its report, *Darfur Destroyed*, Human Rights Watch (2004) reports that "Especially since the beginning of the conflict in 2003, members of the Zaghawa, Fur, and Masalit communities have used these terms [black Africans and Arabs] to describe the growing racial and ethnic polarization in Darfur perceived to result from discrimination and bias emanating from the central government" (p. 1, "The Background").

Such testimony also includes one comment after another in regard to the fact that during their attacks the *Janjaweed* frequently scream racial epithets at their black Africans victims, including *zurega* (which is roughly the equivalent of "nigger"). Other comments that the perpetrators have spewed at the black Africans are: "You are not a real Sudanese, you're black....We are the real Sudanese. No blacks need stay here"; "We are going to cut off your roots"; "The President of Sudan ordered us to cleanse Darfur of the dirty slaves so we can have the beginning of the Arab Union" (quoted in Totten and Markusen, 2006, p. 98). Emily Wax (2004), a *Washington Post* correspondent in Africa, reported that as a twenty-two-year old black African woman was grabbed and about to be raped by six Janjaweed, they spat out: "Black girl, you are too dark. You are like a dog. We want to make a light baby" (p. 1).

While the Sudanese government readily admits that its troops responded to attacks on government facilities (including military bases) by black African rebels, it has claimed, time and again, that the *Janjaweed, alone,* are responsible for the subsequent and sustained scorched earth attacks against the black Africans and that it (the government) does not have the means to rein them in as they (the *Janjaweed*) are loose cannons. Such assertions are disingenuous, at best; again, ample evidence exists that the vast majority of the attacks on the black African villages have been carried out by both GoS troops and the *Janjaweed* (Human Rights Watch, 2004a; Physicians for Human Rights, 2005; U.S. State Department, 2004).

There is also evidence that the GoS purposely hired the Janjaweed to join GoS troops in carrying out the attacks because GoS military troops were already overstretched in its war in southern Sudan and thus did not have enough soldiers available to address the crisis in Darfur (Human Rights Watch, 2004b). Furthermore, a large contingent of the soldiers in the GoS military were black African and the GoS didn't trust the latter to carry out attacks on their (the black African soldiers') own people's villages.

Tellingly, in the early to late 1990s, some villages were attacked up to three, four and more times. In certain cases, African villages were partially burned down by the marauders; in others, villages were utterly destroyed. Almost always, the villages were pillaged and then the black Africans' herds were stolen. Black Africans were often forced out of their village only to be chased down in the desert and beaten and/or killed. Desirous of remaining on their land, most survivors returned to their villages once the marauders had left, rebuilt the destroyed sections, and carried on with life as best they could.

In 2001 and 2002, before the conflict became widely known to the outside world, a rebel movement of non-Arabs in Darfur formed. In early May 2002, a group of Fur politicians complained to Sudanese President Omar al Bashir that 181 villages had been attacked by Arab militias, with hundreds people killed and thousands of animals stolen (Flint and de Waal, 2005, pp. 77-78). As such attacks continued unabated, the black Africans' disenchantment with the government increased in intensity.

The first rebel group to appear called itself the Sudanese Liberation Movement/Army (SLM/A), and on March 14, 2003, it issued the following political declaration: "The brutal oppression, ethnic cleansing and genocide sponsored by the Khartoum government left the people of Darfur with no other option but to resort to popular political and military resistance for purposes of survival. This popular resistance has now coalesced into a political movement known as the Sudan Liberation Movement and its military wing, the Sudan Liberation Army (SLM/SLA)" (The Sudan Liberation Movement and Sudan Liberation Army, 2003, pp. 1-2). Within a relatively short period of time, the group splintered, and from the split emerged a rebel group calling itself the Justice and Equality Movement (JEM).

In what De Waal and Flint (2005) call a "pivotal point" in the conflict between the black African rebels and the GoS troops, the SLM/A and JEM forces struck, on April 25, 2003, the government air force base at el Fasher. In doing so, they killed at least seventy-five people, destroyed several airplanes and bombers, and captured the base's commander (Flint and de Waal, 2005, pp. 99-100). In quick succession, numerous other attacks were carried out. In fact, "The rebels were winning almost every encounter—34 out of 38 in the middle months of 2003. [At this point in time, the GoS purportedly] feared it would lose the whole of Darfur..." (Flint and De Waal, 2005, p. 101).

Any government whose military bases and/or other government facilities are attacked is to going to retaliate and attempt to suppress future attacks. Governments will either arrest the perpetrators or, if the situation degenerates into violence, shoot and then apprehend them, or, outright kill them. What the GoS did, however, was something vastly different and, ultimately, criminal. Using the argument that it believed that black African villagers were harboring rebels, the GoS (along with the *Janjaweed*) began attacking village after village after village of black Africans. Thus, instead of solely tracking down and attacking the black African rebel groups, the GoS and *Janjaweed* began carrying out a widespread and systematic scorched earth policy against non-Arab villagers. In doing so, the GoS troops and the *Janjaweed* slaughtered men and boys (including infants), raped, mutilated, and often killed females, looted household goods and animals, and then burned the homes and villages to the ground (Physicians for Human Rights, 2005; UN Commission of Inquiry into Darfur, 2005; U.S. State Department, 2004). In a report of its findings, the UN Commission of Inquiry on Darfur (2005) stated that "...the large majority of attacks on villages conducted by the [*Janjaweed*] militia have been undertaken with the acquiescence of State officials" (paragraph 125). The attacks led to the forcible displacement of, at first, tens of thousands, then hundreds of thousands and, ultimately (or at least through today) over two and a half million people in Darfur alone (and between 275,000 and 300,000 in Chad).

By late 2003, a flood of black Africans had either been forced from their homes as a result of GoS and *Janjaweed* attacks or had left out of sheer fear. By September 2003, the United Nations (UN) reported that some 65,000 refugees from Darfur had fled to Chad. By December 9, 2003, the United Nations estimated that there were up to 600,000 internally displaced people (IDP) in Darfur as a result of the attacks on the black Africans' villages. In November 2004,

Médecins Sans Frontières (Doctors Without Borders) estimated that some 1.8 million Darfurians had been displaced from their homes, with 200,000 of them in refugee camps in Chad (with the rest in internally displaced (IDP) camps in Darfur) (*Médecins Sans Frontières* , 2004, p. 1).

Between 2003 and today, the GoS has repeatedly denied that its troops have taken part in the scorched earth actions against the black Africans of Darfur. Indeed, while the rest of the world asserts that at least over 250,000 have been killed in Darfur over the past four years (with certain activist organizations claiming that the number is closer to 400,000 or more), the GoS asserts that just 9,000 have been killed, mostly as a result of rebel actions. Ample evidence, though, from a broad array of sources (e.g., the black African survivors of the attacks, African Union troops deployed in Darfur as monitors, numerous humanitarian organizations working in the IDP camps, numerous human rights organizations, including Human Rights Watch, Physicians for Human Rights, and Amnesty International, and the investigations conducted by the United States in 2004 and the UN in 2004 and 2005), have provided evidence that clearly and definitively refutes the GoS' claims and denials.

International Attention: Lots of Humanitarian Help, Little to No Protection

By late 2003, various NGOs (nongovernmental organizations) and the UN scrambled to help the internally displaced persons (IDPs) and the refugees flooding across the Sudan/Chad border, and began getting the word out about the escalating carnage in Darfur. In December 2003, Jan Egeland, UN under-secretary for humanitarian affairs, asserted that the Darfur crisis was possibly the "worst [crisis] in the world today" (United Nations, 2004, p. 1). That same month, Tom Vraalsen, the UN Security General's special envoy for humanitarian affairs for Sudan, claimed that the situation in Darfur was "nothing less than the 'organized' destruction of sedentary African agriculturalists —the Fur, the Massaleit and the Zaghawa" (quoted in Reeves, 2003, p. 1).

In early 2004, scores of activist organizations—especially in the United States, but also in Canada and Europe—began rallying around the Darfur issue, variously, decrying the lack of action to halt the atrocities against the black Africans of Darfur, preparing and issuing reports, calling on the United Nations and/or the U.S. government to be proactive in addressing the crisis, and issuing calls for citizen action.

On June 30, 2004, U.S. Secretary of State Colin Powell visited IDP camps in Darfur and a refugee camp in Chad. While visiting the IDP camp, Abu Shouk, where malnutrition was rife among the 40,000 or so black Africans, Powell said, "We see indicators and elements that would start to move you toward a genocide conclusion but we're not there yet" (quoted by the BBC, 2004, p. 2).

In July and August 2004, the United States—in a joint effort involving the U.S. State Department, the Coalition for International Justice (CIJ), and the United States Agency for International Aid (USAID)—sent a team (the Atrocities Documentation Team or ADT) of twenty-four investigators to Chad to conduct interviews with Sudanese refugees from Darfur for the express purpose of collecting evidence to help ascertain whether genocide had been perpetrated by the GoS and the *Janjaweed*. The Atrocities Documentation Project (ADP), which was the first ever official field investigation of a suspected genocide by one sovereign nation into another sovereign nation's actions while the killing was underway, conducted more than one thousand interviews with Darfurian refugees in camps and settlements on the Chad side of the border with Sudan. Evidence collected by the ADT led U.S. Secretary of State Colin Powell, on September 9, 2004, in a hearing before the U.S. Senate's Foreign Relations Committee, to publicly accuse the GoS of genocide.

Under Chapter VII of the UN Charter, the United States referred the Darfur matter to the United Nations. Subsequently, on September 18, 2004, the UN established the UN Commission of Inquiry into Darfur (COI), whose express purpose, as outlined in UN Security Council Resolution 1564, was to conduct its own investigation into the Darfur crisis. The COI conducted its inquiry in November and December 2004 and January 2005, and submitted its report to the Security Council in late January 2005. In its final section, "Conclusions and Recommendations," the COI report states: "...the Commission concludes that the Government of the Sudan and the *Janjaweed* are responsible for a number of violations of international human rights and humanitarian law. Some of these violations are very likely to amount to war crimes, and given the systematic and widespread pattern of many of the violations, they would also amount to crimes against humanity" (UN, 2005, para 603). While many scholars agreed with the conclusions of the COI, others were taken aback that—based on the COI's own findings—it concluded that genocide had not been perpetrated (see, for example, Fowler, 2006, pp. 127-139; Stanton, 1996, pp. 181-188; Totten, 2006, pp. 199-222).

For the next four years the GoS lied about its actions, the rebel groups split and split again (as of early 2010 it is estimated between that some thirty-one rebel groups now operate in Darfur), peace conferences were held only to have the agreements broken (sometimes the very next day) by one party or another, and chaos slowly but surely began to engulf Darfur. Periodically, the GoS continued its attacks against black African village's, and GoS troops and the *Janjaweed* continued to rape females, now living in IDP camps, as they went in search of wood and water.

The international community looked on and did little to nothing to protect the IDP camps or few remaining black African villages in Darfur (with the exception, that is, of first supporting a very weak African Union force, and second, establishing and supporting an equally weak African Union/UN Hybrid Force). For example, between 2004 and early 2009, the UN Security Council issued over twenty resolutions vis-à-vis the ongoing crisis in Darfur. The results of the resolutions were, at best, mixed. Some were acted on, but most were not. Various resolutions were revised time and again, along with ever-increasing threats, but largely to no avail due to a dearth of action. Tellingly, in July 2006, a senior Sudanese government official was quoted as saying that "The United Nations Security Council has threatened us so many times, we no longer take it seriously"[3] (cited in Nathan, 2007, p. 249).

In June 2004, Sudan allowed the African Union (AU) to deploy a small ceasefire monitoring team in Darfur comprised of representatives from the AU, the GoS, two (later, three) rebel groups, along with the European Union, the UN and the U.S. From a tiny force of 300 troops, the AU force slowly increased to—and eventually leveled off at (up through December 2007)—about 7,000 troops. "As violence against civilians continued, the African Union Mission in Sudan (AMIS) force's mandate was expanded in October 2004 to protecting 'civilians whom it encounters under imminent threat and in the immediate vicinity, within resources and capability" (Human Rights Watch, 2007, p. 5). The new mandate, though, constituted little more than a paper tiger. The AU had neither the resources nor the capability of truly protecting anyone, let alone themselves.

Finally, after immense international pressure, Sudan, in mid-June 2007, agreed to allow the deployment of a special force into Darfur, the UN/AU Hybrid (UNAMID) force. Ultimately, that was followed, on July 31, 2007, by the passage of UN Security Council Resolution 1769 which authorized a combined AU/UN Hybrid force for deployment in Darfur. The resolution called for "the immediate deployment of the United Nations Light and Heavy Support packages to the African Union Mission in the Sudan (AMIS) and a [AU/UN] Hybrid operation in Darfur [UNAMID].... [The] UNAMID ... shall consist of up to 19,555 military personnel" (n.p.). In addressing the mandate of UNAMID, the resolution asserted that: "Acting under Chapter VII of the Charter of the United Nations: ...UNAMID is authorized to take the necessary action, in the areas of deployment of its forces and as it deems within its capabilities in order to: (i) protect its personnel, facilities, installations and equipment, and to ensure the security and freedom of movement of its own personnel and humanitarian workers, (ii) support early and effective implementation of the Darfur Peace Agreement, prevent the disruption of its implementation and armed attacks, and protect civilians, without prejudice to the responsibility of the Government of Sudan" (n.p.). To this day, the hybrid force is sorely undermanned, under-resourced and incapable of providing the sort of protection that was envisioned for it.

Ultimately, *realpolitik* was at the center of the dithering, the watering down of certain sanctions, and the decision not to follow through on numerous resolutions and sanctions. More specifically, various members of the Permanent Five in the UN Security Council (the United States, Great Britain, France, the Russian Federation, and China) had vested interests in Sudan and wanted to protect them.[4] China, for example, has an enormous petroleum deal with Sudan, and engages in significant weapons sales to Sudan; Russia also has a major arms deal with Sudan; and the United States has, off and on, taken advantage of GoS' offers to help shut down terrorist cells within Sudan and prevent potential terrorists from traveling through Sudan on their way to Afghanistan and Iraq to battle the United States in the latter's efforts to, respectively, capture Osama Bin Laden (terrorist mastermind of the September 11, 2001 attacks on the World Trade Center in New York City and the Pentagon in Washington, D.C.) and to stabilize Iraq following the U.S.'s overthrow of dictator Saddam Hussein, which resulted in internecine conflict that ripped the fabric of Iraq apart.

Genocide or Not?

Scholars, individual governments, politicians, activists, and others hold varying views in regard to whether the GoS and *Janjaweed* attacks on the black Africans constitute genocide or not. For example, and as previously mentioned, following a U.S. State Department-sponsored investigation, on September 9, 2004, U.S. Secretary of State Colin Powell declared that genocide had been perpetrated and was possibly still being perpetrated in Darfur.

Conversely, a subsequent investigation conducted by the United Nations (The UN Commission of Inquiry into Darfur) (November 2004/January 2005) concluded that "crimes against humanity," not genocide, had been perpetrated by the GoS. The UN left the door open that upon subsequent study of the crisis and/or additional investigations by other bodies (presumably the International Criminal Court), it was possible that genocide might be found to have been perpetrated. (For a discussion of the ADT and COI findings, see Samuel Totten's "The U.S. Investigation into the Darfur Crisis and Its Determination of Genocide: A Critical Analysis.")

In a May 7, 2004 report ("Sudan: Government Commits Ethnic Cleansing in Darfur") and later, in an October 2007 paper (Q & A: Crisis in Darfur), Human Rights Watch declared that the GoS had committed both ethnic cleansings and crimes against humanity in Darfur. Amnesty International deemed the killings cases of crimes against humanity and war crimes, but did not take a stand in regard to whether the atrocities amounted to genocide or not. Following two on-the-ground investigations in Darfur (2004 and 2005) and an in-depth analysis of the data collected in such investigations (see, respectively, *Assault on Survival: A Call for Security, Justice and Restitution*, and *Destroyed Livelihoods: A Case Study of Furawiya Village, Darfur*), Physicians for Human Rights declared that the GoS had committed genocide in Darfur.

Among those scholars who have asserted that the atrocities perpetrated in Darfur do not constitute genocide are: Mahmood Mamdani (2006), who asserts, in an article entitled "The Politics of Naming Genocide: Genocide, Civil War, Insurgency," that the situation in Darfur appears to be more a case of insurgency and counter-insurgency versus genocide; Alex de Waal (see *Newsweek*, 2007), who perceives the crisis in Darfur as a war and not genocide; and Gerard Prunier (2005 and 2007), who wavers between calling the crisis in Darfur "an ambiguous genocide" (2004), and in a later article, both a genocide and a case of ethnic cleansing (2007).

On the other hand, such scholars as Kelly Dawn Askin (2006), Gerald Caplan (2006), Stephen Kostas (2006), Eric Markusen (2006), Gregory Stanton (2006), and Samuel Totten (2004 and 2006) assert that the crisis in Darfur constitutes genocide. Furthermore, the noted anti-genocide activist Jerry Fowler (2006), a Stanford Law School graduate, has also concluded that the atrocities perpetrated by the GoS and *Janjaweed* in Darfur constitute genocide.

To establish whether a crisis/event is genocide or not, it is imperative to use the language of the UNCG as a lens for examining the facts. Among the most critical words, phrases and conditions set out in the UNCG are located in Article II:

In the present Convention, genocide means any of the following acts committed with intent to destroy, in whole or in part, a national, ethnical, racial or religious group, as such:

(a) Killing members of the group;
(b) Causing serious bodily or mental harm to members of the group;
(c) Deliberately inflicting on the group conditions of life calculated to bring about its physical destruction in whole or in part;
(d) Imposing measures intended to prevent births within the group;
(e) Forcibly transferring children of the group to another group.

In asserting that the crisis in Darfur constitutes a genocide, certain scholars argue that there is ample evidence that the attacks by the GOS and *Janjaweed* clearly resulted in conditions a through c of Article II of the UNCG. The group that is under attack, they argue, constitutes a racial group, and the issue of intent can be inferred from the events on the ground (e.g., what has taken place during the course of the attacks on the black African villages).

The arguments of such scholars, though, go far beyond the above argument:

• Stephen Kostas (2006), discussing Colin Powell's (with the assistance of, among others, Pierre Prosper, former U.S. Ambassador-at-Large for War Crimes) finding of genocide based on the analysis of the data collected by the U.S. State Department's Atrocities Documentation Project (ADP), writes as follows:

> First, they [Powell, Prosper, et al] noted that villages of Africans were being destroyed and neighboring Arab villages were not. Large numbers of men were killed and women raped. Livestock was killed and water polluted. In IDP camps, the GOS was preventing medicines and humanitarian assistance from going in despite persistent international calls for access. Examining these factors, they concluded there was a deliberate targeting of the group with the intent to destroy it.
> Prosper recalls the group examining the concepts of unlawful killing, causing of serious bodily and mental harm, and "the real one that got us,…was the deliberate infliction of conditions of life calculated to destroy the group in whole, or in part." Looking at the IDP camps, Prosper and Powell could not find any "logical explanation for why the Sudan government was preventing humanitarian assistance and medicine" into the camps "other than to destroy the group." The GoS was seen as offering unbelievable excuses, leading Powell to conclude that there was a clearly intentional effort to destroy the people in the camps who were known to be almost exclusively black African (pp. 121-122).

- Gregory Stanton (2006) asks and then asserts, "Was the killing [in Darfur by the GoS and Janjaweed] 'intentional'? Yes. According to the elements of crimes defined by the Statute of the International Criminal Court, genocide must be the result of a policy, which may be proved by direct orders or evidenced by systematic organization. Was the killing in Darfur systematically organized by the al-Bashir regime using government-armed *Janjaweed* militias, bombers, and helicopter gunships? Yes. Were the victims chosen because of their ethnic and racial identity? Yes. Fur, Massalit, and Zaghawa black African villages were destroyed, while Arab villages nearby were left untouched….Does this conclusion constitute the intentional destruction, in part, of ethnic and racial groups? Yes. In short, the violence in Darfur is genocide…" (pp. 182-183).

- Jerry Fowler (2006) argues the following regarding the issue of intent as it relates to the GOS and *Janjaweed's* actions in Darfur: "U.S. Secretary of State Colin Powell concluded that intent could be inferred from the Sudanese Government's deliberate conduct. Inferring intent from conduct in the absence of direct evidence is widely accepted. The International Criminal Tribunal for Rwanda (ICTR) has delineated numerous circumstances that are relevant to determining 'intent' to destroy, many of which are present in the case of Darfur:

'The general context of the perpetration of other culpable acts systematically directed against the same groups'
'The scale of atrocities committed'
'The "general nature" of the atrocity'
'Deliberately and systematically targeting members of some groups [black Africans] but not others [Arabs]'
'Attacks on (or perceived by the perpetrators to be attacks on) the foundations of the group' [especially, the rape of the girls and woman, thus creating "Arab babies" and resulting in girls and women being considered "damaged goods" by their families and thus ostracized, which, in turn, generally, and automatically, precludes them from having children with their husbands or, if single, from getting married and having children]
'The use of derogatory language toward members of the targeted groups'
"The systematic manner of killing'; and
'The relative proportionate scale of the actual or attempted destruction of a group' (International Criminal Tribunal for Rwanda, 1998, paras. 523-524; International Criminal Tribunal for Rwanda, 2000, para. 166) (p. 131).

- Kelly Dawn Askin (2006), a lawyer and a specialist on international law and rape, argues then notes the following: "Rape as an instrument of genocide most often invokes subarticle (b) [of the UNCG] intending to 'destroy a protected group by causing serious bodily or mental harm to members of that group,' and (d) 'imposing measures intended to prevent births within a group'.... The Akayesu Judgment of the ICTR [International Criminal Tribunal for Rwanda] is the seminal decision recognizing rape as an instrument of genocide" (p. 150). Continuing she asserts that "There is every indication that the official policy of the GoS and *Janjaweed* forces is to wage, jointly or separately, concentrated and strategic attacks against black Darfurians by a variety of means, including through killing raping, pillaging, burning and displacement. Various forms of sexual violence regularly formed part of these attacks....Rape crimes have been documented in dozens of villages [now, in 2010, it is more like scores and probably hundreds] throughout Darfur and committed in similar patterns, indicating that rape itself is both widespread and systematic" (Askin, 2006, p. 150).

  Askin (2006) also comments on the epithets made by the attackers during the course of the rapes, which, she argues, indicates a desire to "deliberately inflict on the group conditions of life calculated to bring about its physical destruction in whole or in part; and 'impose measures intended to prevent births within the group': 'We want to change the color. Every woman will deliver red. Arabs are the husbands of those women' (quoted on p. 147); and 'We will take your women and make them ours. We will change the race'" (quoted on p. 147).

The Critical Challenge and Issues Facing Darfur Today

Among the most critical challenges facing Darfur and the international community today are the following: stabilizing Darfur by (1) halting GoS and Janjaweed attacks; (2) ending the fighting between the rebel groups and the GoS; (3) ending the fighting between and amongst the various rebel groups; (4) ending the fighting between various Janjaweed groups; (5) bringing to an end all attacks on the people in the IDP camps; (6) providing the AU/UN Hybrid force with the full complement of troops needed to bring the Darfur conflict under control; (7) providing the AU/UN Hybrid Force with the materiel and resources needed to operate in a fully functional manner in Darfur; (8) widening the participation of various groups in the peace talks and then ensuring that there is a respected and effective leader heading up such peace talks—one that has the confidence of most, if not all, of the actors involved, as well as the will to bring the talks to fruition; (9) developing a sound mechanism for returning the IDPs and refugees to their land; (10) solving the problem of Arab groups now inhabiting, at the urging of the GoS, much of the land once owned by black Africans; and (11) helping Sudan and the people of Darfur effectively address the many systemic issues that led to the fighting in the first place (disenfranchisement of the people of Darfur, land needed by both the nomadic and sedentary peoples, and the even more complex issues relating to the problems created by drought and famine in the area). Finally, the international community must support the International Criminal Court in its warrant for the arrest of Sudanese President Omar al-Bashir and help it to arrest al-Bashir and any other alleged perpetrators that are indicted by the ICC.

What are the Real Probabilities of Progress in Darfur?

The real probabilities of progress vis-à-vis the Darfur crisis are, for now, rather bleak. Since the international community has shown that it, once again, is more prone to issuing words versus taking action to halt ongoing atrocities, it is dubious that anything concrete anytime soon will be done to end the ongoing fighting and chaos that now engulfs Darfur. Certainly more personnel and equipment will trickle in for the AU/UN Hybrid force, but the operable term is trickle. Whether it will ever get its full complement of personnel and all of the equipment it needs remains a question mark. Until it does, there is little hope to bring the situation in Darfur under control. Even then it's dubious that the situation will be brought under control for the truth is, UNAMID is working under a compromised Chapter VII mandate.

As for the peace talks, until both the GoS and the many rebel groups get serious about working out a peace any future peace talks are likely to result in little to nothing. Certainly the major rebel groups need to step up and allow representatives from the other key rebel groups to take part in the talks, otherwise the latter are likely to continue their fighting.

One of the most sensitive and complex issues facing the GoS and international community is the fact that the GoS has allowed, indeed, encouraged, Arabs to take over much of the land that the black Africans were forced off of over the years. The refugees and IDPs are intent on returning to their land, and how and when they will actually be able to do that without sparking another all out battle has not been considered yet. The first step, of course, is to end the chaos in Darfur, the second is for the GoS to agree to allow the return of the black Africans to Darfur, and the third is to decide whether the black Africans should return to the land they were forced to vacate or be given the same amount of land somewhere else—land that allows them, at the least, a livelihood that is comparable to what they had prior to being chased off by the GoS and *Janjaweed*.

The two most complex problems of all, of course, are the GoS' iron-fisted governance of Sudan and the abject disenfranchisement of black Africans of Darfur. In all likelihood, this situation is not going to be addressed/ameliorated anytime soon. Certainly al-Bashir and his cronies are not about to make any radical changes in the way they operate. Furthermore, even if al-Bashir is arrested and tried by the ICC little to nothing may change for those newly in charge may well retain the status quo (e.g., grasping all the power and wealth they possibly can).

As for the arrest of al-Bashir and other alleged perpetrators, only time will tell. The ICC seems intent on arresting him, but much of the rest of the world seems rather blasé, if not against such a move. Some assert that his arrest will contribute to an even more unstable and dangerous situation in Sudan, others are in favor of seeing the ICC follow through on its commitment to try those allegedly guilty of crimes against humanity, if not genocide.

Conclusion

As the international community continues to dither, innocent people in Darfur continue to suffer greatly: be murdered; perish as a result of malnutrition, dehydration and/or lack of medical attention; and/or suffer rape at the hands of the GOS troops and *Janjaweed* (and, increasingly, at the hands of members of the rebel groups). Seven long years have gone by since the "official" start of the crisis in Darfur, and the international community continues to engage in talk versus real action in an "effort" to ameliorate the problems that beset Darfur. Unfortunately, Darfur is a stark reminder that the world is no closer to halting, let alone preventing, genocide than it was during the Ottoman Turk genocide of the Armenians (1915-1923), the manmade famine in Ukraine (1933), or the Holocaust perpetrated by the Nazis (1933-1945).

Notes

1. Colloquially, according to the black Africans of Darfur, *Janjaweed* means, variously, "hordes," "ruffians," and "men or devils on horseback."
2. Deaths due to starvation, dehydration, and unattended injuries has been referred to as "genocide by attrition." The latter phrase/concept was coined by genocide scholar Helen Fein and first used in regard to Sudan by Alex de Waal in his description of the GoS treatment of the Nuba peoples.
3. After considerable debate, compromise, and dithering, the United States and the UN Security Council finally imposed some sanctions on Sudan. For example, on April 25, 2006, the UN Security Council passed a resolution imposing sanctions against four Sudanese individuals, all for whom have been accused of war crimes in Darfur.
4. With a vote of "no," any member of the Permanent Five of the UN Security Council can singly defeat any motion or vote on an issue. The Permanent Five are the only members of the UN Security Council with such power.

References

Amnesty International (2004). *Darfur: Rape as a Weapon of War: Sexual Violence and its Consequences*. London: Author. Accessed at: http://web.amnesty.org/library.

Anonymous (2000). *The Black Book: The Imbalance of Power and Wealth in Sudan*. Khartoum: Author(s).

Askin, Kelly Dawn (2006). "Prosecuting Gender Crimes Committed in Darfur: Holding Leaders Accountable for Sexual Violence," pp. 141-160. In Samuel Totten and Eric Markusen (Eds.) *Genocide in Darfur: Investigating Atrocities in the Sudan*. New York: Routledge.

BBC News (UK Edition) (2004). "Sudanese Refugees Welcome Powell." June 30, 4 pp. bbc.co.uk

de Waal, Alex (2004a). "Darfur's Deep Grievances Defy All Hopes for an Easy Solution." *The Observer* (London). July 25. p. 1. Accessed at: www.guardian.co.uk/sudan/story/0,14658,1268773,00.html

de Waal, Alex (2004b). *Famine That Kills: Darfur, Sudan*. New York: Oxford University Press.

de Waal, Alex (2004c). "Tragedy in Darfur: On Understanding and Ending the Horror." *Boston Review: A Political and Literary Forum*. October/November, n.p. Accessed at bostonreview.net/BR29.5/dewaal.html

Flint, Julie (2004). "A Year On, Darfur's Despair Deepens." *The Daily Star* (Regional, Lebanon). December 30, p. 1. Accessed at: www.dailystar.com.lb/article.asp?edition_id=10&categ_id=5&article_id=11388

Flint, Julie, and de Waal, Alex (2005). *Darfur: A Short History of a Long War.* New York: Zed Books.

Fowler, Jerry (2006). "A New Chapter of Irony: The Legal Definition of Genocide and the Implication of Powell's Determination," pp. 127-139. In Samuel Totten and Eric Markusen (Eds.) *Genocide in Darfur: Documenting Atrocities in the Sudan.* New York: Routledge.

The Guardian (2006). "The Rape of Darfur. Special Reports." *Guardian Unlimited.* January 18, n.p. Accessible at: www.guardian.co.uk/sudan

Human Rights Watch (2007). *Chaos by Design: Peacekeeping Challenges for AMIS and UNAMID.* New York: Author.

Human Rights Watch (2002). "Biography of Hassan al Turabi." New York: Author. Accessed at: www.hrw.org/press/2002/03/**turabi**-bio.htm

Human Rights Watch (2004a). *Darfur Destroyed: Ethnic Cleansing by Government and Militia Forces in Western Sudan.* New York: Author. Accessed at: hrw.org/reports/2004/sudan0504/

Human Rights Watch (2004b). "Darfur Documents Confirm Government Policy of Militia Support: A Human Rights Watch Briefing Paper." New York: Author. July 20. Accessed at: hrw.org/English/docs/2004/07/19/darfur9096

Human Rights Watch (2007). "Q & A: Crisis in Darfur." New York: Author. Accessed at: www.hrw.org/english/docs/2004/05/05/darfur8536.htm

Human Rights Watch (2004c). *Sudan: Government Commits 'Ethnic Cleansing' in Darfur.* New York: Author.

Kostas, Stephen A. (2006). "Making the Determination of Genocide in Darfur," pp. 111-126. In Samuel Totten and Eric Markusen (Eds.) *Genocide in Darfur: Investigating Atrocities in the Sudan.* New York: Routledge.

Mamdani, Mahmood (2004). "How Can We Name the Darfur Crisis? Some Preliminary Thoughts." *Black Commentary*, p. 2. Accessed at: www.neravt.com/left/pointers.html

Mamdani, Mahmood (2007). "The Politics of Naming: Genocide, Civil War, Insurgency." *London Review of Books.* Book of Reviews. March 8. Accessed at: www.wespac.org/WESPACCommunity/DiscussionMessages/tabid/124/forumid/7/postid/408

Médecins Sans Frontières (2005). *The Crushing Burden of Rape Sexual Violence in Darfur.* March 8. Paris: Author.

Médecins Sans Frontières (2005). "Persecution, Intimidation and Failure of Assistance in Darfur. *MSF Reports.* November 1. Paris: Author. Accessed at: www.msf.org/msfinternationa/invoke.cfm?objectid

Nathan, Laurie (2007). "The Making and Unmaking of the Darfur a Peace Agreement," pp. 245-266. In Alex De Waal (Ed.) *War in Darfur: And the Search for Peace.* Cambridge, MA and London: Global Equity Initiative, Harvard University, and Justice Africa, respectively.

Newsweek (2007). "Dueling Over Darfur: A Human Rights Activist and an African Scholar Disagree—Vehemently—on the Best Way to Help Sudan." *Newsweek Web Exclusive*, November 8. Accessed at: www.newsweek.com/id/69004/output

Physicians for Human Rights (2006). *Assault on Survival: A Call for Security, Justice and Restitution.* Cambridge, MA: Author. Accessed at: physiciansfor**humanrights**.org/ library/report-sudan-2006.html

Physicians for Human Rights (2005). *Destroyed Livelihoods: A Case Study of Furawiya Village, Darfur.* Cambridge, MA: Author. Accessed at: physiciansforhumanrights.org/sudan/news

Reeves, Eric (2003). "'Ethic Cleansing' in Darfur: Systematic, Ethnically Based Denial of Humanitarian Aid Is No Context for a Sustainable Agreement in Sudan." SPLM-Today.com, the official website of the SPLM/A, December 30, p. 1.

Refugees International (2007). *Laws Without Justice: An Assessment of Sudanese Laws Affecting Survivors of Rape*. Washington, DC.

Stanton, Gregory H. (2006). "Proving Genocide in Darfur: The Atrocities Documentation Project and Resistance to Its Findings," pp. 181-188. In Samuel Totten and Eric Markusen (Eds.) *Genocide in Darfur: Investigating Atrocities in the Sudan*. New York: Routledge.

U.S. State Department (September 9, 2004). *Documenting Atrocities in Darfur*. State Publication 11182. Washington, D.C.: Author. 4 pp.

Sengupta, Somini (2004). "In Sudan, No Clear Difference Between Arab and African." *The New York Times. Week in Review*. October 3, p. 1. Accessed at: www.nytimes.com/2004/10/03/weekinreview/03seng

The Sudan Liberation Movement and Sudan Liberation Army SLM/SLA) (2003). "Political Declaration." March 14. 4 pages. Accessed at: http://www.sudan.net/news/press/postedr/214.shtml

Sudan Tribune (2006). "'Darfur Will be Foreign Troops' Graveyard' – Bashir." *Sudan Tribune*, February 27, p. 1. Accessed at: www.sudantribune.com/spip.ph?

Totten, Samuel (2006). "The U.S. Investigation into the Darfur Crisis and Its Determination of Genocide: An Analysis," pp. 199-222. In Samuel Totten and Eric Markusen (Eds.) *Genocide in Darfur: Investigating Atrocities in the Sudan*. New York: Routledge.

United Nations (2004). "Sudan: World's Worst Humanitarian Crisis—Press Release." March 22. New York: Author, p. 2

United Nations Commission of Inquiry (2005). *UN Commission of Inquiry: Darfur Conflict*. New York: Author.

Wax, Emily (2004). "'We Want to Make a Light Baby': Arab Militiamen in Sudan Said to Use Rape as Weapon of Ethnic Cleansing." June 20. *Washington Post*, pp. A01-02. Accessed at www.washingtonpost.com/wp-dyn/ articles/A16001-2004Jun29.html

Annotated Bibliography

Amnesty International (2008). *Displaced in Darfur—A Generation of Anger*. London: Author. 26 pp.

This report discusses the terrible state of insecurity in internally displaced peoples' (IDPs) camps in Darfur; and in doing so, it examines the potential consequences of such insecurity and suggests possible remedies.

Amnesty International (2004). *Sudan—Darfur: Rape as a Weapon of War: Sexual Violence and its Consequences*. London: Author. 46 pp.

This report, based on first-person accounts by some 250 black African females, addresses how rape has been used as a weapon of war by Government of Sudan troops and the *Janjaweed* against the black African population of Darfur. It also addresses such issues as the social stigmatization of being raped; the economic, social and health ramifications black African females face as a result of having been sexually assaulted; and how and why sexual assaults result in the destruction of the social fabric of the black African peoples' communities.

Amnesty International (2004). *Sudan: Darfur: "Too Many People Killed for No Reason."* London: Author. 48 pp.

This AI report examines the immense and serious problems posed by the various "armed political groups" in Darfur and the serious human rights abuses perpetrated against civilians.

Apsel, Joyce (Ed.) (2005). *Darfur: Genocide Before Our Eyes.* New York: Institute for the Study of Genocide. 81 pp.

This booklet is comprised of six essays on various aspects of the crisis in Darfur: "Teaching About Darfur Through the Perspective of Genocide and Human Rights" by Joyce Apsel; "Evolution of Conflict and Genocide in Sudan: A Historical Survey" by Jerry Fowler; "Darfur: Genocide Before Our Eyes" by Eric Reeves; "Twelve Ways to Deny a Genocide" by Gregory Stanton; "Investigating Allegations of Genocide in Darfur: The U.S. Atrocities Documentation Team and the UN Commission of Inquiry" by Eric Markusen and Samuel Totten; and "The Human Impact of War in Darfur" by Jennifer Leaning.

Beardsley, Brent Major (2006). "The Endless Debate over the 'G Word'." *Genocide Studies and Prevention: An International Journal* (Special Issue: Genocide in Darfur edited by Samuel Totten and Eric Markusen), 1(1):79-82.

Beardsley decries the international community's tendency to waste precious time debating whether a violent conflict is genocide or something else before acting in an effective manner. He touches on what he believes needs to be done to halt the violence in Darfur. His insights are particularly interesting as he served as General Dallaire's personal staff officer with UNAMIR prior to and during the 1994 Rwandan genocide.

Bureau of Democracy, Human Rights and Labor and Bureau of Intelligence and Research (2004). *Documenting Atrocities in Darfur*. Washington, DC: United States Department of State. 8 pp.

This is the official report of the U.S. State Department's project in July and August 2004 that involved conducting interviews of Sudanese refugees living in refugee camps in Chad along the Chad/Sudan border. The ultimate analysis was based on semi-structured interviews with 1,136 randomly selected refugees. The findings of the study were used by U.S. Secretary of State Colin Powell to declare that genocide had been (and possibly still was being) perpetrated in Darfur by Government of Sudan troops and the *Janjaweed*.

Daly, M. W. (2007). *Darfur's Sorrow: A History of Destruction and Genocide*. New York: Cambridge University Press. 368 pp.

A historian and a specialist on Sudan, Daly provides a detailed historical analysis of the Darfur region, including the events leading up to and culminating in the current crisis in Darfur.

The book is comprised of the following chapters: 1. "The 'Abode of the Blacks'"; 2. "Lords of Mountain and Savanna: The Origins and History of the Fur State to 1874"; 3. "The Ends of the Turkish World"; 4. "Darfur at the End of Time: The Mahdiyya, 1885-1898"; 5. "Between an Anvil and a Hammer: The Reign of Ali Dinar, 1898-1916"; 6. "'Closed District': Anglo-Egyptian Colonial Rule in Darfur, 1916-1939"; 7. "Unequal Struggles, 1939-1955"; 8. "Colonial Legacies and Sudanese Rule, 1956-1969"; 9. "Darfur and 'The May Regime,' 1969-1985"; 10. "Third Time Unlucky: Darfur and the Restoration of Parliamentary Rule"; 11. "The State of Jihad"; and 12. "The Destruction of Darfur."

de Waal, Alex (2005). *Famine That Kills: Darfur, Sudan*. Second Edition. New York: Oxford University Press. 258 pp.

Famine That Kills: Darfur, Sudan is a seminal account of the famine that hit Darfur in the mid-1980s. In this new edition of the book, de Waal discusses the origins of the current crisis in Darfur, including the political landscape, the conflict over land, and the ongoing impoverishment of the people in the region.

de Waal, Alex (Ed.) (2007). *War in Darfur and the Search for Peace.* Cambridge, MA and London: Global Equity Initiative, Harvard University, and Justice Africa. 430 pp.

This highly informative book examines the causes of the conflict in Darfur (which the editor calls a war versus a genocide or scorched earth process), and the international efforts to bring about peace in Darfur.

The book is comprised of the following chapters: 1. "Sudan: The Turbulent State" by Alex de Waal; 2. "Native Administration and Local Governance in Darfur: Past and Future" by Musa Abdul-Jalil, Adam Azzain Mohammed, and Ahmed Yousuf; 3. "Darfur: A War for Land?" by Jerome Tubiana; 4. "Islam and Islamism in Darfur" by Ahmed Kamal El-Din; 5. "The Origins and Organization of the Janjawiid in Darfur" by Ali Haggar; 6. "Darfur's Armed Movements" by Julie Flint; 7. "The Unseen Regional Implications of the Crisis in Darfur" by Roland Marchal; 8. "The Comprehensive Peace Agreement and Darfur" by Adam Azzain Mohammed; 9. "The African Union Mediation and the Abuja Peace Talks" by Dawit Toga; 10. "The Making and Unmaking of the Darfur Peace Agreement" by Laurie Nathan; 11. "Darfur's Deadline: The Final Days of the Abuja Peace Process" by Alex de Waal; 12. "Darfur After Abuja: A View from the Ground" by Abdul-Jabbar Fadul and Victor Tanner; 13. "Narrating Darfur: Darfur in the U.S. Press, March-September 2004" by Deborah Murphy; 14. "Not on Our Watch: The Emergence of the American Movement for Darfur" by Rebecca Hamilton and Chad Hazlett; and 15. "Prospects for Peace in Darfur" by Alex de Waal.

Flint, Julie, and de Waal, Alex (2005). *Darfur: A Short History of a Long War.* London and New York: Zed Books. 152 pp.

This book by two individuals (Flint, a journalist and filmmaker, and de Waal, a scholar and fellow with The Global Equity Initiative at Harvard University) who have spent years in Sudan conducting research provides a solid overview of the crisis in Darfur. It is comprised of the following chapters: 1. "The People of Darfur"; 2. "The Sudan Government"; 3. "The Janjawiid"; 4. "The Rebels"; 5. "The War"; and 6. "Endgame."

Gingerich, Tara, and Leaning, Jennifer (2004). *The Use of Rape as a Weapon of War in the Conflict in Darfur, Sudan.* Washington, DC: U.S. Agency for International Development with Physicians for Human Rights. 56 pages.

This report makes extensive use of interviews and published literature to qualitatively assess the nature, circumstances and context of rape as a weapon in Sudan's ongoing war against the black Africans of Darfur. It is comprised of the following parts: Overview of Darfur Conflict; Use of Rape as a Weapon of War (Historical Overview, Military Utility of Rape as a Weapon of War; The Strategic Use of Rape; Other Uses of Rape in Conflict; Codification as a Crime Under International Law); Use of Rape as a Weapon of War in the Darfur Conflict (Circumstances Under Which Rape Occurs; Prevalence of Rape in the Darfur Conflict; Strategic Use of Rape as a Weapon of War in Darfur; Other Issues Regarding Rape in the Darfur Conflict; Sexual Abuse of Males; Participation of GoS Forces in Darfur Rape); Individual and Community Effects of Rape in Darfur (Short-Term Effects on Individuals; Physical Effects; Psychological and Psychosocial Effects; Short-Term Effects of Rape at the Community Level; Longer-Term Effects on Individuals and Communities); and Major Findings and Recommendations.

Grzyb, Amanda (Ed.) (2009). *The World and Darfur: International Response to Crimes Against Humanity in Western Sudan.* Montreal: McGill-Queen's University Press. 349 pp.

The World and Darfur is an interdisciplinary collection of essays about the world's response to genocide and crimes against humanity in Darfur. It is comprised of the following parts and sections: "Introduction: The International Response to Darfur" by Amanda Grzyb; Part One: From Rwanda to Darfur (1. "What Darfur Teaches Us About the Lessons Learned from Rwanda" by Gerald Caplan; 2. "Lessons Learned and Not Learned from the Rwandan Genocide" by Brent Beardsley; 3. "Media Coverage, Activism, and Creating Public Will for Intervention in Rwanda and Darfur" by Amanda Grzyb); Part Two: The Crisis in Darfur (4. "Three Empirical Investigations of Alleged Genocide in Darfur" by

Eric Markusen; 5. "Mass Atrocity Crimes in Darfur and the Response of the Government of Sudan Media to International Pressure" by Frank Chalk and Danielle Kelton; 6. "Death in Darfur—Total Mortality from Violence, Malnutrition, and Disease—April/May 2006" by Eric Reeves); and Part Three: Representation and Response (7. "Saving Lives in Darfur 2003-2006? Talk, Talk, and More Talk" by Samuel Totten; 8. "Visual Advocates: Depicting Darfur" by Carla Rose Shapiro; 9. "Rhetoric, Rights, and the Boundaries of Recognition: Making Darfur Public" by Daniel Listoe; and 10. "Preventing Genocide and Crimes Against Humanity: One Innovation and a New Global Initiative" by H. Peter Langille).

Hagan, John, and Rymond-Richmond, Wenona (2009). *Darfur and the Crime of Genocide*. New York: Cambridge University Press. 269 pp.

Using criminological concepts, the authors examine empirical evidence to argue that the crisis in Darfur constitutes a case of intentional state-supported genocide. The book is comprised of the following eight chapters, epilogue and appendix: 1. "Darfur Crime Scenes"; 2. "The Crime of Crimes"; 3. "While Criminology Slept"; 4. "Flip-Flopping on Darfur"; "5. "Eyewitnessing Genocide"; 6. "The Rolling Genocide"; 7. "The Racial Spark"; 8. "Global Shadows"; "Epilogue: Collective R2P"; and Appendix: "Genocidal Statistics."

Hassan, Salah M., and Ray, Carina E. (Eds.) (2009). *Darfur and the Crisis of Government in Sudan: A Critical Reader*. Ithaca, NY: Cornell University Press. 528 pp.

This mammoth book is comprised of two parts and five sections that contain twenty-one essays and fifteen appendices, a set of acronyms/abbreviations, a glossary, and two bibliographies.

Part I is comprised of the following: Section One (Origins and Evolution of the Conflict): "Darfur : A Problem within a Wider Problem" by Mansour Khalid; "Ideological Expansionist Movements versus Historical Indigenous Rights in the Darfur Region of Sudan: From Actual Homicide to Potential Genocide" by Atta El-Battahani; "Marginalization and War: From the South to Darfur" by Benaiah Yongo-Bure; "Darfur People: Too Black for the Arab-

Islamic Project of Sudan" by Abdullahi Osman El-Tom; and "The Darfur Conflict: A Natural Process or War by Design?" by Ali B. Ali-Dinar; Section Two (Representations of the War in Darfur): "Who Are the Darfurians? Arab and African Identities, Violence and External Engagement" by Alex de Waal; "The Politics of Naming: Genocide, Civil War, Insurgency by Mahmood Mamdani; Naming the Conflict: Darfur and the Crisis of Governance in Sudan" by Salah M. Hassan; "Darfur in the African Press" by Carina E. Ray; Section Three (Gender, War, and Violence): "Competing Masculinities: Probing Political Disputes as Acts of Violence against Women from Southern Sudan and Darfur" by Rogaia Mustafa Abusharaf; "The Darfur War: Masculinity and the Construction of a Sudanese National Identity" by Karin Willemse; and "Sudanese Civil Society Strategizing to End Sexual Violence against Women in Darfur" by Fahima A. Hashim; Section Four (Darfur: Law, Human Rights, and Prosecution) "The Erroneous Confrontation: The Dialectics of Law, Politics, and the Prosecution of War Crimes in Darfur" by Kamal El-Gizouli; "Sudan's Legal System and the Lack of Access to Justice for Survivors of Sexual Violence in Darfur" by Adrienne L. Fricke and Amira Khair; and "Locating Responsibilities: National and International Reponses to the Crisis in Darfur" by Munzoul A. M. Assal; and Section Five (Sudanese Civil Society, the State, and the Struggle for Peace in Darfur): "The End of Violence: Against Civil Society" by Grant Farred; "Power-Sharing or Ethnic Polarization: The Role of Schoolteachers in Conflict Management in North Darfur" by Musa Adam Abdul-Jalil; "A Civil Society Approach to the Darfur Crisis" by Al-Tayib Zain Al-Abdin; and "On the Failure of Darfur Peace Talks in Abuja: An SLM/A Insider's Perspective" by Abaker Mohamed Abuelbashar.

Human Rights Watch (2006). Darfur: *Humanitarian Aid Under Siege*. New York: Author.

This report provides an examination of the humanitarian crisis that resulted from the fact that the Sudanese government and rebel groups in Darfur greatly hindered humanitarian agencies from reaching hundreds of thousands of civilians dependent on international aid in many areas of Darfur.

Human Rights Watch (2005). *Entrenching Impunity Government Responsibility for International Crimes in Darfur*. New York: Author. 88 pp.

This report "documents the role of more than a dozen named civilians and military officials in the use and coordination of 'Janjaweed' militias and the Sudanese armed forces to commit war crimes and crimes against humanity in Darfur since mid-2003."

Human Rights Watch (2008). *Five Years On: Sexual Violence Still Rife in Darfur*. New York: Author. 44 pp.

This report addresses the ongoing and widespread prevalence of sexual violence throughout Darfur, and delineates cases of rape in which victims were as young as eleven years old. Human Rights Watch (HRW) asserts that the government of Sudan has utterly failed to halt the sexual attacks, many of which are perpetrated by GoS troops and their allies, the *Janjaweed*. HRW also addresses the fact that due to being under-resourced, UNAMID, the international peacekeepers in Darfur, have been "unable to protect women and girls from rape and other forms of violence."

Human Rights Watch (2008). *Rhetoric vs. Reality: The Situation in Darfur*. New York: Author. 22 pp.

A very powerful and eye-opening report vis-à-vis what the Government of Sudan says is happening in Darfur versus the reality on the ground. The report focuses on four key aspects of the situation in Darfur: 1. Continuing insecurity for civilians; 2. The humanitarian situation; 3. Justice and accountability; and 4. The deployment of the African Union-United Nations Hybrid Operation in Darfur (UNAMID).

Human Rights Watch (2005*). Sexual Violence and Its Consequences Among Displaced Persons in Darfur and Chad*. New York: Author. 18 pp.

This report is based on two Human Rights Watch fact-finding missions carried out in February 2005, one to displaced persons camps in South Darfur and one to refugee camps in Chad, to "conduct research on patterns of sexual and gender-based violence and the response of local and international actors." While the research does not constitute a comprehensive assessment of the numerous and complex issues related to sexual and gender-based violence or provide an evaluation of all of the humanitarian groups' efforts underway in Darfur and Chad, it does highlight some of the most significant "elements in the patterns of sexual and gender-based violence—including the urgent need for protection from ongoing violence—and stresses the need for an appropriate response."

Iyob, Ruth, and Khadiagala, Gilbert M. (2006). *Sudan: The Elusive Quest for Peace.* Boulder, CO: Lynne Rienner Publishers. 224 pp.
This book includes a chapter entitled "Flashpoint Darfur" (pp. 133-166), which focuses on the crisis in Darfur. More specifically, according to the authors, "adjusting lenses to take into account historical and sociopolitical factors, this chapter highlights the intricate linkages between past and present that led to the articulation of the desiderata of equitable citizenship and the launching of the militant and rebellious defiance against the central government" (p. 15). Among some of the many issues addressed are the following: politics of exclusion (1956-2006), ethnicization of local dissent and center-periphery dynamics, the attempt at conflict resolution, initial confrontation and reactions, and international engagement and the Abuja negotiations (August 2004-May 2006).

Lippman, Matthew (2007). "Darfur: The Politics of Genocide Denial Syndrome." *Journal of Genocide Research*, June, 9(2):193-213.
A thought-provoking article by a professor in the Department of Criminal Justice at the University of Illinois at Chicago.

Marlowe, Jen with Aisha Bain and Adam Shapiro (2006). *Darfur Diaries: Stories of Survival.* New York: Nation Books. 259 pp.
This book is about the trip three independent filmmakers made into Darfur, where they spoke with dozens of black African Darfurians in an effort to learn about their history, the ongoing conflict there, and what the victims have experienced.

Mayroz, Eyal (2008). "Ever Again? The United States, Genocide suppression, and the Crisis in Darfur." *Journal of Genocide Research*, September, 10(3):359-388.

Herein, the author examines the United States policy vis-à-vis the Darfur crisis, which asserted on September 9, 2004 that the crisis in Darfur constituted a case of genocide. In doing so, he "proposes that constraining effects of the war in Iraq, a deadlocked Security Council, a multifaceted defensive Sudanese government campaign against intervention aided by the existence of at least two key American interests in the country, and the perceived risks of military intervention have combined to impede a meaningful US action to stop the first genocide of the twenty-first century. It is however also argued that while the US government could and should have been much more active, *non-militarily*, on the issue of Darfur, its rhetoric and actions during 2004 did exhibit a certain increase of willingness, although for as yet uncertain motives, to attempt engagement in acts of genocide suppression. The study discusses the motives, obstacles and political realities that have led to a policy of, in fact, non-intervention."

Médecins Sans Frontières (2005). "The Crushing Burden of Rape: Sexual Violence in Darfur — A Brief Paper." Paris: Author. 8 pp.

Based on Médecins Sans Frontières' (MSF) work in Darfur between October 2004 and February 2005, this report addresses a host of issues related to sexual assault, including but not limited to the following: sexual assaults perpetrated against girls and women as they go about their daily activities (versus being sexually assaulted during an attack carried out on a village by GOS troops and/or the *Janjaweed*); multiple rapes and abductions; the medical and social effects of rape; how victims who are sexually assaulted are treated as criminals; and how MSF provides assistance to those who have been sexually assaulted.

Prunier, Gerard (2005). *Darfur: The Ambiguous Genocide*. Ithaca, NY: Cornell University Press. 212 pp.

Prunier provides a solid analysis of the origins and history of the current crisis in Darfur. In doing so, he addresses a host of critical issues in the six chapters that comprise the book: 1. "Independent Darfur: Land, People, History"; 2. "Darfur and Khartoum (1916-1985): An Unhappy Relationship"; 3. "From Marginalization to Revolt: Manipulated 'Arabism' and 'Racial' Anarchy (1985-2003)"; 4. "Fear at the Centre: From Counter-Insurgency to Quasi-Genocide (2003-2005)"; 5. "The World and the Darfur Crisis" and 6. "Conclusions: Darfur and the Global Sudan Crisis." His conclusion that Darfur is an "ambiguous genocide" is poorly argued as he relies on a definition of genocide (other than that found in the United Nations Convention on the Prevention and Punishment of Genocide) that assumes that a "true" genocide must be all-consuming and thus he overlooks the importance of the wording in the UNCG that reads "in whole or in part."

Physicians for Human Rights (2006). Darfur: *Assault on Survival—A Call for Security, Justice and Restitution*. Cambridge, MA: Author. 67 pp.

Based on a series of interviews conducted between May 2004 and July 2005 with eyewitnesses from the villages of Furawiya, Terbeba, and Bendisi, Physicians for Human Rights investigators "randomly surveyed dozens of survivors and documented...compelling evidence of a destroyed way of life and means of survival." The report includes a section entitled "Rape," and while relatively short it is packed with significant information. The authors also delineate how the rape of the black African females constitutes genocide under the UN Convention on the Prevention and Punishment of Genocide.

Reeves, Eric (2007). *A Long Day's Dying: Critical Moments in the Darfur Genocide*. Toronto: The Key Publishing House. 360 pp.

Written by one of the most indefatigable activists working on the Darfur issue, this book presents a detailed examination of the ongoing genocide in Darfur. The book is comprised of the 150 analyses Reeves produced and issued over the internet and in printed commentaries over a three year period (2003 through 2006). The book's contents include the following: 1. "Introduction (Maps)"; 2. "Sudan's Killing Fields Move Westward"; 2. "Rwanda Redux (Pictures)"; and 4. "Genocide by Attrition."

Straus, Scott (2005). "Darfur and the Genocide Debate." *Foreign Affairs*. January/February, 84(1):123-133.

In his introduction to this essay, Straus says: "Despite a decade of hand-wringing over the failure to intervene in Rwanda in 1994 and despite Washington's decision to break its own taboo against the use of the word "genocide," the international community has once more proved slow and ineffective in responding to large-scale, state-supported killing. Darfur has shown that the energy spent fighting over whether to call the events there "genocide" was misplaced, overshadowing difficult but more important questions about how to craft an effective response to mass violence against civilians in Sudan. The task ahead is to do precisely that: to find a way to stop the killing, lest tens of thousands more die" (p. 123).

Straus, Scott (2006). "Rwanda and Darfur: A Comparative Analysis." *Genocide Studies and Prevention: An International Journal* (Special Issue: Genocide in Darfur edited by Samuel Totten and Eric Markusen), 1(1):41-54.

Straus presents a comparative analysis of genocide in Rwanda (1994) and Darfur. In so doing, he examines the patterns and origins of violence in both cases and "uses the comparisons to generate some theoretical inferences about the causes of genocide.... The analysis finds that both cases demonstrate a similar character of violence, but that in Rwanda the violence was more intense, more exterminatory, and more participatory than in Darfur." The article also examines the international response to genocide in both situations. Ultimately, Straus argues that "focusing too intently on a 'genocide' determination may be counterproductive, that international politics matter yet mobilization on Darfur outside of North America was weak, and that protocols for the use of force to prevent genocide should be clarified" (p. 41).

Totten, Samuel (2009). "The Darfur genocide," pp. 555-607. In Samuel Totten and William S. Parsons (Eds.) *Century of Genocide: Critical Essays and Eyewitness Accounts*, third edition. New York: Routledge.

This chapter presents a detailed analysis of the Darfur crisis and why it constitutes genocide. It is accompanied by interviews conducted by the author with survivors of the genocide who now reside in refugee camps in eastern Chad.

Totten, Samuel (2010). "Genocide in Darfur." Special Issue *Genocide Studies and Prevention*. In 2006, for the inaugural issue of Genocide Studies and Prevention (GSP), Samuel Totten and Eric Markusen edited a special issue on Darfur. Almost four years later, Totten edited a second special issue for GSP on Darfur. This new issue includes the following articles: "Darfur: Strategic Victimhood Strikes Again?" by Alan Kuperman; "The International Criminal Court, the Security Council, and the Politics of Impunity in Darfur" by Victor Peskin; "Should Omar al-Bashir President of Sudan be Charged and Arrested by the International Criminal Court: An Exchange of Views" by Alex de Waal and Gregory H. Stanton; and "The UN International Commission of Inquiry: New and Disturbing Findings" by Samuel Totten.

Totten, Samuel (2009). "The Mass Rape of Black African Girls and Women in Darfur," pp. 137-168. In Samuel Totten (Ed.) *The Plight and Fate of Women During and Following Genocide*. New Brunswick, NJ: Transaction Publishers.
    Presents an overview of the Darfur crisis, and then focuses on the pervasiveness of the sexual assaults by Government of Sudan troops and the Janjaweed against black Africans girls and women. In doing so, it discusses the issue of "rape as genocide," and Sudanese law and rape. It concludes with a set of recommendations.

Totten, Samuel, and Markusen, Eric (2006). "Genocide in Darfur." Special Issue. *Genocide Studies and Prevention*, Summer, 1(1).
    This inaugural issue of *Genocide Studies and Prevention: An International Journal* deals exclusively with the crisis in Darfur. It is comprised of the following articles: "Unsimplifying Darfur" by Rene Lemarchand; "Holding Leaders Accountable in the International Criminal Court (ICC) for Gender Crimes Committed in Darfur" by Kelly Dawn Askin; "A New Chapter of Irony: The Legal Impli-

cations of the Darfur Genocide Determination" by Jerry Fowler; "Rwanda and Darfur: A Comparative Analysis" by Scott Straus; "The US Investigation into the Darfur Crisis and the US Government's Determination of Genocide" by Samuel Totten; and "The Endless Debate over the "G Word" by Major Brent Beardsley.

Totten, Samuel, and Markusen, Eric (Eds.) (2006). *Genocide in Darfur: Investigating Atrocities in the Sudan.* New York: Routledge. 284 pp.

Genocide in Darfur: Investigating Atrocities in the Sudan presents an insider's view of the U.S. State Department's Atrocities Documentation Project. Data collected by the project was used by U.S. Secretary of State Colin Powell to make his determination that the Government of Sudan had perpetrated genocide in Darfur. The book includes essays by primary investigators, members of the U.S. State Department and USAID, officials from the Coalition of International Justice, and outside analysts.

UN Commission of Inquiry (2005). *Report of the International Commission of Inquiry on Darfur to the United Nations Secretary-General, January 25, 2005.* New York: United Nations. 176 pp. Also available at: www.un.org/News/dh/sudan/com ing.darfur.pdf

Following the United States declaration on September 9, 2004, that Sudan had committed genocide and the U.S.'s referral of the Darfur matter to the United Nations, UN Secretary General Kofi Annan authorized, under Chapter VII of the UN Charter, a UN investigation into the crisis. During November and December 2004 and January 2005 a team of investigators conducted a commission of inquiry that took them to Darfur, Khartoum, the refugee camps in Chad, among other countries, for the express purpose of ascertaining whether the atrocities amounted to the crime of genocide. In the final report issued by the Commission of Inquiry on Darfur the authors assert that "There is no doubt that some of the objective elements of genocide materialized in Darfur.... Some elements merging from the facts including the scale of atrocities and the systematic nature of the attacks, killing, displacement and rape, as well as racially motivated statements by perpetrators that have targeted members of the African tribes only, could be indicative of the genocidal intent. However, there are other more indicative elements that show the lack of genocidal intent.... The Commission does recognize that in some instances, individuals, including Government officials, may commit acts with genocidal intent. Whether this was the case in Darfur, however, is a determination that only a competent court can make on a case-by-case basis..." (pp. 129, 130). Ultimately, though, the COI found that the actions of the GoS troops and *Janjaweed* did not amount to a genocide but rather crimes against humanity. (For a critique of the UN COI's investigation and ultimate findings, see Samuel Totten's (2009) article in the December issue of *Genocide Studies and Prevention: An International Journal*: "The UN International Commission of Inquiry: New and Disturbing Findings.")

Van Ardenne, Agnes; Salih, Mohamed; Grono, Nick; and Mendez, Juan (2006). *Explaining Darfur: Lectures on the Ongoing Genocide*. Amsterdam: Vossiuspers UvA. 60 pp.

The four short lectures in this book are entitled: "The Road to Darfur Leads Through Khartoum" by Van Ardenne; "Africa's Governance Deficit, Genocide and Ethnocide" by Salih; "Darfur: The International Community's Failure to Protect" by Grono; and "Possibility for Genocide Prevention" by Mendez. While each lecture has its strong points (that is, they are informative in various ways), each also has its weak points (lack of adequate explanation, dubious assertions). The weakest lecture is by Mendez, the then special adviser to the U.N. Secretary General on the prevention of genocide, as it typifies political palaver at its worst in that it includes all of the "stock phrases" that sound good but are largely bereft of real insight.

Vanrooyen, Michael; Leaning, Jennifer; Johnson, Kirsten; Hirschfeld, Karen; Tuller, David; Levine, Adam C.; and Heffernan, John (2008). "Employment of a Livelihoods Analysis to Define Genocide in the Darfur Region of Sudan." *Journal of Genocide Research*, September, 10(3):343-358.

This analysis examines the ways in which the crisis in Darfur has resulted in large-scale destruction of livelihoods in Darfur, the impact of such vis-à-vis long-term social survival, and the relevance of a livelihoods analysis to a key clause in the Genocide Convention. To carry out the study, Physicians for Human Rights carried out three field investigations in Darfur and refugee camps in Chad in order to ascertain "the destruction of lives and livelihoods and the means of survival. Survey teams selected a random sample of refugees from three pre-identified villages in Darfur, each representing one of the three major non-Arab Darfurian ethnic groups in the region. The teams employed structured key informant interviews and focus groups to collect both quantitative and qualitative data to explore the loss of livelihoods and lives to establish patterns of attack." Based on interviews with forty-six respondents and six focus groups, the teams collected systematic data on the impact of the violent attacks on villages, the close coordination of government military forces with the *Janjaweed* militia, and the patterns of destruction of livelihoods. Ultimately, the researchers conclude that "the government of Sudan and its proxy militia, the *Janjaweed*, have created conditions of life for many thousands of non-Arab Darfurians that guarantee the destruction of their livelihoods, lives and communities. They have deliberately inflicted on the non-Arabs of Darfur conditions of life calculated to bring about their physical destruction in whole or in part. These actions constitute genocide as such under the UN Genocide Convention, which obliges nations to both prevent and punish the crime."

Vehnmki, Mika (2006). "Darfur Scorched: Looming Genocide in Western Sudan." *Journal of Genocide Research*. March, 8 (1): 51-82.

Discussion of the scorched earth policy of the government of Sudan in Darfur.

10

Genocide in Guatemala

Samuel Totten

Introduction

Throughout the early to mid 1980s, over 200,000 Guatemalan people, primarily impoverished indigenous Mayans[1] residing in small countryside villages in the western highlands, were the victims of a vicious state-driven counterinsurgency and genocide. The latter involved extrajudicial killings, hundreds of massacres, and the displacement of approximately one million people. In the process, some 440 villages were utterly destroyed. The attacks and killings also resulted in roughly 200,000 orphans and 80,000 widows.

This chapter examines the root causes of the genocide, the actions comprising the genocide, the ramifications of the latter, and the post-genocide period.

Roots of the Violence

For centuries in Guatemala, unequal treatment of the indigenous peoples by ladinos (the Spanish conquerors) plagued the social and political landscape. Part and parcel of the latter was conflict related to race, ethnicity, and class that played out in overt prejudice, discrimination, economic exploitation, and disenfranchisement. In this regard, Green (1999) argues that "the relationship between

271

political violence and the deeply rooted and historically based structural violence of inequality and impunity suffuses Guatemalan society, [and is] expressed through class, ethnicity, and gender divisions and experienced by Mayas as virulent racism" (p. 10).

The U.S. Sponsored Overthrow of a Democratically Elected Government in Guatemala and Its Continued Undermining of Democracy and Freedom in Guatemala

In the midst of the Cold War, the United States was obsessed with the spread of communism worldwide, and was averse to any communist or socialist state in "its backyard."

In 1951, a left of center politician, Jacobo Arbenz Guzman, was elected president of Guatemala. In 1952, his government passed a law, Decree 900, "Law of Agrarian Reform," that proved to be extremely controversial in some quarters. As Wilkinson (2002) notes, the "overarching aim [of the law], set forth in its opening paragraph, was to 'overcome the economic backwardness' of the country and 'improve the quality of life of the great masses'" (p. 83). Arbenz' politics and policies were particularly looked askance at by the U.S. government as it feared their "impact on national politics, [believing] that the reform's success would benefit the communists" who were suspected of being behind the reforms[2] (Wilkinson, 2002, p. 166). Subsequently, in 1951, the United States Central Intelligence Agency (CIA) organized a coup, and replaced Arbenz with a right-wing military regime. From that point forward, a series of U.S.-supported right-wing governments and their policies resulted in a vicious cycle of government-sponsored repression and violence. Indeed, as Manz (2004) notes, "The growing political realities of the cold war and the United States foreign policy toward Central America gave the Guatemalan military and economic elites complete license to rule in an increasingly authoritarian way. Anti-communism served to justify and conceal the most heinous of crimes, and the United States—except for the [Jimmy] Carter administration—eagerly funneled millions of dollars to military regimes decade after decade, showing no concern for the brutality committed by the armed forces"[3] (p. 21).

In 1960, a military uprising failed. Some rebel officers fled to the mountains in eastern Guatemala, where, inspired by the Cuban Revolution, they studied Marxism-Leninism and formed the initial guerrilla groups that would carry out an insurgency in the years ahead. The movement became known as Fuerzas Armadas Rebeldes (FAR) or Rebel Armed Forces.

In 1966, the United States sent U.S. Army Green Berets to Guatemala and spent millions of dollars to train the Guatemala Armed Forces[4]. Subsequently, FAR suffered a major setback and defeat as a result of the 1966-1968 counterinsurgency campaign carried out by the Guatemalan army. It was during this period that army-organized death squads were formed and became active. More than 8,000 people, largely unarmed civilians, were reportedly killed in the subsequent counterinsurgency effort at that time.

Taking a step back, the insurgency movement set out to reconstitute itself, and that, in part, involved building a "political support base in the western highlands" (Jonas, 2009, p. 380). After doing so, it returned, in the 1970s, to armed combat against the government.

Tellingly, after he became president in 1971, General Carlos Arana Osorio, who oversaw an increase in killings and disappearances, asserted that "If it is necessary to turn the country into a cemetery in order to pacify it, I will not hesitate to do so."

A Series of Paradoxes and Their Impact on the Highland Mayas

Key events between 1960 and 1980 proved to be pivotal in regard to the clash between the indigenous peoples and the Guatemalan government. In regard to the latter, Susanne Jonas (2009), a specialist on Guatemala, reports the following:

Structural transformations of the 1960s-1980s changed the overall situation of Guatemala's indigenous highlands populations in their class definition and profoundly affected their self-conception and identities as indigenous; here lay the basis for the widespread Mayan uprising in the late 1970s and early 1980s. Economic growth followed by economic crisis broke down the ... barriers that had kept the Mayas relatively isolated in the highlands.

...In the countryside, structural contradictions—the crisis in subsistence agriculture, compounded by the massive 1976 earthquake—uprooted and displaced thousands of indigenous peasants, causing them to redefine themselves in both class and cultural terms. As producers, they were being semi-proletarianized as a seasonal migrant labor force on the plantations of the Southern Coast, meanwhile often losing even the tiny subsistence plots of land they had traditionally held in the highlands. The combination of their experiences of being evicted from their own lands and their experiences as a migrant semi proletariat radicalized large numbers of highlands Mayas. Even the more developmentalist influences were contradictory, in that they raised hopes and expectations in the 1960s only to dash them in the 1970s. The clearest examples of this dynamic were those peasants who received land from the government's colonization programs in the 1960s, only to have it taken away again in the 1970s, as the powerful army officers grabbed profitable lands in colonization areas. (Pp. 377, 378)

Throughout the 1960s and 1970s the highlands Mayans came into ever-increasing contact with the ladino society, and that too had a transformational effect. In this regard, Jonas (2009) asserts that "Increased contact had the paradoxical effect of reinforcing their defense of their ethnic/cultural identity, as expressed in the languages, customs, community and religious practices, claims to the land and other rights, and their overall worldview. These elements of their identity became a factor in mobilizing their resistance to the ladino-dominated state" (p. 378).

At one and the same time, the Guatemalan army continued to oppress indigenous peoples by attacking their villages, and shooting and killing Mayan civilians—sometimes in massive numbers. Be that as it may, the government's goal of terrorizing the highlands into a state of passivity backfired in that by the late 1970s, hundreds, and then thousands, of Mayas began fighting back.

As Jonas (2009) notes, "all of these [aforementioned paradoxical experiences of the 1970s] coincided with the transformation of grassroots organizations of the Catholic Church, and the rise of Christian based communities, and the gradual emergence of a 'Church of the Poor'" (p. 379). This resulted in village priests joining the local people in social justice movements. Subsequently, the actions of the priests influenced the church hierarchy to move away from its conservatism and join the effort as well. Ultimately, both the priests' actions and that of the Church in Guatemala were perceived by the Guatemalan government as part and parcel of the "subversive movement"—a movement that the government was intent on stanching at all costs.

The Reign of Terror Carried Out by the Rios Montt Government

Over time, the guerilla uprising grew in size and spread across the country. More specifically,

> [t]he guerrilla armed uprising reached its height in 1980-1981, gaining 6-8,000 armed fighters and 1/4-1/2 million active collaborators and supporters (Adams, 1988, p. 296), and operating in many parts of the country. By the early 1980s, entire Mayan highlands communities were turning to the insurgents for arms, to defend themselves from army incursions and massacres.... The new wave of armed struggle was taken very seriously by Guatemala's elites and army as heralding a possible seizure of power by the insurgents. (Jonas, 2009, p. 380)

Fearful of a leftist take-over (largely as a result of the guerrillas' actions), the Guatemalan government, in 1981, undertook a scorched earth effort to destroy the insurgency. As fierce as the initial counterinsurgency effort was, it was ratcheted up in 1982, following the March 1982 coup d'etat by the military, which saw General Efrain Rios Montt become president of Guatemala. More specifically, throughout 1982 and 1983 the counter-insurgency became more vicious and more brutal as government forces ravaged hundreds of villages, killing tens of thousands of innocent people. Manz (2004) reports that "[t]he military's concept of an internal enemy [was] anyone who was not a fervent military supporter..., and the lines blurred between armed combatants, collaborators, sympathizers, and civic democratic participants" (p. 18). Quoting a Ladino villager, Manz (2004) writes: "The military would say, 'That child is a guerilla,' Sabas recalled. 'A child in the womb of the mother was already a guerilla. So they applied the scorched earth, because not even the seed was to be left.' Thus, children, along with everyone else, would be tortured and murdered" (p. 104).

Even as the leftist guerrillas attracted many people from extremely different groups in Guatemala, thus forming a more inclusive and stronger revolutionary movement, "a change in balance of forces between the insurgents and the army began during the second half of 1981, as the army initiated an unprecedented counteroffensive against the civilian support base of the insurgents" (Jonas, 2008, p. 380). The slaughter by government forces was indiscriminate, except for the fact that it was largely aimed at those of Mayan descent. According to Jonas (2009), "…the army openly acknowledged [that the] goal was literally to 'drain the sea' in which the guerrilla movement operated and to eradicate its civilian support base in the Mayan highlands" (p. 381). It was during this period that "[e]ntire sectors of the Maya population became military targets" (Jonas, 2009, p. 381). It was largely the latter philosophy and actions that led both various human rights activists and scholars to deem the government's actions "genocidal." It is estimated that between 1981 and 1983 some 100,000 to 150,000 civilians (both unarmed and primarily of Mayan descent) were murdered. Based on the actions of the government and the resulting destruction and death, human rights organizations and scholars concluded that "the army's policies were *systematically directed to destroy some ethnic sub-groups in particular, as well as the Mayan population in general*" (emphasis in the original) (Jonas, 2009, p. 381).

But the death and destruction did not end in 1983. As Jonas (2009) notes, "The next phase of the counterinsurgency campaign, from 1983 to 1985 (under the military regime of General Oscar Majia Victores), was also violent and devastating for the highlands Mayas. The most obvious goal was to consolidate military control over the population through a series of coercive institutions: (a) mandatory, involuntary paramilitary 'civilian self-defense patrols…'; (b) rural resettlement camps known as 'model villages…'; and (c) Inter-Institutional Coordinating Councils, which centralized administration of development projects at every level of government (local, municipal, provincial, national) under military control" (pp. 383-384).

In an attempt to counter the insurgency, the Guatemalan military began conscripting Mayan boys as foot soldiers and using Mayan men as civil patrollers[5] and military commissioners "to carry out surveillance on their neighbors and at times to commit murder" (Green, 1999, p. 31). Green (1999) notes that the latter

led to severe ruptures in family and community social relations. Not only [did] it undermine the sense of trust and cooperation among family members and neighbors, but the dividing of such loyalties [was] instrumental in perpetuating fear and terror, as family members themselves [were] implicated in acts of violence. This complicity, not surprisingly, [had] a devastating impact on the special potency of kinship and community relations" (p. 31).

A Shaky Peace

In March 1994, the Guatemalan government and leftist gueril-las signed a human rights accord. In late December 1996, a peace treaty was signed between the leftists and the government to end the thirty-six-year war.

A significant aspect of the peace agreement was to be the imple-mentation of earlier agreements to establish social equality via economic and agrarian reforms, the protection of human rights, and the establishment of a "Truth Commission" to investigate the crimes committed during the period of conflict. It was also sup-posed to result in the resettlement of refugees, recognize Indian rights, reform election laws, disarm and demobilize rebels, and consider future of the Guatemalan military.

Speaking of the limitations of the peace agreement, Green (1999) argues that "…the Guatemalan Peace Accords that resulted from the negotiations defined peace and security in its narrowest terms equating peace with the absence of war and security with the absence of military threat. These restricted definitions both overlook the multifaceted problems that circumscribe Guatemalan society—economic ecological, demographic, narcotic, and gender issues—and discount their importance in constructing lasting peace and justice in Guatemala" (p. 51).

A National Reconciliation Law was ratified and took effect in December 1996 that protected rebels from arrest. Concomitantly, in late 1996 the Guatemalan government issued a blanket amnesty for those involved in many crimes (the exceptions being torture, genocide and forced disappearance). Human rights activists, though, criticized the law, asserting that the vagueness in its language could prevent prosecution of those accused of perpetrating atrocities throughout the 1980s and early 1990s. In fact, throughout the 1990s and first decade of 2000, prosecution of the guilty has been rare and prosecutors seem particularly reluctant to challenge the military.

What has not been rare is the exhumation of hundreds of mass graves. The Catholic Church in Guatemala, alone, has identified

442 massacre sites. Upon the exhumation of the graves, the victims' family members and friends have been able to retrieve the remains of the murdered and bury them in proper graves.

To the chagrin, if not outright despair, of many, Efrain Rios Montt was elected speaker of Guatemala's Congress in December 1995. His ultimate aim was to be elected president of the country, but he was not successful in that effort.

In 1995, a United Nations Human Rights Commission in Guatemala sharply criticized the human rights record of the government of President Ramior de Leon Carpio. While not directly implicating the government, it presented extensive evidence of ongoing military involvement in human rights violations such as torture and cited complicity in cases of harassment, torture and murder. It particularly emphasized the point that authorities frequently and systematically failed to investigate such cases.

In June of 1996, a United States presidential panel, the Intelligence Oversight Board, issued a report based on a study that documented the fact that the CIA "did not keep Congress adequately informed of its activities in Guatemala and was insensitive to human rights abuses there" (n.p.). Furthermore, the report asserted that "several CIA assets [agents] were credibly alleged to have ordered, planned, or participated in serious human rights violations such as assassination, extrajudicial execution, torture or kidnapping while they were assets—and that that the CIA was contemporaneously aware of many of the allegations" (n.p.).

In 1998, the Recovery of the Historical Memory Project (Recuperacion de la Memoria Historica) published *Guatemala No Mas!* (*Guatemala Never Again!*). *Guatemala No Mas!* reported the findings of a study undertaken by the Human Rights Office of the Archdiocese of Guatemala concerning the violence that engulfed Guatemala between 1960 and 1996. Ultimately, *Recuperacion de la Memoria Historica* conducted 6,500 individual and collective interviews. Ninety two percent were interviews of victims.

Guatemala No Mas! addresses a host of critical issues, including but not limited to the following: the historical context of the period; the perpetrators; the methods of torture and killing that were carried out; the extent of the massacres, torture, and rape;

the destruction of entire communities; the forced cooptation of civilians by the military to carry out its dirty work; and the fact of clandestine prisons and cemeteries.

In February 1999, the Commission for Historical Clarification (in Spanish, *Comisión para el Esclarecimiento Histórico,* or CEH),[6] which was sponsored the United Nations, issued a report on the tragedy that had engulfed Guatemala. It concluded that more than 200,000 people were killed, 93 percent of them by government forces. In part, the report stated that "The massacres, scorched earth operations, forced disappearances and executions of Mayan authorities, leaders, and spiritual guides were not only an attempt to destroy the social base of the guerrillas, but above all, to destroy the cultural values that ensured cohesion and collective action in Mayan communities" (CEH, 1999, p. 23). Notably, the report asserts that some of the states's counterinsurgency operations could accurately be deemed genocide. More specifically, the report stated that

> The CEH is able to confirm that between 1981 and 1983 the Army identified groups of the Mayan population as the internal enemy, considering them to be an actual or potential support base for the guerrillas.... In this way, the Army, inspired by the national Security Doctrine, defined a concept of internal enemy that went beyond guerrilla sympathizers [sic], combatants or militants to include civilians from specific ethnic groups....
> The CEH concludes that the reiteration of destructive acts, directed against groups of the Mayan population, within which can be mentioned the elimination of leaders and criminal acts against minors who could not possibly have been military targets, demonstrates that the only common denominator for all the victims was the fact that they belonged to a specific ethnic group and makes it evident that these acts were committed "with the intent to destroy, in whole or in part" these groups [Article II, first paragraph of the UN Convention on the Prevention and Punishment of the Crime of Genocide].
> The CEH concludes that agents of the State of Guatemala, within the framework of counterinsurgency operation carried out between 1981 and 1983, committed acts of genocide against groups of Mayan people. (CEH, 1999, pp. 39, 41)

Tellingly, the CEH report dismissed the military's assertion that the massacres were the result of rogue solders, and it found that there was an explicit strategy to terrorize the population and that it was organized, planned and directed from the highest levels of the Guatemalan government. It further asserted that the state had resorted to serving the purpose of protecting a racist and unjust economic order.[7]

In the decade and a half after the peace agreement, the situation in Guatemala remains strained, tentative and not a little violent.

Critical Challenges Facing the Field Today

A number of critical challenges continue to face Guatemala vis-à-vis the government's past genocidal actions as well as the human rights situation in Guatemala today. Among the most significant are: securing the rule of law in Guatemala, securing the protection of human rights, ending impunity and bringing to justice the perpetrators of the past and current abuses, and providing safety for those Guatemalans who are seeking justice for past abuses.

Despite all of the talk and all of the promises, Guatemala has seen minimal progress in establishing the rule of law. Guatemala has also seen equally minimal progress in providing the protection of human rights for all of its citizens. Until both are established, there is little hope that Guatemalan citizens will experience the freedoms that all peoples across the globe are entitled to under the UN Declaration of Human Rights.

As for the issue of impunity, according to Human Rights Watch (2006),

> A dozen years after the end of Guatemala's brutal civil war, impunity remains the norm when it comes to human rights violations. Ongoing violence and intimidation threaten to reverse the little progress that has been made toward promoting account-ability. Guatemala's weak and corrupt law enforcement institutions have proved incapable of containing the powerful organized crime groups that, among other things, are believed to be responsible for attacks on human rights defenders, judges, prosecutors, and others. (182)

Tellingly, "of the 626 massacres documented by the truth commission [*Comisión para el Esclarecimiento Histórico*] only three cases have been successfully prosecuted in the Guatemalan courts. The third conviction came in May 2008, when five former members of a paramilitary 'civil patrol' were convicted for the murders of 26 of the 177 civilians massacred in Rio Negro in 1982" (Human Rights Watch, 2009, p. 182).

Exacerbating the matter is the fact that "The army and other state institutions resist cooperating fully with investigations into abuses committed by current or former members. And the police regularly fail to provide adequate protection to judges, prosecutors, and witnesses involved in politically sensitive cases"[8] (Human Rights Watch, 2009, p. 182).

In regard to providing safety for those seeking justice (meaning, those survivors providing testimony at pre-trial hearings and at the trials of alleged perpetrators and/or seeking compensation in a court of law, et al.; and those human rights activists working on the behalf of victims and survivors), it is bound to be a long and difficult road. Tellingly, Human Rights Watch (2009) reported that "The [Guatemalan] Human Rights Ombudsman's Office documented nearly 200 attacks and threats against human rights defenders in 2007, [alone]" (p. 183).

Complicating and exacerbating this situation is the fact that "[t]here is widespread consensus among local and international observers that the people responsible for many of these acts of violence and intimidation are affiliated with private, secretive, and illegally armed networks or organizations, commonly referred to in Guatemala as 'clandestine groups.' These groups appear to have links to both government officials and organized crime, which give them access to considerable political and economic resources" (Human Rights Watch, 2009, p. 184).

The Real Probabilities of Progress in the Field

The real probability of progress remains a question mark. Only time will tell if local human rights activists in Guatemala in conjunction with international human rights activists, along with nudging by the United Nations and individual states, are able to move Guatemala towards a freer and more open society that truly honors the various human rights agreements it has ratified. The same is true of expanding the peace agreement so that it truly addresses the grievances and needs of those who suffered (as well as those who continue to suffer) so grievously at the hands of the Guatemalan government.

Conclusion

The tragedy that unfolded in Guatemala between 1954 and the mid-1990s (and whose profound ramifications continue through today) was (and is) tied directly to U.S. policies, decisions, and actions. It is a history that many are not familiar with, and a genocide that, until relatively lately, has largely been overlooked. Concomitantly, many of the ills that plague Guatemala today are a direct result of the policies, decisions and actions that various military juntas carried out during those years. Indeed, the legacy of human rights abuses, impunity for crimes against humanity and genocide, and the oppression of the "common" person lives on in infamy. This is not likely to change anytime soon unless the nations of the world that truly care about the human rights of people everywhere apply hard and sustained pressure on Guatemala to both right its wrongs and change its aberrant ways.

Notes

1. Manz (2004) reports that "about half of Guatemala's eleven million are Mayan. Twenty-two ethnolinguistic groups exist. Some are small in number. The largest of the Mayan groups is the K'iche, who live primarily in El Quiche, the province most targeted by the military. Thus they suffered a disproportionate number of deaths during the civil war and more than half of the massacres" (p. 249).
2. Ironically, the U.S. supported exactly the same sort of reforms in other countries, but feared that communists had their hand in the reform in Guatemala.
3. President [Ronald] Reagan was particularly supportive of General Efrain Rios Montt, a born-again Evangelical Christian who was responsible for some of the worst massacres after he seized power in a coup in March 1982. "On December 4, 1982, President Reagan met with Guatemalan President Rios Montt in Honduras and dismissed reports of human rights abuses in Guatemala published by Americas Watch, Amnesty International and others as a 'a bum rap.' The following month, the Reagan administration announced that it was ending a five-year embargo on arms sales to Guatemala and had approved sale of $6.36 million worth of military spare parts to that country. This sale was approved despite U.S. law forbidding arms sales to governments engaged in a consistent pattern of gross violations of internationally recognized human rights" (Manz, 2004, p. 23).
4. The United States also trained numerous Guatemalan military leaders at its School of the Americas. Many of these "leaders" went on to oversee the counterinsurgency comprising assassination, torture, terror, summary execution, massacres, "disappearances" (of approximately 40,000 people), and genocide.
5. "During 1982-1983, one million peasants were conscripted into the civil patrols, practically the entire rural adult male population" (Manz, 2004, p. 161).
6. The CEH's objective was to "clarify with objectivity, equity and impartiality, the human rights violations and acts of violence" (CEH, 1999, p. 11).
7. On a related but different front, Human Rights Watch (2009) reports that in a landmark ruling, Spain's Constitutional Court held in September 2005 that, in accordance with the principal of "universal jurisdiction," cases of alleged genocide committed during Guatemala's civil war could be prosecuted in the Spanish courts. In July 2006 a Spanish judge issued international arrest warrants for eight Guatemalans and the Spanish government requested their extradition in late 2006.

However, in December 2007 the Guatemalan Constitutional Court ruled that two of the accused could not be extradited to Spain. Nevertheless, the Spanish court has pushed ahead with the case: in February, May, and October 2008 it collected testimony from witnesses, victims, and experts on the conflict. Meanwhile, in Guatemala, the case continues to be held up by defense motions, while witnesses and experts are subjected to harassment and threats" (p. 185).

8. Human Rights Watch (2009) reports that "The July 2005 discovery of approximately 80 million documents of the disbanded National Police, including files on Guatemalans who were murdered and 'disappeared' during the armed conflict, could play a key role in the prosecution of those who committed human rights abuses during the conflict" (p. 182).

Human Rights Watch (2009) further reports that "In February 2008 President Álvaro Colom announced that he would open the military archives spanning Guatemala's civil war. However, the minister of defense has since delayed handing over the files, arguing that the constitution protects the confidentiality of documents related to national security. A new law passed in September 2008 challenges this argument: Article 24 of the Law of Access to Public Information orders that 'in no circumstances can information related to investigations of violations of fundamental human rights or crimes against humanity' be classified as confidential or reserved. The military archives remain closed, however" (p. 183).

References

Commission for Historical Clarification (1999). *Guatemala: Memory of Silence: Report of the Commission for Historical Clarification*. Guatemala City: Author.

Green, Linda (1999). *Fear as a Way of Life: Mayan Widows in Rural Guatemala*. New York: Columbia University Press.

Human Rights Watch (2009). *World Report 2009*. New York: New York: Seven Stories Press.

Jonas, Susanne (2009). "Guatemala: Acts of Genocide and Scorched-Earth Counterinsurgency War," pp. 376-411. In Samuel Totten and William S. Parsons (Eds.) *Century of Genocide: Critical Essays and Eyewitness Accounts*. New York: Routledge.

Manz, Beatriz (2004). *Paradise in Ashes: A Guatemalan Journey of Courage, Terror, and Hope*. Berkeley and Los Angeles: University of California Press.

Perera, Victor (1995). *Unfinished Conquest: The Guatemalan Tragedy*.

Recuperacion de la Memoria Historica (1998). *Guatemala No Mas!* [*Guatemala Never Again!*]. Guatemala City: Author.

Wilkinson, Daniel (2002). *Silence on the Mountain: Stories of Terror, Betrayal, and Forgetting in Guatemala*. Boston, MA: Houghton Mifflin Company.

Annotated Bibliography

Afflitto, Frank M., and Jesilow, Paul (2007). *The Quiet Revolutionaries: Seeking Justice in Guatemala*. Austin: University of Texas Press. 206 pp.

Based on interviews with more than eighty survivors of the state-sanctioned violence that tore apart Guatemala throughout the 1980s and early 1990s, this book reveals the efforts of those men and women who worked to bring about "change in politics, law and public consciousness" in Guatemala. The titles of the last four chapters provide a solid sense of the major topics and issues addressed in the book: "Seeking Justice"; "The Social Movement to End Impunity"; "The Movement is Fragmented by the Peace Accords"; and "Identity, Rule of Law and Democracy."

Americas Watch (1986) *Civil Patrols in Guatemala.* Washington, DC and New York: Human Rights Watch. 105 pp.

This report highlights and examines the Guatemalan government's practice of forcing hundreds of thousands of civilians to serve in so-called civil patrols, which were basically paramilitary groups, as a way to control the citizens and force them to assist in the fighting of the internal war that was being fought throughout the 1980s and the 1990s. All males, as young as eight years old, were conscripted, upon the threat of beatings and even death if they refused, into the ranks of the civil patrols. Many in the civil patrol were forced, against their will, to beat, torture, and kill so-called "subversives."

Americas Watch (1987). *Human Rights in Guatemala: No Neutrals Allowed.* New York: Human Rights Watch. 108 pp.

Herein, the authors examine three categories of violations of the right to life under the then current Guatemalan government: rural massacres (the government's so-called "guns and beans" strategy); selective killings; and executions. The authors assert that "We devote the major part of our attention to rural killings because they reflect the nature of military efforts to eliminate unrest and because of the extraordinary proportions of the abuses being committed." The report includes the discussion of "testimony gathered by reliable sources, testimony and interviews conducted by the researchers, and the review of statements issued by the government and articles in the press."

Carmack, Robert M. (Ed.) (1992). *Harvest of Violence: The Maya Indians and the Guatemalan Crisis.* Norman: University of Oklahoma Press. 334 pp.

This book is comprised of ten case histories vis-à-vis the institutional violence, discrimination and atrocities visited upon the

Maya-speaking peoples of Guatemala by the Guatemalan government, particularly the period ranging from the 1960s through the late 1980s.

The book includes the following parts and chapters: Part One: Generalized Violence (1. "Introduction: Sowing the Seeds of Violence" by Shelton H. Davis; 2. "The Story of Santa Cruz Quiche" by Robert M. Carmack; 3. "The Transformation of La Experanza, an Ixcan Village" by Beatriz Manz; 4. "The Evangelicals, Guerillas, and the Army: The Ixil Triangle Under Rios Montt" by David Stoll); Part Two: Selective Violence (5. "The Operation of a Death Squad in San Pedro la Laguna" by Benjamin D. Paul and William J. Demarest; 6. "Story from a Peaceful Town: San Antonio Aguas Calientes" by Sheldon Annis; 7. "When Indians Take Power: Conflict and Consensus in San Juan Ostuncalco" by Roland H. Ebel); Part Three: Indirect Violence. (8. "Tourist Town Amid the Violence: Panajachel" by Robert E. Hinshaw; 9. "Destruction of the Material Bases for Indian Culture: Economic Changes in Totonicapan" by Carol A. Smith); and Part Four: Refugees of Violence (10. "Struggle for Survival in the Mountains: Hunger and Other Privations Inflicted on Internal Refugees from the Central Highlands" by Richard Falla; 11. Mayas Aiding Mayas: Guatemalan Refugees in Chiapas, Mexico" by Duncan M. Earle; and 12. "Conclusions: What Can We Know About the Harvest of Violence?" by Richard N. Adams).

Commission for Historical Clarification (Comisión para el Esclarecimiento Histórico, or CEH) (1999) (Eds.). *Guatemala: Memory of Silence: Report of the Commission for Historical Clarification.* Guatemala City: Author.

The editors of the report state the following in their introduction: "The Report begins with a description of the mandate and the methodology it followed in carrying out its work, and subsequently enters into an examination of the causes and origins of the internal armed confrontation, the strategies and mechanisms of the violence and its consequences and effects. The conclusions are then presented and are followed by recommendations, the third component of the CEH's mandate. Finally, there are annexes that include the findings on specific illustrative cases of the events of the past; a listing with a brief description of each and every case presented to the Commission; and various other elements utilized in the fulfillment of the mandate.

"The conclusions summarize the results of almost a year of investigation and are based on testimonies received directly by the CEH, together with a wealth of information from the Parties to the confrontation, other governments and a variety of secondary sources. These were complemented by historical analysis and statistical information from the CEH's database.

"The conclusions are structured in three complementary sections: general conclusions, conclusions regarding acts that constitute violations of human rights and acts of violence, and conclusions related to the process of peace and reconciliation. To aid understanding, there are also annexes relating to the conclusions which include: a chronology of the governments of Guatemala and of the armed confrontation, basic maps, and statistical information."

Cullather, Nicholas (1994, declassified in 1997). *Operation PBSUCCESS: The United States and Guatemala, 1952-1954.* Washington, DC: Center for the Study of Intelligence, Central Intelligence Agency. n.p.

A history of the Central Intelligence Agency's (CIA) role in planning and implementing 1954 the coup d'etat that removed democratically elected Guatemalan President Jacobo Arbenz Guzman from the office of president. It is based on CIA records and declassified secret operational files. Cullather examines the social, political and economic forces that resulted in Arbenz being elected president in 1951 and examines how and why the Cold War influenced U.S. President Dwight David Eisenhower to give his imprimatur for the coup.

Esparza, Marcia (2005). "Post-war Guatemala: Long-term Effects of Psychological and Ideological Militarization of K'iche Mayans." *Journal of Genocide Research*, September, 7(3): 377-391.

In this article, the author argues that "persisting militarization [in Guatemala] continues the genocidal destruction of indigenous peoples' traditional communal bonds by setting army loyalists against human rights workers and the left-oriented wing of the Catholic Church." In doing so, she identifies "three interrelated post-war outcomes of this polarization and militarization among the K'iche: (i) community conflicts arising from dehumanization of the 'other,' (ii) economic breakdown, and (iii) the spreading of a perception of the army as guardian and protector." The study is based on extensive field work (including in-depth interviews with army collaborators) conducted in Guatemala from 1997 through 2000.

Falla, Ricardo (1983). *Masacre de la Finca San Francisco Huehuetenango, Guatemala (17 de Julio de 1982)*. Copenhagen: IWGIA. 117 pp.

Written and published in Spanish, this is an early and important report on the massacre carried out by the Guatemala military in Huehuetenago.

Gleijeses, Piero (1991). *Shattered Hope: The Guatemalan Revolution and the United States, 1944-1954*. Princeton, NJ: Princeton University Press. 464 pp.

This book presents a thorough examination of a revolution that brought about landmark agrarian reform, but subsequently spawned a CIA-sponsored a coup d'état that overthrew the democratically-elected President Jacobo Arbenz Guzman in 1954—which, ultimately, resulted in massive disenfranchisement of the poor (especially that of the Maya), insurrection, and a Guatemalan government-scorched earth policy involving the destruction of hundreds of villages and the mass murder of hundreds of thousands of Maya people.

Grandin, Greg (2000). *The Blood of Guatemala: A History of Race and Nation*. Durham, NC: Duke University Press. 343 pp.

In the *Blood of Guatemala*, Grandin takes the long view of Guatemalan history to help explain the violence that engulfed the life of the Maya people in the 1970s and 1980s. In doing so, he presents the complex history of the region, exploring such issues as caste, gender and politics amongst and between various peoples (including Maya and Ladinos) in the eighteenth and nineteenth centuries; elite politics and popular protests between 1786 and 1826; land, labor and "the commodification of community"; race, class, and "the nationalization of ethnicity"; "Mayan modernism"; class struggle and "the death of K'iche' nationalism"; and the 1954 U.S.-supported coup and its myriad and violent ramifications (1954-1999).

Grandin, Greg (2004). *The Last Colonial Massacre Latin America and the Cold War.* Chicago, IL: University of Chicago Press. 311 pp.

   In this case study, Grandin, associate professor of history at New York University, argues "the Latin American Cold War was a struggle not between political liberalism and Soviet communism but between two visions of democracy—one vibrant and egalitarian, the other tepid and unequal. And ultimately the conflict's main effect was to eliminate home-grown notions of social democracy." Grandin bases his study on a wide range of personal testimonies as well as archival research, including declassified U.S. documents. His indictment of the United States' insidious involvement in Guatemala (including its part in the 1966 secret execution of over twenty Guatemalan leftists, which prefigured later disappearances in Chile and Argentina) is scathing.

Green, Linda (1999). *Fear as a Way of Life: Mayan Widows in Rural Guatemala.* New York: Columbia University Press. 229 pp.

   Fear as a Way of Life is an ethnographical study of "how the intricacies of violence are inextricably linked to the widows survival in Xe'caj." Green asserts that "Violence is not simply the historical background for this ethnography, as I had initially imagined it; it is implicated in the ways in which the women refashion social memory and cultural practices, both as a consequence of and in response to the fear that circumscribes their lives" (p. 6).

   The book is comprised of the following chapters: Part One: A Legacy of Violence (Chapters 1. "In the Aftermath of War: An Introduction"; 2. "The Altiplano: A History of Violence and Survival"; 3. "Living in a State of Fear"); and Part Two: A Legacy of Survival (4. "From Wives to Widows: Subsistence and Social Relations"; 5. "The Embodiment of Violence: Lived Lives and Social Suffering"; 6. "The Dialectics of Cloth"; 7. "Shifting Affiliations: Social Exigencies and Evangelicos" and 8. "Mutual Betrayal and Collective Dignity").

Hayner, Priscilla B. (2001). *Unspeakable Truths: Confronting State Terror and Atrocity*. New York: Routledge. 340 pp.

In the course of critically examining a host of truth commissions conducted across the globe in the aftermath of state terror and atrocity, Hayner discusses various aspects of Guatemala's effort to come to terms with its recent violent past. In part, the author addresses the focus and efforts (including, variously, successes, barriers, setbacks and failures) of Centro Internationacial para Investigaciones en Derechos Humanos (CIIDH), the Commission to Clarify Past Human Rights Violations and Acts of Violence that Have Caused the Guatemalan People to Suffer, the Recovery of Historical Memory Project of the Catholic Church's Human Rights Office (REMHI), the Unidad Revolucionaria Nacional Guatemalteca, the Guatemalan Foundation for Forensic Anthropology, and the Guatemala Project at the National Security Archive.

Higonnet, Etelle (Ed.) (2008) *Quiet Genocide: Guatemala 1981/1983*. New Brunswick, NJ: Transaction Publishers. 335 pp.

Quiet Genocide: Guatemala, 1981-1983 contains essays that address a host of historical and legal issues that make a case that the Guatemalan Government's actions against its Mayan citizens in between 1981-1982 constituted genocide. Essentially, the book constitutes a critical review and translation of the Guatemalan Truth Commission's findings on genocide. It includes contributions from Juan Mendez (former Advisor on Genocide to UN Secretary General Kofi Annan), Marcie Mersky (field coordinator for the Catholic Church Project Report on Guatemalan Historical Memory (REMHI) and coordinator of the Final Report for the UN-sponsored Commission on Historical Clarification, and currently the

Transition Manager for the United Nations Verification Mission in Guatemala), and leading scholars from Guatemala.

Jonas, Susanne (1991). *The Battle for Guatemala: Rebels, Death Squads, and U.S. Power.* Boulder, CO: Westview Press. 288 pp.

Herein, Jonas, a professor of Latin American and Latino Studies at the University of California, Santa Cruz, presents a contemporary history of Guatemala's thirty-year war. "Using a structural analysis that takes critical events and changes in the nation's economic and social structure as the starting point for understanding its political crises, [Jonas] unravels the contradictions of Guatemalan politics and illustrates why, in the face of unmatched military brutality and repeated U.S. interventions, popular and revolutionary movements have arisen time and again."

Jonas, Susanne (2000). *Of Centaurs and Doves: Guatemala's Peace Process.* Boulder, CO: Westview Press. 297 pp.

Jonas examines the decades-long internal war in Guatemala, the United States' insidious involvement, and the peace process of the 1990s, and the so-called "democratization process." The chapter titles of this hard-hitting book provide a good sense of the breadth of issues addressed: 1. "Background: Guatemala's Thirty-Six-Year Civil War"; 2. "The Mined Road to Peace"; 3. "The Terms of Peace"; 4. "Can Peace Bring Democracy or Social Justice?"; 5 "The U.S. Role: The Cold War and Beyond"; 6. "Implementation Wars"; 7. "High Hopes and Stark Realities: Obstacles to Sustainable Development"; 8. "The Hijacking of the Constitutional Reforms"; and "Conclusion: 'Reinvention' or Lost Opportunity: Global, Comparative, and Imaginary Perspectives."

Jonas, Susanne (2009). "Guatemala: Acts of Genocide and Scorched Earth Counter-Insurgency War," pp. 377-411. In Samuel Totten and William S. Parsons (Eds.) *Century of Genocide: Critical Essays and Eyewitness Testimony*, third edition. New York: Routledge.

This chapter provides a succinct but solid overview of the genocide perpetrated against the Maya people by the Guatemalan government. It also includes powerful and informative first-person accounts by survivors of the genocidal actions.

Krueger, Chirs, and Enge, Kjell (1985). *Security and Development Conditions in the Guatemalan Highlands*. Washington, DC: Washington Office on Latin America. 74 pp.

This report basically examines the impact of political violence that was perpetrated in Guatemala between 1980 and 1984. The authors, both anthropologists and consultants to the U.S. Agency for International Development, report, in part, the following: "50 to 75 thousand persons have been killed or disappeared; 440 villages have been destroyed; several hundred thousand people have been temporarily displaced for periods of several months to three years and more; 50 to 75 thousand people relocated to 'model' villages; economic destruction and impoverishment has been massive; through the expansion of military bases and outposts, populations in rural and small urban areas have been under continuous and highly militarized surveillance and the adult male population has been forced to participate in civil patrols" (p. v).

Manuel, Anne and Eric Stover (1991) *Guatemala: Getting Away with Murder.* New York: Americas Watch and Physicians for Human Rights. 89 pp.

The authors discuss two forensic missions undertaken to analyze the flawed medical and scientific procedures applied in the miniscule number of death investigations of suspected cases of torture, extrajudicial killings and massacres by Guatemalan government authorities.

Manz, Beatriz (2004). *Paradise in Ashes: A Guatemalan Journey of Courage, Terror, and Hope.* Berkeley and Los Angeles: University of California Press. 311 pp.

Manz, a professor of geography and ethnic studies at the University of California at Berkeley, provides a moving and detailed account of the repression and violence that engulfed Guatemala during the civil war of the 1980s. More specifically, she relates the story of the people in the village of Santa Maria Tzeja, near the Mexican border, and in doing so "places the saga [of the village] in a broad framework that encompasses Guatemala's tortured history, the conflicts of the Cold War, and the tensions of contemporary globalization." The book is based on her interviews with peasants, community leaders, guerillas and members of the paramilitary forces.

Manz, Beatriz (1988) *Refugees of a Hidden War: The Aftermath of Counterinsurgency in Guatemala.* Albany: State University of New York Press. 283 pp.

    Among the issues Manz addresses are: the relationship between the Mayas and the Guatemalan government, Mayas as internally displaced peoples inside Guatemala, Mayas as refugees in Mexico, and the "return migration to Guatemala."

McClintock, Michael (1985). *The American Connection.* Volume 2, *State Terror and Popular Resistance in Guatemala.* London: Zed Books, n.p. Based in part on official U.S. documents, this study takes to task, from a leftist perspective, the U.S. government's policies in Guatemala from 1950 through the early 1980s. It is particularly scathing of "the United States doctrine of counterinsurgency and its programmes of security assistance since 1960...."

Melville, Thomas (2005). *Through a Glass Darkly: The U.S. Holocaust in Central America.* Philadelphia, PA: Xlibris Corporation. 652 pp.

    In this self-published book, Melville relates the events of the genocidal attacks on the Mayans in during the 1970's and 1980's, and does so via the life story of Ron Hennessey, a U.S. citizen and Maryknoll priest who worked in El Petén and later in San Mateo Ixtan. The story traces Hennessey's life as he moves from being a deeply patriotic American to becoming a stanch critic and opponent of U.S. policies in Central America.

    Hennessey first arrived in Guatemala in 1964 and served in several parishes in the Quetzaltenango area (near Huehuetenango) with Mayans. A fellow priest and colleague of Hennessey's has reported elsewhere that "As the massacres began to increase Ron actively sent eyewitness accounts to his three nun sisters in Iowa and asked them to publicize the atrocities in the US press. His later conversations with the US Embassy officials who try to get him to change his statements to a 'more balanced' view are right out of Alice in Wonderland. Embassy officials then proceed to misquote him out of context."

Montejo, Victor (1999). *Voices from Exile: Violence and Survival in Modern Maya History.* Norman: University of Oklahoma Press. 287 pp.

Montejo, who is a Maya expatriate and an anthropologist, presents the story of one group of Mayas from the Kuchumatan Highlands who fled to Mexico as the Guatemalan governments carried out a counterinsurgency war throughout the late 1970s and 1980s that resulted in the destruction of some 440 Maya communities and the mass murder of tens of thousands of civilians and the upheaval of hundreds of thousands who fled the killing and destruction.

Montejo, Victor (1987) *Testimony: Death of a Guatemalan Village.* Willamantic, CT: Curbstone Press. 113 pp.

An eyewitness account of a violent and deadly attack by Guatemalan government forces against a Mayan village. At the time, Montejo, from Huehuetenango, was a school teacher. He is now a professor of anthropology at the University of California, Davis.

Nelson, Craig W. and Kenneth I. Taylor (1983*) Witness to Genocide: The Present Situation of Indians in Guatemala.* London: Survival International. 44 pp.

A short booklet report that argues that the Guatemalan governments' actions against its indigenous peoples constituted genocide.

Oficina de Derechos Humanos del Arzobispado de Guatemala (1988). *Guatemala: Nunca Mas.* Four Volumes. Guatemala City: Recuperacion de la Memoria Historica (REMHI).

This major report, undertaken by the Human Rights Office of the Archdiocese of Guatemala, documents the violence that engulfed Guatemala between 1960 through 1996. Some 600 people from rural areas were trained to conduct interviews for the project. Ultimately, they conducted 6,500 individual and collective interviews, 92 percent of the interviewees were victims of the violence.

The report, which places the violence that engulfed Guatemala for thirty-six years in historical context, addresses a host of critical issues, including but not limited to the following: the perpetrators, the method of torture and killing that was carried out, the massacres, torture, and rape to which victims were subjected; the fact of clandestine prisons and cemeteries; the destruction of entire communities; and the forced cooptation of civilians by the military to carry out its dirty work. It includes a wealth of powerful first-person testimony that provides a close-up view of the horrors to which the victims were subjected.

Organization of American States (1994) *Special Report on the Human Rights Situation in the So-Called "Communities of Peoples in Resistance" in Guatemala.* Washington, DC: General Secretariat: Organization of American States Inter-American Commission on Human Rights. n. p.

This report is comprised of the following chapters: I. Introduction; II. Historical Background of CPRs; III. Major Recent Complaints and Government's Position About Them; IV. Other Spontaneous Settlements Without Contact with the Outside World ("The Lost Communities); V. Conclusions.

Perera, Victor (1995). *Unfinished Conquest: The Guatemalan Tragedy.* Berkeley and Los Angeles: University of California Press. 392 pp.

This book examines the historical, cultural and economic factors that resulted in Guatemala's civil war, which Perera refers to as "the third conquest" of the Mayan people. As Perera notes, this book is a combination of "journalistic reportage, personal narrative, oral testimony and ethnographic investigation." Basically Perera focuses on four regions of the conflict: Santiago Atitlan, Huehuetenango, the Ixil Triangle (all of which are located in the "highlands"), and the Peten lowland. As interesting and informative as the book is, it is weakened by its absence of footnotes.

Perlin, Jan (2000). The Guatemalan Historical Clarification Commission finds genocide. *ILSA Journal of International and Comparative Law*, Spring, 6(2): 389-414.

A brief overview of the genocide finding by the Historical Clarification Commission.

REMHI (1999). *Guatemala: Never Again! The Official Report of the Human Rights Office, Archdiocese of Guatemala*. Maryknoll, NY: Orbis Books. 332 pp.

This work is an abridged English translation of *Guatemala: Nunca Mas*, the latter of which was published by the Oficina de Derechos Humanos del Arzobispado de Guatemala in Guatemala City, Guatemala. (See Oficina de Derechos Humanos del Arzobispado de Guatemala (1988). *Guatemala: Nunca Mas*. Four Volumes. Guatemala City: Recuperacion de la Memoria Historica [REMHI]).

Sanford, Victoria (2003). *Buried Secrets: Truth and Human Rights in Guatemala*. New York: Palgrave Macmillian. 313 pp.

An extremely powerful book that chronicles the efforts of Maya survivors of the genocidal campaign against the Maya people by the Government of Guatemala to seek truth, justice and healing. Ultimately, the book provides a detailed examination of the Commission for Historical Clarification and is based on more than 400 testimonies from, among others, the survivors of the massacres, and members of the forensic teams who carried out exhumations of clandestine cemeteries, human rights leaders, military officers, guerillas, and government officials.

The book is composed of the following: "'The Bones Don't Lie'"; "The Silencing of Maya Women"; "'It Fills My Heart with Sadness': Ethnography of Genocide Part I"; "The Exhumation and the Anti-Christ: Ethnography of Genocide Part II"; "The Phenomenology of Terror"; "Guatemalan Army Campaigns of Genocide"; "From Survivor Testimonies to the Discourse of Power"; "The Power Effects of Declaring the Truth"; "Excavations of the Heart: Healing Fragmented Communities"; and "Genocide and the 'Grey Zone' of Justice."

Schirmer, Jennifer (1998). *The Guatemalan Military Project: A Violence Called Democracy.* Philadelphia: University of Pennsylvania Press. 345 pp.

In this remarkable book, Schirmer, a lecturer in social studies at Harvard University, examines the Guatemalan military's role in human rights violations in which 200,000 deaths and disappearances were perpetrated, primarily against Guatemala's Maya people. In their own words, high-ranking military officials relate their thoughts and feelings about the violence, the political opposition, national security doctrine and issues, democracy, human rights and law. The work is also based on interviews with high ranking Guatemalan government officials, lawyers, social scientists, and journalists.

Schlesinger, Stephen; Kinzer, Stephen; and Coatsworth, John (1995). *Bitter Fruit: The Story of the American Coup in Guatemala.* Cambridge, MA: David Rockefeller Center for Latin American Studies, Harvard University. 358 pp.

First published in 1982, *Bitter Fruit* explores the U.S. Central Intelligence Agency's operation to overthrow the democratically elected government of Jacobo Arbenz of Guatemala in 1954. The authors base their analysis and findings on both U.S. government documents as well as extensive interviews with former CIA and other government officials.

Sieder, Rachel (Ed.) (1999). *Guatemala after the Peace Accords.* Washington, DC: Brookings Institution Press. 269 pp.

The various chapters in *Guatemala after the Peace Accords* evaluate the progress made as a result of the implementation of the peace agreements "and signal some of the key challenges for future political and institutional reform." Following an introductory chapter by Gustavo Porras, the government's main negotiator in the peace process, the other chapters address the following issues: demilitarization; indigenous rights in the peace process; the challenges of nation-state and citizenship construction; issues of truth, justice, and reconciliation; an assessment of the value of the Truth Commission; and an analysis of different aspects of political reform in Guatemala.

Sieder, Rachel (2003). "War, Peace, and the Politics of Memory in Guatemala," pp. 209-234. In Nigel Biggar (Ed.) *Burying the Past: Making Peace and Doing Justice After Civil Conflict*. Washington, DC: Georgetown University Press. This chapter provides a succinct overview of the violence Guatemala has suffered since the U.S. backed overthrow of the reformist government of Jacobo Arbenz Guzman in 1954, particularly focusing on the mass killing perpetrated by government troops from the late 1960s through the 1980s; the difficulty and complexity of coming to a negotiated settlement to the armed conflict; the efforts of various actors to get at the truth of what transpired over the years and the problem of bringing the perpetrators to justice; and the thorny and ongoing problem of democratization of all facets of Guatemalan society.

Simon, Jean-Marie (1987). *Guatemala: Eternal Spring Eternal Tyranny*. New York: W.W. Norton & Company. 256 pp.

This book by Simon, who spent six years in Guatemala, is comprised of more than 130 colored photographs that document the horrific human rights situation.

Stoll, David (1993). *Between Two Armies in the Ixil Towns of Guatemala*. New York: Columbia University Press. 383 pp.

"This book challenges how the human rights movement thinks about a country notorious for rightwing terrorism. David Stoll's reinterpretation of the civil war in Guatemala focuses on the Ixil Mayas of the Western highlands. Based on their testimony, he attributes Ixil support for guerrillas in the early 1980s not to revolutionary impulses but to dual violence—the coercive pressures of military confrontation which Ixils describe as 'living between two fires.'"

Streeter, Stephen M. (2001). "Interpreting the 1954 U.S. Intervention in Guatemala: Realist, Revisionist, and Postrevisionist Perspectives." *History Teacher*, November, 34(1): 61-74.

An interesting and informative historiographical overview of the intervention and overthrow of the democratically elected government of Jacobo Arbenz Guzman by the U.S.

Wilkinson, Daniel (2002). *Silence on the Mountain: Stories of Terror, Betrayal, and Forgetting in Guatemala.* Boston, MA: Houghton Mifflin. 373 pp.

Wilkinson, who works with Human Rights Watch, relates the horrors of Guatemala's 36-year internal war that resulted in the murder of some 200,000 people, massive destruction of Maya villages, and the displacement of hundreds of thousands of Mayans. He does so through the investigation of the burning down of the manor of a major coffee plantation by a rebel group. During the course of his investigation he interviewed a wide-range of Guatemalans—coffee plantation workers, former guerrillas, small town mayors, and high and powerful government officials—and in relating the story he uncovers the long sordid history of Guatemala, including the U.S. government's involvement, reaching back to the land-reform movement that was cut short by a U.S.- sponsored military coup in 1954.

Zer, Judith (2001). *Violent Memories: Mayan War Widows in Guatemala.* Boulder, CO: Westview Press. 338 pp.

Examines a host of issues relating to the scorched earth policies of the Guatemalan government against the Mayan people in the 1970s, 1980s, and 1990s, including but not limited to the following: social conditions faced by the Quiche Indians, the social, political, and economic situation faced by Maya women during the period of internal warfare, the sort of violence to which the Maya people were subjected and the plight and fate of war widows.

Index